That
Flipping
Book

An All-Inclusive Guide to All Niches of Real Estate Investing

That

Flipping

Book

An All-Inclusive Guide to All Niches of Real Estate Investing

Charity Woods

That Flipping Book

"For my Rillas."

TABLE OF CONTENTS

Preface

How do I write a preface? What is a preface, really? I am a real estate investor not an author.....at least I was...until now.

That moment that changes your life, when you are in it you rarely know that THIS MOMENT is going to be the life changer. My fingers touched the keyboard and I had so much and nothing to say all at once. I felt like I was both empowered and vulnerable at the same time. Then I did it... the first word...sentence...paragraph...and chapter. I became an author.

I was not alone. My friends and family never said "This is a ridiculous idea" or asked me "What do you know of writing?" I was so hyper-focused that we barely avoided a campaign to put my face on wine bottles as a missing person. I mean, nobody I know drinks milk....

Two people not only encouraged me but REALLY gave me that push and I was either going to fly or stumble out into traffic and be hit by a bus. (What is the statute of limitations on pushing...just in case? The bus could be running late.)

I was once told that I have more Johns than a five-dollar hooker. I prefer to say that I have a Johntourage. It seems that if you are going to be a dude that has a consistent roll or impact in my life there is a good chance that your name will be John. My uncle, my mechanic, the owner of one of my favorite restaurants, two realtors that I write deals with on the regular, an ex, a guy in my favorite local band, and two of my close friends.

The last two pretty much know all of my business and still ~~love~~ ~~like~~ tolerate me. These two guys have been pivotal in my transition from being a full-time real estate investor to being a real estate investor, mentor, coach, teacher, author, and blogger. They are two of the most intelligent, motivated, ambitious, badass people that I know. So I am going to dedicate my preface to them. (Nobody reads these anyway, right?)

John Dixon has tolerated me the longest (he wouldn't have it any other way!!). We have been friends through seven years of crazy bfs and gfs, career and financial ups and downs, and just everyday life.

Although he has a background in law enforcement his education is in business. It was he who really gave me that push to start mentoring and training people. He was tired of hearing me say "I am going to start coaching and teaching" so he brought me my first student and I was forced to get started.

He also made me realize that I needed a training manual for my clients, which turned into this book. He has given me a lot of insight on how my mindset, and the entrepreneur mindset in general, differs from the general population. He has contributed to the majority of the section "Now What?" of the book and I am proud to call him my partner in the Wealth Warriors program teaching business and entrepreneurialism to my students.

John Cucci has not had the pleasure of putting up with me as long as his homonymous counterpart but might have more to deal with at times. His wisdom allows me to bring my dilemmas to him expecting resolution. (Poor guy, but he loves it. He does. Idc what he tells you.)

When I was at a point where I was complaisant and comfy in my "empire" that I had built over the years, it was his energy and intellectual creativity that reminded me that I do not want to stop dreaming, building, and constantly creating a better version of myself. He inspired me and continues to do so.

This guy took time out of his double military career, fulltime job in finance, fitness training, and being a super captivating writer to review and edit my book. It was also he who had to talk me out of my feelings of vulnerability about blogging. John actually made me feel like I was not just conveying information but also entertaining people at the same time.

In closing I want to just say that I am grateful to have the support and assistance of two, real-life, American, heroes. JD has served in law enforcement for many years including the FBI and an NYPD officer on 9/11. JC has served his country in not one but two branches of the U.S. armed forces. He served proudly in the United States Army and now honorably defending our country in the Air Force. I am very lucky to have them both in my life. Thank you John!!

Introduction to the Wealth Warriors Lifestyle

Why are you here? What made you sacrifice this time from your life to come here today, to read these words? Take a look at your life. How happy are you really?

Happiness is defined as a feeling of pleasure and excitement because of your life situation. What is your life situation? Are you punching a clock, trading your time for money?

Is time not our most valuable commodity? What is yours worth? Are you trading an hour of your time for $8.00, $10.00, or even $30.00? Are you trading a year of your life for $25,000, $50,000, or $75,000?

If you were facing your last days and could buy more time with your family, more time to fall in love, more time to travel, what would it be worth to you? It would be *priceless*. Time is so valuable you cannot put a monetary amount on it. So why allow corporate America to tell you the value of your time; of your life?

I am not going to tell you that transforming your life into being an investor is easy or that it will happen overnight. That would be untrue; for most of us we will have to work hard and struggle. We will have to make sacrifices. Give up weekends, nights, even take on or quit a second job in order to be able to sever the chains that tie you to the slavery of what society tells us we need, and give you the freedom to be.

Be?

Be what you ask. Be free. Be able to go to all of your daughter's games, heck free to coach. Be able to actually stay home and take care of your son when he is sick without worrying about money or being reprimanded for calling in. Be able to care for your aging parent in their final days. Be able to travel the world. Be able to spend time with the love of your life. Be able to find the love of your life without having to worry about their income or yours. Be able to know that you, male or female, are independent, self-reliant, and able to sustain on your own.

There is a quote that says:

> *"Entrepreneurship is doing today what others won't so that you can live tomorrow like others can't."*

This could not be truer. As an entrepreneur you have the power to set your salary. Do you want a bigger house? Put more time in. Are you comfortable with your income but want more time? Cut your work load back. You have the power. Your earning potential belongs to you. Gone are the days of hoping to get noticed for a promotion or begging for a 3% raise.

When I bought my first house, I wanted an elevated herb garden. I was so excited about walking out the door and picking herbs fresh out of my very own garden to season my Gourmet cuisine I was planning to learn how to cook. I went to the local hardware store and bought lumber, soil, seeds, and fertilizer. I was ready to roll. I got this stuff home and realized that I had no tools nor did I know how to use them even if I had them. Now I just had a dream, a desire, and a pile of stuff, but then no way to implement it.

I will give you the tools and knowledge to build your herb garden. Is your herb garden an empire or just a comfortable business allowing your time to be truly yours? This is for you to decide.

You will be given the tools to fix and flip homes making fast cash. You will have an arsenal of options for acquiring a home with no money required and no credit consideration. You will learn how to make money off real estate that you never even own. You will know how to maximize being a landlord in any environment.

Of course, if I had the tools and knowledge but did not want to spend my weekend digging out the plots to lay the foundation for my garden, I would still have nothing but a waste of money.

Now, are you going to use your tools to cultivate your garden? Unfortunately most of you will not take the next steps to begin severing your chains of dependency to the mindset of trading time for money. Most of you will leave here today excited and motivated only to get back into the usual daily routine. Rather than spending your evenings cultivating leads, you will watch your favorite TV shows. When you could be taking real steps to build a future, on the weekend you would rather do yard work or grab a drink with your friends. It is these choices that keep us a slave to the grind. You will have to make the choice to work to live; not to live to work.

Being an investor means changing the way you think. It means looking at the long and short term. It means throwing away what you have always been told about how to live and die in America.

When we were children, we were asked what we want to be when we grow up. Most of us had answers like doctor, lawyer, fireman, police officer, teacher, maybe even a ballerina. We were taught that we will trade time for money. We are told to put our money into a 401K or IRA and hope we have enough to supplement social security, if it still exists when we retire. We hope that the mutual funds our brokers chose for our life savings do well. What if the market crashes again? What happens to all of our safety and security?

If we go to work we will be rewarded with a paycheck. The amount of that paycheck depends on how valuable you are to the society, right? Not really, this is a damaged system. Why does an athlete make millions but those who are willing to give their life for the safety of others or the country make only a few thousand? I think we would all agree that having athletes is less important than having emergency responders. So in reality we have to realize that we are paid according to a skill set. If you are replaceable at your job you are paid as such. Not only are you paid that way but you are viewed as such as well. You could show up at work tomorrow and find that you have been laid off or that your department has been eliminated. What do you do? You depended on that money to pay for all of your things that have made your lifestyle what it is.

Most of us live with an existence of debt which is offset by the perceived security of a job and retirement. We just realized that both of those things can disappear in an instant. How do we safeguard ourselves from the potential disaster of a job loss or poor decision with our 401K?

Create your own future. Minimize dependency on debt. Work for the only person that you know won't fire you tomorrow, you. Build your retirement out of tangible assets. Change the way you think to include knowing that your health and happiness are as important for you as for those you love.

Create your own future by letting go of conventional wisdom that you are a good person if you have a respectable job for a respectable company earning a respectable wage. Give all of that respect to your ability to ensure the very best future for you and your family.

Begin the process of minimizing debt by letting go of the idea that you need "things" to be happy. Things will come later. Make the sacrifice of driving a less expensive car, making your coffee at home rather than going to Starbucks in the morning, and spending your free time developing the foundation for your future.

Work towards knowing that you will be the one in control of your destiny and that you will **NOT BE REPLACEABLE** because you are working for you. You will not decide that you are making too much and give your job to another with less experience. You will not decide that you had a bad couple of months in production so you are going to let yourself go. You will look out for yourself and the things most important to you. Even if your goal is not to be a full time investor you can create enough passive income that being fired is not a worry. Why put your retirement in the hands of a stranger when you can control your own destiny?

How does a 401K work? A third party pools your savings in with others and tries to make the best investment she can for her clients. She has been educated in this field. She has been adequately trained. But she is human. The stock market can be volatile. It is dependent upon trends that are predictable but also things which are not. Natural disasters, terrorist attacks, and so on. Stocks are a good place to grow your money once you have it but probably not the best place to create your wealth.

If you are just saving for your future and putting away 10% of an average salary of $50,000, you will only be saving $5,000 per year. If you are 25 right now and you plan to retire when you are 65 you will be saving for 40 years. Granted, at 25 you probably do not make $50,000 and at

65 you might make more than that. We can just use this as a rough estimate for now.

If you save $5,000 per year for 40 years you will have $200,000. You would have earned simple interest of less than 1% over the last 40 years. Assuming that you will earn 1% on your savings you will have a little less than $250,000. Not too shabby until you look at how long that will last.

How much do you need to maintain your lifestyle and do a few things you want to do? $5,000 per month? Great. You are covered for four years. What if you want to live past your 60's?

Now let us assume you have an average salary of twice that, say $100,000? What if you are able to find a great money market at 3%. Now you have about three quarters of a million dollars to use. Still only good for twelve and a half years. So unless you plan to die at 77 you are in a tough spot.

What if you bought a piece of real estate at 25 and it was paid off at 55? What if that real estate brought in a monthly revenue of $1,000. Would that help? Sure. What if you did that for the next 5 years? You could retire forever. You could be immortal on your retirement. A shiny, pale vampire.

Are you thinking, "Charity, I am not 25!! Hell, My kids are 25!!" That's OK!! You can start to acquire assets and wealth that will follow you for the rest of your life. You may have to be more aggressive or use it to supplement what you already have in place. Either way it helps, a lot.

What if you could do this with very little upfront cost? What if you can take advantage of the same tax advantages as an IRA?

That's what am talking about!!!

We are all living in our physical body and psychological mind. Our physical and mental health is more important than our financial health. ***What is wealth without health***? Would the richest man in his final days not give it all up for the opportunity to be healthy? This is not a health and fitness course, this is not a self-help class. This is a real estate investment class called **Wealth Warriors**. A warrior is strong. A warrior is determined.

Am not suggesting that you cannot achieve success without a six pack abs and the clarity of Buddha. This is unrealistic and I would not be leading by example. I am suggesting a healthy diet, exercise, and letting go of external factors that create negative influences on you. This will help you to maximize your true potential.

The world is full of negative influences. There are the naysayers who told you that you are silly for going to a real estate investing workshop or buying a book on real estate investing. The ones that tell you that you will lose money, that you will fail. How much real estate are they doing? Do they even use real estate as a verb? What do they know about it? Are they active real estate investors? Are they even financially secure? Are they able to work only 10-20 hours a week to support their family?

Imagine, you have been framed for a serious crime. You need help badly. The cards are stacked against you. You walk into the office and sit down sick with anticipation. You are riding everything on this guy's ability to defend you. Your family, finances, and freedom. He walks in; you look at him and talk a deep breath and say "Doctor, what is my defense?"

You wouldn't let your chiropractor give you legal advice, would you? I mean, he is a smart guy, highly educated, and not in jail himself, must be qualified. No, of course not. Let those who know real estate advise you on real estate.

Do not fall prey to those who either do not know enough or do not want to see you succeed. This is a common deterrent from success. In fact, it is the number one reason people don't try to do something new.

The second problem I have encountered in people who are not making the most of their situation is distraction. I will not lie. I too have fallen prey to this monster. Even when I wanted to begin this program, I spent a year just messing around and procrastinating until one of my friends pushed me into getting started and another friend asked me to teach him. One is now my partner.

You are only going to be as successful as the people closest to you. You have to get into the investor mindset.

It is my hope that each person who signs up for a class, request a personal mentor, or reads these words applies all of their new knowledge. I wish for each one to have the freedom to be....

They say opportunity only knocks once. Why are you sitting and waiting for opportunity to come to you? This isn't the publishers clearing house sweepstakes! Go wake Opportunity up!!! Bang on its door!!! Take control!!! Make things happen do not wait for things to happen to you.

Be a Wealth Warrior.

What is Real Estate Investing?

Everyone wants to be a real estate investor but why? What is investing in real estate really? Is it for everyone? Is it for you?

Real Estate investing is defined as all transactions that involve the purchase, ownership, management, rental, or sale of real estate for profit.

But what is real estate investing to you?

When girls are small they daydream about their wedding and being a princess. They draw ball gowns and ponies. Not this girl. I drew houses with hip roofs and two story bay windows. I drew floor plans and picked the interior for my imaginary home. Real estate has always been in my blood. I have no idea where it came from as my dad owned a commercial kitchen and bathroom remodeling company and my mom worked for a psychiatric hospital. Neither sibling caught the investors bug. My sister is a banker who likes to play it safe and my brother just likes to play.

Getting back to the question, what is Real Estate Investing? To me it is a world of infinite possibilities. It is the career that is ever evolving but remains constant. It is the only way I know that one can work 10-20 hours a week and live very well. It is the maker of more self-made millionaires than any other industry. To me real estate investing is a magical world where creativity is rewarded but you can follow a consistent plan and do amazing things.

Through real estate I have been able to ease the mind of a single mother who was facing foreclosure by buying her home and saving her credit then putting her and her children in a home that they could afford.

I was able to provide financing to a mother of three teen boys who had been diagnosed with cancer and just wanted something to pass on to them. The bank denied her. I did not. That was in 1999. Her eldest son now lives in that home with his children and wife. A final gift from his mother.

I have wiped tears of joy from grown men and held the grateful hands of an elderly woman giving thanks in prayer for her new home.

The most profound value of my career choice has been very recent. In 2013 my father became ill with a heart disease. I was fortunate enough to be in a position where I was able to be at the hospital every day as I only had to work a few hours a week to maintain my lifestyle. I was able to see that there was a serious lack of care at that hospital and demanded a transfer. After being told that because the transfer was requested rather than ordered by a physician he would be responsible for the payment. I had the financial freedom to offer to pay for treatment.

As luck would have it, my father was the third recipient of a surgery which at that time was a clinical trial and this happily saved his life. We also did not have to bear the brunt of the medical bills as he qualified for the trial.

The aftercare was pretty extensive and he was scheduled for PT, OT, and cardiology appointments several times a week. My mother was in a panic as to how to be able to accommodate this schedule and her job.

I was able to find a home with a little apartment for him so that he could stay with me part time and go to his cardiac therapy and his other numerous appointments. We were able to hang out and have fun. He really looked forward to his visits as did I.

In December 2014, a little over a year and a half from his heart surgery I took him to the hospital for the last time. On December 16th we found out that he had stage IV pancreatic cancer that had progressed beyond the reach of treatment. We spent that day together playing games and exploring the hospital. I spent the night there that night and many nights over the next few weeks. On January the 3rd 2015 he took his last breath. I was able to be there almost every day. If I was punching a clock I would not have been able to be there for him or if I was I would have had to worry if I was going to be able to make ends meet. This is the freedom of Real Estate Investing.

There are a multitude of ways to invest and we will cover all of them in the contents herein. You will learn in detail each way to find and make an offer. Let's go over the various styles for investing that you can make.

We have all heard of **Flipping**. It is featured on shows like Flip This House and Flip Men. Flipping is the practice of buying a house that is in bad shape and renovating it to become the best house on the block. The investor will then sell the house and hope to make a profit.

Wholesaling is when an investor gets an offer accepted on a property but does not intend to buy it. Rather, he will sell the contract to another investor for a profit. This is a virtually risk free way to earn money in real estate.

Buyer Wholesaling is when the investor acts as a marketing consultant for other investors by matching buyers seeking lease purchases and owners financing with the properties and investors with those options available. This is different from a realtor as they are only showing properties which are not for sale in a conventional fashion.

Landlording is the practice of owning real estate with the intention of renting it out to make a monthly profit. This creates a residual monthly income. This is called passive income; the ability to make money without actively working.

Owner Financing is buying and/or selling without the use of banks or financial institutions. This allows one to purchase property without any credit restriction. This can create a continued passive income without the hassle of maintenance and repair on a home.

A **Lease Purchase** is when one enters into a contract with the rights and responsibilities of a landlord but the ownership remains with the seller for a set term. Upon the expiration of the agreement the buyer has the right to purchase at a predetermined price.

A **Purchase Subject To** is a purchase where one buys a home and uses the financing that is already in place as the method of payment. This is not the same as an assumable loan.

In the next few pages you will become fully aware of each of these methods and when they are best used. You will know how to find homes to match the type of transaction you desire.

In a few years when someone asks you, "What is real estate investing?" I look forward to hearing what real estate investing is to **_you._**

Before You Get Started

I know that you are ready to just jump right in headfirst and get started! YAY!! No. There are many things that need to happen before you can begin. You need to set yourself up for success first.

Remember being a kid and you rip into that giant birthday present and it is a bike!!!! You always wanted a brand new bike, not your big sister's old bike but your very own shiny, new bike. YAY!!!! Wait. You have to put it together. You pull the instructions and all of the pieces out of the box and hop into it. Ultimately you just want to ride the bike but you know that you cannot ride it if it is not put together.

Right now we are going to put the bike together.

Forming Your Business

When you get started in real estate investing you are starting a business. You are not just buying a house to rent out or to fix and flip. It is extremely important for you to separate everything you have worked for your entire life from the assets you are going to acquire in real estate. How do we do this?

We must form an LLC, or Limited Liability Company. The creation of this entity will be the force field between you and any legal liability that may come your way. Let's face it, you are dealing with people's homes and houses which are being renovated. This by its nature you are at risk of lawsuits. This is an unfortunate side effect of investing. I do not say this to scare you from investing but to help you to see the importance of forming an LLC.

This is a lesson I learned the hard way once. I personally entered in to a lease purchase agreement for an investment property with a senior attorney from one of the biggest law firms in the Richmond area. Everything went well for the first two and a half years when suddenly there was a ton of new development in that area. This caused the values to increase. Like any fiercely savvy attorney, she saw the investment become more valuable back in her hands. She wanted the property back.

Meanwhile, my tenants had stopped paying rent and were doing a great job at manipulating the legal system. So they were enjoying a rent free lifestyle for the past couple of months. As the non-emotionally attached investor I am now, I see this as a perfect opportunity to dump a *non-preforming property with bad tenants* on a lawyer who can handle that herself.

Guess what? I was personally invested both on paper and emotionally. Two major NO's. So I decided to be a stubborn ass and go toe to toe with this hot shot lawyer over a couple hundred dollars a month (which I am not even getting right then) and a potential sale in a couple of years.

She, of course decides that litigation is the best option and proceeded full force. I was literally receiving a motion daily. On top of that, if they were asking for my personal information like *MY* bank account statements, *MY* monthly income, *MY* personal business because I had become the *ONE* entity responsible. This put my personal assets and credit not only at risk but open to inquiry.

I soon realize that I am going to spend more in legal fees than I would even make off of the home in the remaining term of the agreement. At his point a reasonable person would let her have the stupid house. I was obviously lacking in the reason department so…you will love this logic. I decided to tell my attorney that I would handle it myself to save legal fees. (like WTF!!) Seriously, if I could get my hands on a time machine I would use it just to go back and kick my own ass!!! Honestly, I can't believe that I am even telling this story in first person. (SMH. #embarrassingstoriestoldinpublic)

At this point the hot shot attorney is both livid and cruelly amused by my hubris. My situation was going from bad to worse and I didn't even know it. I was out having drinks with my friends laughing about the whole matter the day before court. I was a dumbass. For real!!

I am going toe to toe with one of the top lawyers in VA so there is no surprise ending here. I lost. I lost *BIG*. I not only owed her the house, money (which to this day I cannot figure out how), and I also have the privilege of paying for her billable hours to sue the shit out of me. I did leave with something unexpected though. I had acquired a shiny new judgment in the amount of $17,000. See, if you lose in court it shows up on your credit even if you pay that day.

I personally owed her the money. It hit my credit and stayed there for 7 years. If I had just put the house into the name of a separate LLC I, Charity, would have no liability to this debt. It would never have been on my credit.

Granted, if that was all I changed, I would have still been a dumbass but it would have been easier to hide it.

I actually got lucky. I have heard of people who lost their own homes over business transactions that went awry when they were not protected by the shelter of an LLC.The easiest and recommended way to set up your LLC is to have your real estate attorney do it for you. He will be your registered agent. This means if someone is looking for who controls the company they'll find your lawyer. People rarely look for that info for happy reasons. Let it go directly to the one who is going to handle it.

There is a cost though. It typically cost between $750 and $1500. To me, it is well worth it!

I bet some of you are thinking, *"Charity you said I could invest in real estate with little or no money. We haven't even started to learn about real estate and you are already telling me to drop over a grand!"* I know. I said that. And honestly, there was a time that $1,000 might as well have been $1,000,000,000. I just didn't have it. I will tell you a more affordable way to set up your LLC but I do recommend that if you can pay your attorney to be your registered agent, you should.

You will need a name. I have heard great names, plain names, funny names, adult humor names, and ones that are just ridiculous. I do not care what your company is called. I had a guy name his business Smith Enterprises and his last name was Jones. I don't care. A guy told me he was naming his Tripod Properties (a little adult humor there). Guess what? Don't care. Doesn't matter. Just have a name that no one else in your state is using.

Google the website for the *SCC* for your state. The *SCC* is the **State Corporation Commission**. Once on the site you will just do an entity search to see if anyone else is using the name you want. Once you find one that is not taken you will "*buy*" it. Most states just call it registering it but it cost between $50 and $150. This, my friends, I cannot assist you with, Uncle Sam wants his money.

Next you will need an *EIN*, **Employer Identification Number**, from the IRS. This is what distinguishes your entity from you personally in the eyes of the IRS. Again, this is very important. I have not had an issue with this thank goodness! I do not have an embarrassing story about being a super, giant, asshole for this situation.

This is also the number you will use to establish your bank account, utilities, and so on. You want to be sure to use this number rather than your social security number because you do not to run the risk of seizure of personal funds if you find yourself in a nice little spot like the one I mentioned earlier. Had I used the business name and business account exclusively I would have been offered a lot more protection.

You will need an **Operating Agreement** to accompany your LLC and this is to be on file with the SCC. This is probably not a document that you want to try to create on your own. Below is an actual table of contents from one of my LLCs. The document is about 35 pages and 7500 words. If you are moderately fiscally challenged at the moment you can go to legal sites like *legalzoom.com* and create a reasonable Operating Agreement for between $100 and $200.

If you are super broke. Like you are going to swipe one of those giant rolls of toilet paper from the outdoor restroom at the gas station on the way home because the generic tissue is still $3.00 kind of broke. If that is you right now, you can go through the steps at any of the legal sites and get access to the finished draft of the OA as soon as they are created for review before buying them. You can type that stuff out on your own using theirs as a template. Again, not really my first choice but sometimes you find yourself fishing change out of the couch to buy Ramen for $0.33.

I want to point out that **YOU** are the person I love to see. You have the most drive and potential for super success.

TABLE OF CONTENTS

ARTICLE I

NAME, PRINCIPAL PLACE OF BUSINESS AND PURPOSE

ARTICLE II

TERM AND DISSOLUTION OF THE COMPANY

ARTICLE III

CAPITAL CONTRIBUTIONS AND MEMBERSHIP INTERESTS, GAINS AND LOSSES

ARTICLE IV

INCOME, LOSS AND DISTRIBUTIONS OF AVAILABLE CASH

ARTICLE V

MANAGEMENT, POWERS, DUTIES AND RESTRICTIONS

ARTICLE VI

BOOKS, RECORDS AND FISCAL PERIOD

ARTICLE VII

DISTRIBUTION UPON DISSOLUTION AND TERMINATION

ARTICLE XII

MISCELLANEOUS

Once you have completed these three tasks you are a real life, legit, business owner. Woot Woot!!! Look at you all business ownery. Seriously though, your business will have to become your baby in order for it to grow into a big strong self-sustaining entity. You will need to love it, feed it, and nurture it. You will need to make this business a part of you, interwoven into the very fabric of your soul. Then you can build your dream.

Finding the Personality of Your Business

I park in the deck across the street and start to walk over. I can see Ali, the owner of La Parisienne Bistro, on the patio enjoying a smoke and a glass of wine. He stands and waves as he sees me approach the quaint little French bistro. A smile spreads across his face as I am greeted with a kiss on the cheek and a hand on my back guiding me to a small, quiet table where he joins me.

"*Jamil, a bottle of Chateau de Latour please and the special for the day*." Ali orders my food and wine and I am never disappointed. The conversation and wine flow well past the early closing time, after the employees have closed the store, we sit. Laughing and exploring politics, religion, history, and family; all topics generally left not to be discussed at a dinner table. When I am there I feel as though I am catching up with my dearest friend at a bistro in Bordeaux.

In an eclectic area in Richmond known as Carytown sits a freestanding building with a trellis covered in tiny white lights. This is Stuzzi. When I enter I am greeted at the door with a big hug and an onslaught of compliments from Peter (pronounced ˈpētə like Lois says Peter on *Family Guy*), the owner. He ushers me to the corner of the bar which he occupied with some of his old friends and in those moments I am his old friend as well. We approach the familiar pop of the cork and glug of Gulfi Neromaccarj is barely audible over the energetic roar of the group. The hand of a man of who will surely be a friend by the close of the evening extends the glass of vino he just poured for me.

Peter orders Piccola Piastra after Piccola Piastra with handmade pastas and sauces, meats, and deserts. The food is brought with one plate and many forks. We all share. Sinatra plays a little louder than dinner music should with *The Godfather* silently on repeat on the flat screens about the bar. The conversation is kept light unlike the heavy Brooklyn and Italian accents that spin about me. There is inevitably singing and dancing as "friends" filter in and out of the restaurant. Being there is like going home to my big, New York, Italian family even though I am a mutt from central Virginia.

Am I telling you this so that you now look at your visit to the local Applebee's a little less fondly? No. Well a little, but no. I want you to notice the experience I shared about two of my favorite restaurants had very little to do with the food. The owners, Ali and Peter, created an atmosphere which I wish to be.

Each place is remarkably different but remarkably similar. La Parisienne Bistro offers a quiet experience where I am able to share world views with my Parisian friend. Stuzzi offers a loud whirlwind of sound and flavors, laughing and dancing like a scene out of any good mafia movie. The similarities are that the proprietors "own" the experience you are going to have in their establishment. They take control of making sure that fun is had and food is good. They go about it differently but it gets done all the same. Neither is better or worse than the other.

I want you to take time to consider what experience you want for your clients to have when they work with you. If you are a flipper you should aspire to provide the highest quality home in the area in a price range that is affordable to the people who are looking for a home there. You aren't cutting corners. If you are a wholesaler you will want every buyer to be able to rely on your word again and again. You will be selling to investors so you have potential for repeat customers. They should know that if you give them a value of a home after repairs are made, they can trust that to be true. You aren't elevating value and diminishing the cost of repair to make more money for yourself. If you are utilizing creative financing you should offer the best options available to sellers who are in need while providing a solid path to ownership to people who have been told they are not good enough to own a home.

Think of the promise you want to make to your client of what you will provide them consistently. This is your professional mission and you should do all that you can to provide that experience for each client.

What do you want them to expect from you?

When I go to La Parisienne Bistro I expect a nice quiet meal with a friend. When I go to Stuzzi I expect a party. Was that how they envisioned their restaurant? Probably.

When you come to one of my Wealth Warrior classes I want you to expect a dynamic, entertaining, all-inclusive real estate investment training class. I want you to leave here feeling confident about your skills in real estate, excited to get started, and feel as though you actually had a good time.

Take a moment to write down what you want for your clients to experience when they work with you. Quickly condense that idea to become your mission statement. Here is an example of mine for one of my businesses.

> Mission Statement: *Provide solid, real, tangible solutions to every client by either increasing wealth and assets or reducing burden and debt one situation at a time.*

The bottom line is that you can market your way into new customers but you cannot bullshit your way into repeat customers. Every interaction needs to be filled with respect and a serious interest in finding the solution they seek. In the past few years actively investing almost 100% of my new business came from old business.

Creating the Most Successful "You"

"I do a weird thing when I am nervous where I tilt my head back like I am super confident. This is my attempt to fake it until I make it, or at the very least make it easier for someone to slit my throat." — Amy Poehler, Yes Please

Does that last quote mean that Amy Poehler is insanely funny and extremely successful and hence we should adopt the attitude of "*Fake it until you make it*?" Yes. Absolutely. Not just because Amy says so but because numerous psychological studies agree.

A study in the UK put groups of people together in 4's and asked them to solve mathematical word problems, like the ones we had in school. Their goal was to see if individuals naturally fell into rolls when placed with strangers. What fascinated me was that there was consistently a leader. One person in each group spoke up with confidence and tried to solve the problem. Here is the kicker, post activity, the members in the group were asked to evaluate the skill level of each person. Almost all of them, in every test group, believed the one who appeared most confident to be the most knowledgeable, even after the test administrators stated that (s)he was wrong. Taking that a step further, even the test administrators stated that they felt that the "leader" was more knowledgeable in math even though statistically they were on the same level as the others in the group.

This is known as the *Status Enhancement Theory*. Basically, by elevating the appearance of your status, you appear to others to be superior. Appearing confident is more valuable than actually being the most experienced.

I am by no means suggesting that you go out there and pretend to be a real estate guru that has been in the business so long that you held a land use contract on the Garden of Eden until God called the note and kicked the kids out when in reality; this is your first day at it. I am only suggesting that you feel confident in the skills and techniques you learn here and speak of them with confidence. I want you to propose deals like you have done it a million times before.

Here is a great example of one of my students, John, who made me extremely proud. I am literally reading an exaggerated "*I Quit*" version of a text explaining that being a badass in the Air Force, a financial consultant and a fitness trainer made the dedication of time into real estate difficult. Facing a possible deployment in 3 months he believes that there was insufficient time to really make any money. I heard, "*I am scared to try.*"

Boy was I wrong!!! Literally a couple of seconds later I got "*As we are having this conversation a guy walked in to my office with a house that he has 30 days to get under contract. Owes $166,000 to the bank. The other homes in the area are worth more like $300,000.*"

I pulled comps and realized that the actual value was closer to $325,000. He went after it like a shark. They had a potential to make over $100,000 on the sale if they listed below market conventionally but he went ahead and pitched the shit out of them. Let me remind you that he had never done a real estate deal before. In fact he had not even finished reading the instructional material. But on this day he was an expert. He asked the right questions and made the right offers.

Ultimately they decided to list with an agent and make some moola but he did such a fantastic job utilizing the knowledge he had recently acquired that they really considered the offer of $166,000 as a good offer. They were even appreciative to know the option was there if the conventional methods did not work.

This was not a failure but a success even though the contract did not materialize. It was an excellent opportunity to practice and also opens the door to word of mouth referrals. They came in overwhelmed in the face of a foreclosure looking for answers and he provided them immediately.

Not all offers will be accepted but they can all be a chance to win. Win at building a relationship with a person who may know someone else that needs you. Win at finding creative solutions to the problems of your client. Win at taking every opportunity.

On the flip side of that I called another student and told him that I had just secured $100,000 in private money for him and asked when we could sit down and write offers. He asked me if I would just invest for him because he really doesn't want to make time. Do I look like a stock broker? What?? I am paid to teach you to make money not to make it for you. He had $20,000 to invest and wanted to do a flip. I told him no. But I will give him 12% back in simple interest and allow my students who want to put the time in to use it. He agreed. He was happy to make $200 per month allowing others to make thousands.

He is not wrong. He is just not right. Not right for this business. It does require dedication, drive, and gusto.

What do you think of when you think of a real estate investor? How do they dress? What do they drive? A few folks flipping houses, wearing business casual or some overpriced jeans, and driving an expensive car. Right?

Where does that idea come from? Reality TV? Being an actual investor means being able to discern the difference in a house that needs to be flipped and one that should be held, or sold wholesale. Would creative financing be the best option?

An actual investor needs to dress the part for the type of offer (s)he is going to make. If you are sitting down with your realtor making offers for flips you can wear anything which you feel comfortable in. That is not what this next section is about. The next few paragraphs pertains to when you are meeting with a buyer or seller directly.

When you are meeting with your client, either a buyer or seller, you want to convey several messages.

1. I am a professional and I take this seriously.
2. I am a hard worker who is working hard for you.
3. I am not making a fortune off of you.

You will need to dress for success. Let your client know that you are a professional and they are of the utmost importance to you. Women: slacks, skirts, suits, and dresses are best. Men, I would recommend a suit or dress slacks and a button up at least. I only recommend wearing jeans or any casual item on weekends to meet buyers. Never to meet a seller and never for an open house.

I want to focus mostly here on when you are meeting with a seller. You will be negotiating some pretty unconventional agreements and the entire package needs to say "*I am a confident, knowledgeable, professional whom is offering you the best solution for all of us.*" Remember our buddy John up there? He was working at the bank where the sellers came to seek a solution to their problem. He was at an instant advantage as he was automatically the expert because they came to him. He was already in a suit looking professional. We do not always get this lucky. We have to bring the game to them.

You should immediately create a Professionalism Packet. Basically, you are going to create the first impression that they are working with a business that deals in creative real estate versus a single investor.

Let's talk first about your **Business Cards**. You will want to create a business card as soon as you begin your venture into greatness. The very day you create and make legal your business name; that day is the day you get cards. You can get enough to get started on Vistaprint.Com for pretty cheap when it is your first order.

Below are actual examples of two cards that are very different that are done for two businesses I have. One I am the only owner and the other I am one of three partners. There are several things I want you to notice on each card.

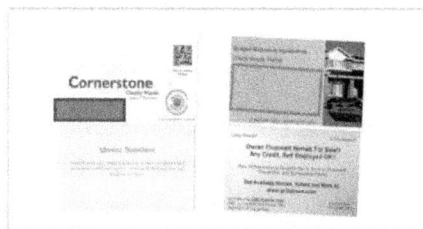

First do you have any idea which card is for my business which I have partners? No, right? You should identify yourself on your card as a managing member, partner or senior partner rather than the owner. Why would you want to do such a thing?

All three titles have enough authority to conduct any business necessary but not ultimate authority. Sometimes you just can't offer the client what he wants and that is ok. If you are the sole decision maker it can be difficult to stay firm. Also, it gives the appearance that you have worked your way to this position.

The general mindset of most people is that if you are working for a company that promotes you or makes you a partner you must be really good at your job. If you go and start a business, well anyone can do that. Obviously, as a business owner I know that as the owner you better be giving 110% every day. People that are actively trading time for dollars are of the opinion that you are better qualified if you are doing the same.

Remember, you want to give the impression of a business not a guy who is making a crazy offer on their house. You will be making offers that often force the seller to put a lot of trust and faith in you doing what you say that you will do. It is easier to have faith in what appears to be an established entity with multiple people ensuring this process goes as planned than it is to put faith in a single person.

Second I want you to notice the different types of cards. The two businesses are basically the same but we have different focuses. So the need for the different styles is necessary. Allow me to explain.

Real estate investors often find a niche that they feel they do best or is the most profitable. You will want to gear your image around that. The focus of Greater Richmond Investments is to buy and sell houses using creative financing; Sub To, Lease Purchase, and Owner Financing. Whereas the focus of Cornerstone Consulting was more broad spectrum and included a strong emphasis on building capital through private investors.

We are going to take a closer look at each card and distinguish the reasons behind the styles. First we will look at the Greater Richmond Investments card, the orange one.

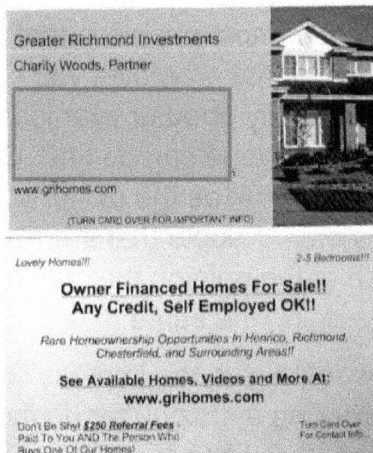

This card is designed to

1. attract attention,
2. convey clearly what we do and,
3. generate one type of client.

How is this done? First you need to know your client. We are looking for people who are in unique situations needing to be rid of their home and for one reason or another are unable or unwilling to sell the home by use of conventional means. We are looking for buyers who are unable to purchase a home using a bank for whatever reason. This business model is pretty specific so the company name and marketing reflects that.

I know I said that I do not care what you name your business. That is partially true. The fact that you have a business name is the most important part. The way you brand your business will have a lot to do with the name and many other factors.

If it is your plan to just flip homes the name does not matter at all so again this section is not really for you, the flipper.

Back to the card. The business name is obviously one where we are involved in real estate investing. We buy and sell houses. We used a color that will stand out. If I meet you in line at the grocery store and give you my card you will most likely remember the color and it will be easier to find when you look for it.

Notice how on the back we explain EXACTLY what we do. Owner financed homes for sale. Any Credit. Pretty straight forward.

Lovely Homes!!!

2-5 Bedrooms

Owner Financed Homes For Sale!!
Any Credit, Self Employed OK!!

Rare Homeownership Opportunities In Henrico, Richmond, Chesterfield, and Surrounding Areas!!

See Available Homes, Videos and More At:
www.grihomes.com

Don't Be Shy! $250 Referral Fees -
Paid To You AND The Person Who
Buys One Of Our Homes!

Turn Card Over
For Contact Info

We also solicit referrals. Put it right out there!! Everything you want to know is right there.

Cornerstone Consulting is a little vaguer and there is a reason for that. With Cornerstone we have a more broad range of things we want to do. We will be buying and selling using creative means like *Greater Richmond Investments*, but also we will be managing property of others and raising private capital to flip. It is important that we have a professional appearance and that we do not isolate ourselves to only one style of investing.

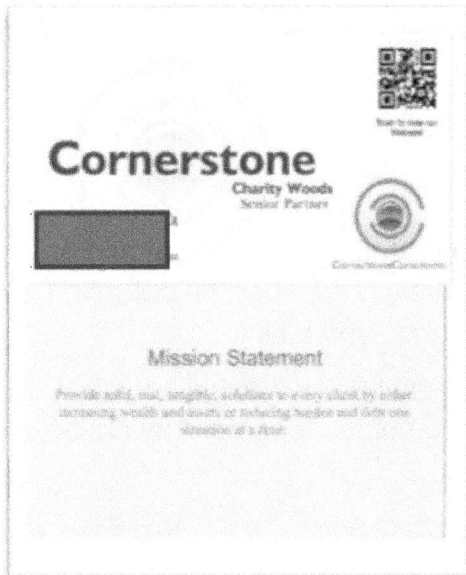

Notice that rather than a photo of a house there is use of a logo. The colors are subtle and professional. Unless you talk to me you really will not know what I do. What is the purpose for that? Because when I am at your home telling you how I can relieve the burden of foreclosure by taking over your payments having a professional card will not hurt me. But when I am trying to convince you that your retirement is better managed in a self-directed IRA allowing me to utilize that money and giving you a guaranteed ROI of 12% a flashy card about owner financing will hurt me.

Before you create your card, you will want to consider how you intend to invest. If you want to be in a niche, create a card that reflects that. If you are planning to be a broad spectrum investor, you may want to go with a card that is adaptable to every style.

If you are working on a really tight budget you are able to get away with good business cards and being prepared for the appointment with a pre written offer if you know what it will be or a blank contract. A **FAQ** about the type of offer you are making is a good thing to include as well.

If you are working with a larger budget, it is a good idea to buy folders with a spot for your card and two pockets. You may even want to have them made with your company name and logo. (Much like the ones we give you in our classes. That alone is worth taking one.)

Place your card in the designated spot. In one pocket you will place the contract and FAQ about the type of offer you are making.

In the other pocket you will place a little package where you basically market yourself and business. You will have more and more options as your business grows and you have actual transactions to speak of. You will want to get this professionally printed on a glossy paper.

Your first page should include your logo (if you have one), a generic picture of a property, a nice pic of you and your partners (if you have any), and contact information including a business website. I am not particularly excited about putting a picture of just you on there as the goal is to be a business and not a dude. Once you acquire clients you will want to add their testimonials to this page.

You can allow that to be a complete professionalism package. Especially if it is just you and you just started. You do have the option of an introduction page to your client. Stating who you are, your background, and so on.

It can be something like this....

Dear Client,

I am happy to be the housing solution specialist that will be working with you today. It is my goal to make each and every meeting the best experience possible by working diligently to ensure that I am able to find the best solutions possible to each and every unique situation.

Thank you for allowing me the honor of working with you. I am looking forward to building a lasting relationship.

Warm Regards,

Charity

CHARITY WOODS

Made Up Company, Senior Partner

Direct Dial: 804-555-1234
charity@madeupcompany.com

Born in Church Hill, Charity is a Richmond native. She has resided in Richmond, Chesterfield, Prince George, and finally settled in Henrico's West End allowing her vast and intimate knowledge of Central Virginia.

For more information please go to www.masonstoybox.org or Facebook.com/MasonsToyBox

Charity heads the Retail Acquisition and Sales Department. She oversees the purchase, renovation, and sale of all cash and creative purchased properties. Charity has been a real estate investor since 2000 with a background in property management, development, and federal, state and local compliance regulation.

So you know to dress as a professional and have your professionalism packet handy. What should you drive, given the option? A nice fancy smancy car? *NO!*

First I want to say that once you get into the investor mindset you will look at an *expensive car as a **liability rather than an asset**.* If you want a super nice car you better be able to pay cash for it and not miss the money.

Back to the place that most of this room is at....

You probably already have a car. Maybe you are 23 and saved up tips from your part time waitressing job for 6 months to be able to afford a 1992 Dodge Aries station wagon with a rust hole in the floor board that goes completely outside. Maybe you are a bit older and have worked hard and rewarded yourself with a nicer new Land Rover Range Sport. Who do you think makes the best first impression when you pull up to meet a client?

The Range Rover of course. It shows that you are good at what you do, right? **WRONG**!!! It shows that you are making a lot of money and they are going to assume that it is off of them. Driving a super nice car give the impression that you are a big, bad, evil, greedy, real estate investor.

Many of you may be realtors and have heard that a nice ride is an investment in your business. This is true for a realtor. A nice car shows that (s)he is highly capable at selling homes and making whatever part of 3 or 6 percent after the broker is paid. People assume that the realtor is not making extra money off of them personally because it is based on volume and the price of houses. This means you are just better at your job than the realtor in the 1992 Dodge.

When you, an investor, pull up in a super nice car the client tends to believe that you are making money by screwing them over. So if you are lucky enough to have a car that cost more than some of the offers you are going to be putting on houses you may want to take a few thousand and buy a little inexpensive knock around car. I personally use a six year old VW Golf two door.

On the flip side, if you are that 23 year old waitress, you may want to make your title "Housing Solution Specialist" on your business cards until you can upgrade a little bit more.

HINT: Driving an average car is the best bet. You should also get magnetic signs made that say "I Buy Houses" along with your phone number to put on the side.

Having a Web Presence

My hairdresser broke up with me. I feel like I need to explain so that you don't think I'm some super diva that is so particular that anyone with self-respect runs as far from me as possible. My best girlfriend's best guy friend married a chic who became my stylist. They divorced and she let me know that we too were parting ways because she is not keeping in contact with people who remain friendly with her ex. Anyway, we are broken up and I have been looking for a new salon. I have tried several and haven't found my new salon home just yet. When I look for the next spot to try I google "hair salons near me." If there is no website or if it is a crappy one I do not try them.

Why? IDK. Really, I have no idea.

All professional companies now have a website. You can buy your domain name super cheap with coupon codes. You can buy your domain name for as little as $0.99. GoDaddy is a popular site for purchasing your domain name.

There are many web design sites that allow you to create your website entirely on your own. They look great and are interactive. It is also really inexpensive to launch.

When you create your website you want to have your Home page with a little brief information about what you do. For example if you are a broad spectrum investor you can say something like:

> *"We are dedicated to finding solutions for buyers, sellers, and investors with dignity and integrity. We provide shelter and home-ownership to buyers who have faced hardships. We relieve the burden of upside-down mortgages, dilapidated houses, and overwhelming mortgage payments to sellers. We ease the anxiety of making the right decisions to ensure the future of all persons from the working class to the elite investor. We do this with pride and compassion for each member of our community to build a better tomorrow, together."*

Put some cool pictures of houses there. Be creative.

Have a section about the houses you have available. I like to have a slide show, description, and map for each one. I have a "button" to inquire about the home.

Coming soon to Short Pump!!!

I WANT THIS HOUSE

- Located conveniently in Short Pump
- 4 bed room
- 2.5 Baths
- 1700 sqft
- $1650 per month
- $259,500

Set up a page for sellers to contact you for a same day offer. Get general information like address, square footage, condition, and why they want to sell. Be sure to have fields for contact information as well.

I find it very valuable and it adds credibility to your business if you link your website to PayPal allowing them to pay online. This is also a preferred payment method for most millennials.

You will want to have a section that caters to the individual who may have interest in becoming a *Private Lender*. You will learn all about this very soon. This section should basically just be a spot that is offering a person a teaser and an opportunity to get more information. We are going to discuss the Private Lender many more times. If you are a bit confused, don't worry, you will know more than you want soon enough.

You will want to immediately begin getting testimonials from each buyer and seller while they are still happy and in love with your real estate magic. You can just record this with your smartphone camera. A raw, real, unrehearsed, testimonial is the best. This lets people know that you don't suck!!

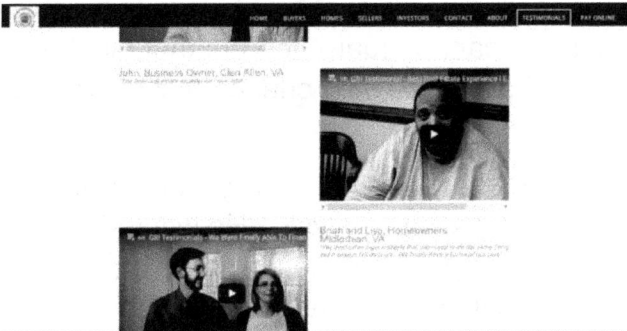

You do not need to create a masterpiece of a website, although you can. You need not spend a fortune on web design, although you have that option. The bottom line is that you just need a web presence to be taken seriously.

Phone Systems

I was trying on summer dresses at the mall wishing that the weather would just get warm and stay that way when my phone rang. It was a person calling about a house. I can tell because I get the prompt saying *"press 1 to accept the call or press 9 to send it to voicemail."* I took the call and it was a man named Mr. Jones. He was interested in a house we had for sale with *owner financing* in a below average part of a high end neighborhood. We were requiring $26,000 as a down payment. I explain this to Mr. Jones and he did not bat an eye. We meet an hour later and he gave me $5,000 to hold the house for a week until we can close. He walked into closing with a bag full with $21,000 in cash in it. We sure would love to be able to replicate him. We cannot guarantee another him but we can work towards having the best chance at it by tracking the leads.

Allow me to rewind. I had an overly analytical partner with an affinity towards statistical analysis. He wanted to track everything. This is really a great idea. Prior to his findings we were spending money on mailers and newspaper ads which proved to be worthless.

My partner wanted to know which signs got the best reply, how many leads came in from banners, craigslist, postlets, backpage (none btw it is for prostitutes we learned that the hard way), and so on. How are we going to accurately track the source of the calls without having to take into consideration human error? Basically, I know that I will forget to ask "*How did you hear about us*?"

After considerable brainstorming, we learned that we needed different phone numbers that we could track and we needed it to be affordable. The solution was using a web based phone system. We used *Ring Central* but now there are so many more options. This provides an affordable way to track lead generation but also gives the appearance of a larger company with several lines, toll free numbers, and extensions.

This is not a deal breaker. You can run a perfectly good real estate investing business from your personal cell phone. It is just a helpful hint that might make your life easier in the long run.

Building a Team

We have all heard that a chain is only as strong as its weakest link. This is something you need to consider in building your team to assist you in creating the life you desire. You will want to be sure that the people you chose are skilled professionals that are accustom to working with investors. Honestly, it is a great position to be in when you are your own weakest link. You are able to be guided by those who know more than you. They want you to win because you are making sure they are able to work. I am speaking of using the right attorney, realtor, accountant, and contractor. These are the most important members of your team.

Imagine working out a really awesome creative financed deal and your attorney tells you that he can't close it. He has no idea what to do. He is not even sure of the legalities. This would be a serious problem for you. You would not be able to make the transaction work with that attorney and would be scrambling to look for another. It is in your best interest to find, interview, and select a team before you need them.

You are going to learn many things within the covers here. You will be able to understand the complexities and multiple variations of the business. Your team should as well.

There are many ways to look for your team. I find one in particular to work the best. Go to a networking event and ask other investors. Word of mouth referrals are really the best way to find who is leading in the industry. Also, many times you will find those who specialize in investor services are already there waiting for you. We will talk about networking events later but this is really the easiest way to find a good team.

I find it to be most important to have an attorney that understands your business because, let's face it, you probably do not understand his too much. He needs to be able to fully understand the ins and outs of what you do, maybe even a little better than you do at first.

To be sure that he knows your business it is good to ask him a set of questions. Right now you will have absolutely no idea what you are saying but very soon you will.

- Are you specifically a real estate attorney?
- Who is your typical client?
- Do you work with many investors?
- Are you familiar with land use contracts? Do you close them? Do you feel confident defending

them in court if needed? Do you have one that you prefer your clients use?

- Are you able to offer a simultaneous closing?
- Do you close homes that are subject to the existing mortgage?
- Will you offer a "closing" type option for a lease purchase?
- Do you do title in house?
- Can you do a 7 or 14 day close?
- Do you have much experience closing owner financed homes? Do you have a mortgage drafted that you use? Do you have a promissory note drafted that you use? Have you had the opportunity to defend these documents in court?
- What is your knowledge in the arena of Landlord Tenant?

An attorney that deals in investor transactions will at the very minimum understand these questions. Many of these questions will stump a conventional real estate attorney.

Finding a realtor or broker that is able to assist you is also very beneficial to your operation running smoothly. This is a very strong truth for those who are going to be flipping. You better not only have a realtor who does an awesome job but also one who you personally like. You two will be spending a lot of time together.

You will want to your realtor to be able to answer the following questions:

- Who is your typical client?
- How many investors do you work with?
- How do you write investor offers?
- How do you feel about blind offers?
- What is your stance on choosing not to ratify an offer after it has been accepted?

- Do you have to hold the EMD or can we send it to the attorney?
- Do you offer flat fee listings? How much?

Having a contractor who is professional, reliable, affordable, and knowledgeable can make the difference between a hit or a miss. Of those four things can you guess which is the least important? It is affordability. You can add cost into the offer. You cannot add shoddy work into the offer.

You will want to ask the contractor the following:

- Who is your typical customer?
- Do you do much for investors?
- Do you do any new construction?
- How many crews do you have?
- Are you a GC or do you operate your crews?
- Do you hold a Class A, B, or C?
- Do you have an EIN?
- How many total renovations have you done in the last 6 months? Who was the typical client? Homeowners or investors? What was the average turnaround time?

You will probably need an accountant unless you happen to be super excited about reading the latest and greatest in tax law. You will look for an accountant who is used to clients that buy, sell, hold, manage, and flip properties.

- What percentage of your clients are actively investing in real estate?
- Are you able to give me some pointers in reducing my tax debt for each type of investing?
- How do you recommend I update you? Monthly, quarterly, annually?

If you find an accountant who is working with many other investors you can bet that she is well versed in the type of deductions that are exclusive to active investors. Many people own a piece of investment property or two but very few conduct real estate transactions regularly.

The Importance of Networking and Education

One day I woke up and called my sister. *"April,"* I said, *"I am going to be a real estate investor."* It was 1999 and my sister was 19 and completely outta flips to give that Saturday morning at 7am. I was 21-22 and knew this was my life path. Obviously, I was met with far less enthusiasm than I had anticipated. Did she even hear me?

I later realized that saying *"I am going to be a real estate investor"* in 1999 was like saying I am going to be an astronaut back them. There was no reality TV about flipping houses…I'm not even sure that there was any reality TV at all. If you are under 30 you are probably like *"What the….What did ya'll watch?"*

Information was more difficult to come by. I went to the library and looked up real estate books. Now the under 30's are really like *"Woah, wait what? You went where?"* Yep a real life library.

What did I find? Some stuff on conventional real estate, a little about investing but not nearly enough. Of course I had no idea that I had no idea and plugged ahead. You don't know what you don't know. By 2000 I was chugging along putting ads in the newspaper, canvasing neighborhoods with flyers, highlighting the map book on the streets I hit…No, this is not a history lesson. This is really how we did stuff.

I learned bits and pieces from others I met along the way, making mistakes, and making mistakes. Did I mention I learned from making mistakes? It wasn't until later when the internet was more available and people were creating groups about mutual interest that I found a meet up group dedicated to real estate investing. This was maybe 2003 or 2004. You would be surprised how much trouble I managed to get into in 4 or 5 years. Remember, I was too stubborn to quit anything. This time I have to say that I am glad because if I had I have no idea what I would be doing instead.

Before public record was available online I physically went into neighborhoods looking for homes. I would drive or walk the streets of flip rich areas looking for the ones that needed me, the ones calling my name. The worse the property, the more I loved them. Then I would go look them up at the courthouse.

One beautiful early summer day I was strolling through the streets of Petersburg, VA. For those of you unfamiliar with this area, it is ranked the #1 least desirable city in Virginia. The crime rate is high and the employment is low. One of every three students there will not graduate high school. There is a heavy population of drug addicts, dealers and those who pay for the drugs through prostitution. Don't get me wrong, there are some really nice parts of Petersburg as well. I was not in one of those unfortunately.

Guess what? I can get a house cheap so I'm there!!! I see this dilapidated building that is absolutely, hideously beautiful. It's was a mess!!! I break in through the back and immediately notice a dog carcass in what appears to be a partially occupied living room. There is a possibility that someone is living here with a dead dog.

If this was a 1990's horror movie, the intelligent brunet and cool black guy would tell me to leave but being a stubborn blonde (at that time) I would not have listened. It was just me so that didn't happen. Either way, I continued to explore.

I walked around the corner to the hall where there was a giant hole in the floor and water actually moving in the basement. I had no idea why the water is moving. The more I know about the mechanics of houses the less I understand this. Was there a sump pump working in this abandoned wretch of a building? I was sure there was no power so that is not likely. Was it rats or snakes? Lochness? Who knows? I am just glad I didn't go to solve the mystery. Based on the choices I was leaning towards Nessie.

Any person who has any common sense about them would look at this house and see that homes are selling in the $40's. Like $40. The house needs about $100k in work. Walk away, right? Canine carcass, Nessie is the best option for what is living in the basement which is exposed thanks to a giant hole in the floor. Not this gal. I went up the stairs.

Up. The. Stairs.

I know that I have to navigate around the sea monster in the floor and possibly trip over a decaying body if I had to make a quick exit. Didn't care. Still going up there.

It smells worse than one could imagine. A strong, hot, odor of feces, urine, and metal hit you in the face. Now at this point I am half expecting to find a slaughter house full of dead bodies but rationalized....this is good now, pay attention...."*if there were bodies here the dog would not have starved to death*".

Perfectly reasonable deduction, you should keep looking.

Suddenly a man appeared in the doorway with his shirt wrapped around his head, his eyes wild and yellow, and his lips dry and chalky. I realize the smell of human excrement is him as his pants appear to be soiled and have been for longer than I would like to imagine. He was 3 feet away and was looking at me like I was the other white meat and what's for dinner.

I realize that I couldn't out run this guy, I'll fall in the loch or end up face down beside poor ole fluffy. I was going to have to use the only weapon I have…

I took a deep breath, looked him dead in the eye, and said *"Oh my goodness. I am so sorry. My agent told me this house is vacant. Butch!!! The owner is still here we need to go!!!"* I apologized and scooted out as calmly as possible. (*Side note, I never had an agent named Butch. It just sounded tough.*)

I am pretty sure that my parents stopped calling me for about a year just because they didn't want to hear the newest level of crap I had stumbled into.

Back to the meet up group in 2003'ish…. a couple of weeks later I attended my very first Real Estate Networking Group. Guess what I found out? There is a company that finds vacant homes and their owners for you. They just send you a list. Do you have any idea the benefit of that knowledge!!???

Networking groups are a perfect place to find like minds, great ideas, what works and what works better. Guess what else you can find? People who are looking for you. Hard money lenders, attorneys who work for investors, accountants who work with investors, and even other investors!!!

Are you a flipper? Maybe Johnny is a wholesaler. You can use each other. Are you interested in creative financing? Maybe Sally is about to let a deal walk because she can't find the solution. Find your networking groups and go.

Make it your social time while you build the foundation for the future you want. You are still making sacrifices while enjoying a few libations and fellow entrepreneurs.

The free exchange of information is priceless. It is also important to grow a sense of comradery in an industry where we tend to work solo most of the time. This keeps us grounded when our heads are too far in the clouds, but also lifts us up when we feel discouraged. This motley group of misfit entrepreneurs become your colleagues and you theirs. *Embrace* it.

Always Raise Capital

I am sure that I will not shock any of you by saying that real estate is fueled by money. In one way or another it is all about the bottom line just like any other business. You, as a small business owner, need to know how to access capital through means other than your own money. Well, if it's not your money whose money is it? **OPM**, *Other People's Money*. You down with OPM? Yea you know me! (Throw back to 1990)

Remember my two students earlier on? The one who decided that he would rather do other things than real estate? That guy is Russ. It's time to give him a name too. So Russ has a more conventional mindset than investors. Russ works at a regular job for a big company and makes a decent living. Russ puts some money in savings and spends the rest on bills and things that make him feel good. Going out with friends, a car that cost more than the cash he has available, entertainment, and so on.

He is a young man in his early 20's and has managed to save $20,000.00. Russ isn't doing badly for himself. He is off to a good start. He thought that he wanted to learn to flip houses but realized that he's not really about that life.

Russ is not so stuck in the conventional mindset that he does not see the value of nonconventional investing. We briefly discussed previously that when we think of traditional investing we tend to think of the stock market, bonds, and so on. Those things have a place but so does a guaranteed high return. We can provide that for folks who do not want to actually try their luck as an investor. They can sit back and earn. Russ is going to earn $2,400 a year on his $20,000. In just over 8 years he has doubled his money if he never reinvests the interest.

We have been told our entire lives to work hard, be responsible, and save for our future. But how can you save for your future when you actually lose 2.65% of your savings to inflation? That means if you had $50,000 in savings in today it would be worth the equivalent of $39,523.48 in ten years. What about stocks? That is always a gamble. Sometimes the outcome is positive but you run the risk of low security. How about a money market or a savings account? The security is great but the returns are far less than the rate of inflation.

You as a real estate investor should always offer the opportunity to EVERYONE of being a private mortgage investor on real estate transactions. They are not the real estate investor, you are. Once they know that you are the professional equipped with the ability to deal with ever changing markets it is a safer bet for them to make the most of their existing capital. They can just be the bank. Your bank.

By offering high return rates at 8-12% they are able to see real growth in their portfolio. They are secured the same way a bank is secured, through a mortgage, a promissory note, and first or second position on the title. This means that if you default on the note they can take the house and all of its equity from you. Since you are going to learn to buy a house with 25% equity, they are pretty well protected.

You will need to create a private investor packet. This can be done in many ways. Some like to create just a small pamphlet that you can leave around creating interest at random. Some prefer a larger scale production. I personally have a bound booklet that I use. I feel that it is most professional and appropriate for the situation. You are asking them for hundreds of thousands of dollars at times. The least you can do is spend $10 on nicely bound marketing material.

I recommend having this done as soon as you can. You never want to be stuck in a position where you have a great deal in the works but can't pay for it.

Let's revisit our other student, John. If the seller had taken his offer for $166,000 are we all to believe that John just had almost $200,000 laying around? No. He would have to raise investment capital. With only 30 days to close, he better have that in his back pocket. Meaning, he should have already found the funds before he needed them.

In addition to a packet you need to know how to get them to have interest in your packet. Humans have a short attention span. You have 20-30 seconds to cultivate curiosity. You need to have a prepared speech that is only a few seconds long that prompt them to ask you how they can get in on this.

> Ralf: Hey Bob I see you have
> been doing a lot of stuff with
> buying and selling houses. Haha.
> You win the lottery big fella?
> (Ralf is obviously a jealous peer.
> Time to switch that up)
>
> Bob: Oh heck no, Ralf. I couldn't
> do it if it wasn't for people just
> like you who want to make 12%
> back on their money.
>
> Ralf: I don't make 12% on
> anything.
>
> Bob: Well I'm sorry to hear that.
> I'll tell you how you can.

Look there. Bob just turned Ralf from a hater to a potential private lender. See how quickly that happened? In a flash Bob explained to Ralf that, yes, he is making money but he is not alone.

> Sage: Fiona, can you believe the
> company is not matching our
> 401K any longer?

> Fiona: I am not really worried about it. I put all of my money in a self-directed IRA and earn 12% guaranteed.
>
> Sage: You put your money where and get how much? What are you talking about?

We just learned two things from Fiona.

1. It takes only a second to stir someone's interest in the right situation.
2. You can be your own investor.

That's right. You do not have to look for brand new investors to start. Your investors do not have to have a ton of money stuffed in a mattress. You sometimes have moola right under your nose. Do you have equity in a home? Take out an **HELOC**. (*Home Equity Line Of Credit*) Do you have a 401K or IRA? Move it to a self-directed IRA. We talk more about this later on. The point is to ABC, always be closing....on *capital*.

I was sitting beside an elderly man in court once waiting for my unlawful detainer case against my tenant to be called and I could see that he was extremely agitated and flustered. Every time a case was called he would grow more anxious. Not sure why he is there I am assuming that he is the defendant. Plaintiffs are generally not concerned as much with the outcome of the case. Virginia is a very pro landlord state. If you do not pay you cannot stay.

His case gets called and he is actually the Plaintiff. He goes before the judge with a young couple that did not even bother to dress appropriately for court. The female literally did not even change from her bed clothes. She wore a hugely oversized shirt, what looks like pajama pants to me and has a cloth tied around her head with pink, squishy curlers (or rollers depending on where you are from) peeking out. The gentleman, I am using this term loosely, was told three times while standing there that he needed to pull his pants past his undergarments by the bailiff.

Beside them sits a little, frail, looking old man in a brown suit. His white curls wound close to his ears and around his neck but the top of his head shown if the bright fluorescent lights of the courtroom. He stood clutching his Sunday hat in one hand and a few papers in another.

I could not hear the case but only the ruling. The judge ruled in favor of the defendant. I was sure this was a technicality. I was also sure that if I follow this man out I will miss my own case. I did anyway. I quickly gave him a card and said "I can get your house back for you" and ran back in.

When I came out of court there was already a message on my phone. I listen it sounds like this, "*What? What? Is there someone there? Hello?*" I had a pretty good idea who it was.

I called the number back and identified myself as the lady he met in court. "*You the little lady lawyer?*"

"*No sir. I am an investor but I can help you.*"

He stops for a minute and says "*Hester, I think it's that lady lawyer I told you about.*"

It was very difficult to get his name and address and I am reasonably sure he thinks a "lady lawyer" is coming to the rental property.

I meet with Henry and Hester and find out that they have no idea what they are doing with the property. It was left to him when his brother passed on. It is owned out right but there is debt associated with Henry's brother's last days and they need to pay it off. They are renting the house out for $300 which is the same as the payment arrangement they made with the hospital and Hester is worried that Henry will go to jail if they can't make that payment. They are taking money out of their social security check that should go for their necessities to give to the hospital when the tenants do not pay and they are about 6 months behind. Hester was cutting their pills in half to cut pharmaceutical cost.

The house was worth about $125,000. Market rent was about $1,100. Needless to say they were getting screwed.

I talked to Henry and Hester about getting a **HELOC** for $100,000 and paying off the $20,000 in medical that remained after life insurance paid out the estate. I offered them 12% on the $80,000 if I could invest it. That gave them $800 per month. I also took control of the property via lease purchase with a payment of $800 as soon as I got a new tenant/buyer in the place. Henry and Hester were very relieved to know that they had a preforming asset versus a huge liability. I had their tenants out in 30 days and new ones in in 45 days.

The point of this story? People often have hidden assets they have no idea they even have access to. Henry and Hester had no idea that they could get cash out of the house without selling it. Guess what? When they did sell it they had 100% of the cash I used back leaving them the full sales price of the house in their pockets.

Always look for a potential Private Lender. Do not be afraid to talk about it. What are your parents doing with their equity? What is your neighbor doing with his retirement account? What is your church doing with the *New Wing Fund* to grow their investment and be able to build sooner? You could be an answer for which someone has been looking like, Henry and Hester.

The Back-Up Plan

What happens when you are unable to secure private capital and you have a really awesome deal on the table? You can sell it to another investor. This is called **wholesaling**. Or you can move forward with private financing from a Hard Money Lender.

A **hard money lender** is a person who knows and appreciates the investment potential in funding real estate investors. (S)he will know the security and safety that comes with this type of investment.

Hard money is intended for flipping only as the interest rates are high, there are usually a few points up front, and the terms are short with escalating interest.

A hard money lender is a friend to the investor. Do not let the name fool you. This is not some guy off the Sopranos that is going to rough you up for not having a house sold in time. He wants you to be successful because your success is his success.

In fact, it is actually a good idea to use a hard money lender the first couple of flips. (S)he is very knowledgeable in the mechanics of fix and flip buying. The lender will evaluate your offer and your intended repairs. (S)he will not fund you if you will not make money in the deal.

We were flipping a beautiful American Four Square style home in a transition neighborhood in Highland Springs. We bought the house with a great spread. We had secured a private lender for the renovation cost but with several flips going used a hard money lender named Tom for acquisition.

When we bought the house the only thing we could see that would slow down the sale was a neighbor with a boat parked across the entire front yard. Otherwise, the neighborhood was a mix of nice homes that had been flipped and ones that were a little run down. A transition neighborhood by its definition.

Day 1 of the renovation I meet my contractor, Brandon, out there and am excited to get to work. The neighbor with the boat comes over and ask me if I bought the house. I tell him that I did. He proceeds to tell me all this stuff that he believes to be wrong with it. We had obviously had an inspection and he was incorrect but I thanked him for the information. I let him know that the house will be better than new before we are done. For some reason this angers him and he is getting very agitated. Brandon knows I am a bit feisty at times and believes it is a good idea to come to my rescue before this gets out of hand. Brandon approaches with a hand out and a country charm that calms the Ogre right on down.

Day 2. We have the guys painting the stucco so we have to spray. There is just no way to get in the texture with a roller. They have taken every precaution to not allow for overspray. This is a professional company providing high quality work.

As soon as I pull up Ogre comes running out of his home all upset yelling at me because there is paint on his new truck. You know what? I'd be upset too!!! Heck yea!! Brandon comes running over to smooth out the situation. I walk away. Come to find out the "paint" is pollen and Brandon has agreed to pay for a mobile detailing company to come and clean the pollen off his car. A win for the Ogre.

He consistently complains about the renovation but nothing serious.

The renovation is complete and our realtor puts a sign on the yard. The neighbor puts the biggest confederate flag I have ever seen in his yard. He moves a couch to the front porch and scatters his yard with seating not intended for outdoors or seating at all. Well this sucks. My partner, the nice one, goes and asks him to take it down and clean up the yard. He gets kicked off the property. I try calling the city about the stuff in the yard. Apparently as long as the grass is cut he is in compliance. My analytical partner tries to bribe him. Nothing is changing his mind. It is his mission to make sure we do not sell the house.

When agents bring their clients in to look at the home he waddles over reeking of beer to tell them that he knows for a fact there is structural damage and there was a murder in the house a few years back.

We host an open house and he sits in his yard couch yelling racial jokes at the guest. As long as he is on his land, he is not breaking the law. Hmmmmph!!

So we are having a really hard time selling the house and the winter is coming up. This could be really bad. Being a flipper is like being a settler in the winter. It is a hard time of year if you haven't prepared. Anything you have not sold, you are just going to eat cost. We are having a tough time getting Tom his money back and are concerned that he is going to want to foreclose. Instead, Tom asked us how he could help. What is the issue with the house? And so on. Did he continue to charge us interest? You becha! But he did not want to take the equity we had built. The house was ultimately purchased by a Marine who I am sure did not tolerate Ogre's behavior. We made a little, Tom made a lot. Winners all the way around.

If you are an active investor it is good practice to be friendly with a hard money lender. By friendly, I mean that you should have one that you know and that knows you before you find the deal you want him to fund. They close fast and don't ask for much.

Remember John and his almost super awesome first flip. He had not secured private money nor hard money. How was he going to make this happen in 30 days? I was going to assist him in finding a hard money lender.

You can find hard money lenders at investor and realtor meet up groups. There are also several that are national and available on line. You will need to qualify the flip, not yourself. Most hard money lenders are less concerned with your credit than with the spread on the loan.

Having access to cash quickly is really the name of the game. Having both private money and hard money available to you puts you at a real advantage.

Putting Your Plan to Action

You have learned the key steps to getting your real estate investing business started and are ready to learn the ropes. Remember, this section might be the most important. You have learned how to protect and represent your business. Going forward you will make mistakes but by having the protection in place and the character of your business secure, you will not lose more than the cost of the one mistake.

I have condensed the items you need to complete into a handy checklist for you.

- **Create your LLC**
- **Get an EIN from the IRS**
- **Have an Operating Agreement**
- **Have business cards made**
- **Write your mission statement**
- **Create your Professionalism Packet**
- **Purchase a domain name (web address)**
- **I recommend getting a web based phone system**
- **Find networking groups in your area and attend**
- **Find your team**
  - **Contractor**
  - **Attorney**
  - **Realtor**
  - **Hard money lender**
  - **Accountant**
- **Create a Private Lender Packet**
- **Look for private lenders**

Remember, once you decide to embrace this you are always a real estate investor. You should be "on" all of the time, ready to pitch. You never know who will want to be a private lender or who will be in need of relief from a house that is a burden.

When you are actively interacting as an investor be professional. Dress and act the part. Exude confidence in every interaction.

Protect and preserve the integrity of your business by determining the personality for your baby and nurturing it in every transaction.

Mistakes will be made. Deals will go wrong. You will not always be happy with the outcome of your transaction. Do not be discouraged. Do not give up. You can never win the game if you do not play.

Fair Housing and ADA

I really do not like to start a section with a disclaimer but I am going to do it today. I am not a certified Fair Housing instructor. This training is not in lieu of a fair housing class that is taught and approved by the regulatory authority in your area.

That said, let's jump in.

Prior to April 11, 1968, landlords, realtors, developers, and pretty much everyone involved in the housing industry could decide who lived where based on the personal preferences of the owner or manager.

Looking at this time period, there was a serious need for such laws as the country was ripe with prejudice over a multitude of things. There were communities that would not allow "colored" residents, single mothers, the elderly, and first generation Americans to name a few. This social bias disproportionately impacted the sect of the population most in need. We are all familiar with the racial inequalities of that time but consider for a moment the other situations that were going on. The Vietnam War was raging with American casualties near 60,000. The U.S. was drafting and recruiting young men in droves and their marketing was targeted towards Latin and African American men 18-24 offering housing, job security, and a future for their families in a culture where those things were often nearly impossible for a person of the wrong ethnic or cultural background.

Many of these young men would rush to marry and start a family with their high school sweetheart or current love as the thought of going to war without someone waiting must have seemed unbearable. Imagine being this young wife and mother finding out that your husband has made the ultimate sacrifice. Already overwhelmed with grief at the loss of your husband you then learn that your housing on base will end and you need to go find a place for you and your baby. This seems horribly difficult in the best situation but that's not all, she is also met with the obstacle of finding housing when most landlords have policies against single mothers, unmarried women who are pregnant, and children in general. If she is a minority she may also not be welcome for that reason.

This is just one example of how housing was streamlined by many to be singularly inclusive of white, traditional, Christian families and if you do not fit that mold you are not welcome.

President Lyndon Johnson had tried unsuccessfully to push a follow up to the Civil Rights Act of 1964 many times with opposition in the House and the Senate. After the assassination of the Reverend Martin Luther King Jr. The country was broken and divided. Riots arose throughout the country. Anti-war demonstrations continued, it seemed that most of the country was angry about something. Utilizing the energy of the country as a catalyst, President Johnson was able to get the *Fair Housing Act of 1968* passed and signed into law on April 11, 1968.

This made it illegal on a federal level to discriminate against a person in regard to housing due to race, color, national origin, religion, sex, familial status, or disability. For most of us born in the 70's, 80's, and 90's this seems so obvious, it seems ridiculous to have to tell people not to discriminate. There had been a culture of elitism for so long that it was not viewed as discrimination, just good business.

Women were considered a risk and were not welcome to rent in many communities. Women could not even apply for credit until 1974. They were paid considerably less than men. The rationale for their lower wages was that their employment could be jeopardized by a pregnancy and they would have to go on maternity leave.

Even now I work with older landlords who do not fully grasp the concept of Fair Housing. These are landlords of all races and ethnic backgrounds. I bought a few houses from a man who was retiring and moving to Florida. He wanted to keep one as a rental. This is common and I cannot fathom why since I am offering guaranteed monthly payments with owner financing but it happens all of the time. Back to the point.

In order to secure the rest of his portfolio, I agree to manage his one property. Immediately he starts to call me repeatedly, worried about the "kind" of tenant in the home. He makes reference to national origin, religion, and familial status all in one sentence.

"You check them against national security don't you? I don't want any terrorist in there. No men that look like they are members of the Taliban. " Are you serious? First what does that look like? Second, if I was a member of a terrorist cell trying to cause harm, wouldn't I try to assimilate? Third, do you even hear yourself?

His thought, *"I am an upstanding American who is trying to ensure the safety of those around me."*

He never took the time to put himself in the shoes of the person of whom he is speaking of. What if this man has fled his country due to civil unrest and wants no part of it? What if this man is here on a student visa and is currently working with top minds to create a cure for cancer? Or even just a man who fought to meet the criteria to come to America so that he can work hard, get a good job and practice the religion he chooses?

I had another landlord say, "I don't want anyone there who is a single mother or a couple that is not married." That is clearly not okay.

She herself was a single mother before the kids grew up and knows the struggle. She is thinking, "*I do not want to have to evict a family so I would rather have a stable married couple.*" To that mother who got turned away this could be devastating. She works and has good credit. She pays her bills but is not good enough. If this type of idealism is acceptable she would have no place to go or at least be very limited.

One guy didn't want an overweight person. Seriously???? This shit is real and still happening. I can't even see where this guy was coming from.

In 1990 the *Americans with Disabilities Act* became law and added a broader spectrum to the expectations and definitions of being a disabled person in America. If any of the three landlords above had made those statements to perspective tenants their lives would have been a lot tougher.

If anyone wanted to file a complaint they could go to a civil rights attorney, an activist group in the area, or to the local *HUD* office. Chances are testers would have been sent out to "read" to the owner in question. This means that they will act as a buyer or renter and see if they are getting the same response as the complainant described.

If it is determined that there is a violation, a charge will be filed against the person or entity in question by the U.S. *Department of Housing and Urban Development* (HUD). This will cause them to have to appear in several hearings. Hiring an attorney is strongly recommended.

The HUD site states that one may be fined up to $16,000 in penalties for the first offence and up to $65,000 for subsequent offences. I have heard of higher fines and I am pretty certain that they are a culmination of multiple offences or the same offence with multiple occurrences.

The Department of Justice may also decide to charge the accused as well. Should this occur you will be looking at additional fines and penalties up to $100,000 per offence. That can add up quickly.

The complainant may also bring suit in civil court. In this situation he will be represented by a private attorney who will seek compensation for his client. The complainant might be awarded compensatory damages. These are actual cost incurred as a result of the discrimination. This can include rent for a new place, hotel and storage cost, legal fees, time missed from work if it directly relates to the discrimination, among other costs that maybe incurred from housing discrimination. The attorney will probably also ask for non-economic damages for mental anguish, humiliation, or psychological injuries. These monies are awarded directly to the complainant.

A judge also has the option to impose punitive damages. These are discretionary and are generally imposed if the court feels there is willful and malicious intent. This is paid to the court not to the complainant.

If you are found to be actively in violation of the Fair Housing Act or the Americans with Disabilities Act, an injunction can be placed on your business disallowing continuance until it is lifted. As you can see this is not a mistake you want to make. Fortunately most things do fall into the category of common sense but not all.

The federal law covers Race, Color, National Origin, Religion, Sex, Familial Status, and Disability which is enhanced further by **ADA**.

One may think "*Ok, easy. I am not going to discriminate against anyone.*" Maybe not intentionally but there are many areas that can be gray as we are often dealing with perception.

Race

noun ancestry, birth, breed, class, cultural group, culture, descent, ethnic group, ethnic stock, family, folk, genealogy, genus, group, kind, line, parentage, people, phylum, stem, stirps, stock, strain (as defined by legaldictionary.com)

 The definition above offers a group of singular words to describe what race "is." The question is what does it mean in America today? As most of us are a cultural and ethnic hodgepodge of components it is nearly impossible to identify most of us as a singular race by use of scientific means like genealogy. We can better find our heritage which is not really a protected class but race is protected.

Allow me to give you my best advice. Race is a matter of perception; how one identifies. You are best served to not mention race at all. It has nothing to do with housing. There is no reason for you to offer any advice, opinion, or otherwise in relation to race. Keep it out of your mouth.

Color

1. the quality of an object or substance with respect to light reflected by the object, usually determined visually by measurement of hue, saturation, and brightness of the reflected light; saturation or chroma; hue.
2. 2. the natural appearance of the skin, especially of the face; complexion:
   (as defined by *dictionary.com*)

Color in this context applies to the pigmentation of one's skin. The same advice applies here as above. There is no reason to mention color. Just because we are not mentioning these things does not mean that we will not need to take them into consideration.

National Origin

Noun
1. The nation of one's birth.
(as defined by yahooanswers.com)

National origin refers to the nation which a person was born. This unfortunately is a topic which I feel I need to elaborate upon because in my experience it is the most frequently violated of the protected classes in current times. With the conflict over immigration and worries about terrorism, many landlords are steering away from certain ethnicities. Citizenship or lack thereof is not a protected class. Nationality and being a legal citizen of the United States are not contingent upon one another. One has nothing to do with the other. If you wish to check the citizenship of applicants feel free to do so. Just be warned, if you verify one person's citizenship you better verify every person who applies. You must also have a written policy. Keep in mind also, you can deny applications due to citizenship status within the U.S. but you cannot pick which nationalities are permissible and which are not. It is all or none.

Marketing all-inclusive to the last three protected classes is an extremely important concept in Fair Housing. You must ensure that all persons feel welcome in your community or to buy or rent through your business. When you use forms of marketing that show people having a great time or just living life, be sure that a variety of races, colors, and nationalities are included in this marketing.

Religion

noun re·li·gion \ri-ˈli-jən\
Popularity: Top 1% of lookups

Simple Definition of *religion*

- : the belief in a god or in a group of gods
- : an organized system of beliefs, ceremonies, and rules used to worship a god or a group of gods
- : an interest, a belief, or an activity that is very important to a person or group

(as defined by Merriam-Webster Dictionary)

When we define religion we need to understand that there is a plethora of belief systems and you may or may not agree with them or even acknowledge them. The reality is that religion, as most protected classes, is a matter of perception at times.

Religious discrimination is generally not intended as disrespect to other beliefs but an intended preference to those who are in the same mindset as you. Statements like "Christians Preferred" or "Bring your Torah to waive your security deposit" is a violation of Fair Housing.

Often, religious discrimination is completely unintentional. Have you ever been to a property that is decorated for a religious holiday like Christmas or Easter? Of course you have. We all have. Technically this is a discriminatory practice. If you decide to have a party for your residents in December, call it a Holiday Party or Winter Party. If you want to send out cards to your clients over the holiday season, make them Thank You or Thinking of You cards. Not cards specific to a holiday.

Growing up in a Jehovah's Witness household we celebrated zero holidays. No Christmas, Chanukah, Kwanza, Ramadan, Easter, birthdays, nothing. I do not remember my parents ever being offended by the multiple displays of the holidays. I, as a kid, felt envious but not as though I was being targeted or hated against. Most people I know who practice a less common faith in the area which they are in are not offended by the numerous displays of the holidays which are more popular. There are some who feel that they are being targeted by not being represented. These are the ones we want to be sure not to offend.

There has been a trend of discriminatory practices against the Muslim population as a result of fear in relation to an increase of Muslim extremism in the Middle East and globally. This of course is isolated to the extremist and should in no way be reflected in your day to day business practices.

Take a second to look at this great example of how to violate Fair Housing. I am sure these people do not know that they are advertising in a way that discriminates in two protected classes.

Sex

One's gender, generally male or female.
(defined according to yahooanswers.com)

I feel as though we all know that sex is gender. More and more people and groups have broadened the definition of gender to include hermaphrodite, trans-gender, and trans-sexual. It is unlawful to solicit exclusively for or against any gender. Period.

Familial status is defined as having one

or more individuals under 18 years of age who reside with a parent or with another person with care and legal custody of that individual (including foster parents) or with a designee of that parent or other person with legal custody. (As defined by California Department of Fair Employment and Housing)

This definition simply states that you cannot deny an applicant due to having in their custody minor children. Once upon a time prior to 1968 there were adult only communities where children were not allowed. This is now against the law. Obviously.

Did you know that you cannot offer a "kiddy pool" or "adult only pool" on your property? This discriminates against the familial status of the residents who are not included in that description. If a middle aged resident wants to lay in six inches of water you have to let them.

My neighborhood offers an "owner's pool" as the adult pool. Technically, kids can't own property so they are excluded. Honestly, I am not sure how legal this is but nobody seems to notice or care. The other pool is way more entertaining to children with fountains, slides, and such. No kid wants to go to the smaller, boring pool. I'm pretty sure they could have not named it at all and the result would be the same.

In situations where you have a fitness center or other location where safety is a concern so you wish to keep kids out, the best I can offer is that it is alright, as far as I know, to use the manufacturer recommendations as guidelines. For example if you install a leg press in the gym the manufacturer might have somewhere in the instructions that it is not recommended for children under 16 years of age. There you have a legal age restriction.

You do not have to install a playground or any other facility geared towards children for multi-family properties.

Again, be sure that your marketing material shows children if you are showing people.

Disability is **defined** as any person who has a physical or mental impairment that substantially limits one or more major life activities; has a record of such impairment; or is regarded as having such impairment. Life activities include walking, talking, hearing, seeing, breathing, learning, performing manual tasks, and caring for oneself. (as defined by ADA.gov)

We probably thought that we all knew what a disability was but the definition is a broad one that has grown and evolved over time through litigation, settlements, and advocacy. First I want to point out the discrepancy in the definition above. It says that one must have a record of impairment OR be regarded as having such impairment. What does that mean? I have heard that argued two ways.

1. If an impairment is obvious you are not to ask for verification. If a man comes to you in a wheelchair as an amputee and asks for a modified unit you need not request verification from his physician that he needs that unit.
2. The other argument here is that one cannot ask for verification at all. If a man walks in to your office, teaches you the wobble, and asks for a wheelchair accessible apartment you need to give him one. When I managed a rather large portfolio of affordable housing apartment complexes this was a real issue as you are required to provide reasonable accommodations and reasonable modifications for disabled persons. I left that decision up to the owners of the properties as

ultimately it was them who bore the brunt of a wrong decision. I would recommend that if you are planning to deal with multi-family properties; consult an attorney that specializes in ADA for your area.

ADA requires that an owner make reasonable accommodations and reasonable modifications for disabled persons if they request. Allow me to point out that you are not to ask if they need any modification or accommodation nor if they have a disability. This can be considered humiliating or disrespectful to some and whilst meaning well you can get into hot water.

You cannot always see a disability and some may surprise you. An example is a person with chronic alcoholism or a person who is or was the victim of domestic abuse. These are considered a disability under ADA in some, if not all, areas.

I had a Vietnam Veteran who was a double amputee and wanted an apartment. I had no first floor units available. I have to be careful how I tell him that I do not have a first floor unit available. I say "*I can show you the two that I have available. They are second floor. Does your preference include a second floor unit?*" He says that it does.

This guy is a real hero if you ask me. His body was forever changed by a land mine at age 19 but never his spirit. He had a positive attitude about his life and there was no obstacle that ever stood in his way. When I thanked him for his service he told me that he was thankful for the opportunity to serve his country.

He was all smiles as we get to the building. He hopped right out of the chair and pulled himself up the stairs with his hands. He took the apartment.

I began a policy of letting my tenants know of all units becoming available as a part of the news letter stating "*you*

can refer a friend or come see me if you are looking for a change of scenery."
He never came to me.

He was in that apartment for years. He was still there when I left. Happy as a lark.

A reasonable accommodation is a change in policy to accommodate a person's specific need. An example of that would be; your tenant has to pull the trash can to a central location for pick up. The tenant is unable due to Muscular Dystrophy. You should then have maintenance pick it up or negotiate an arrangement with the trash company to pick up the trash at the door. Please note that service animals are always accepted and do not have to be registered as such. There is no pet fee or deposit for this animal and you need only the word of the tenant. You can require that the animal is up to date on all shots and meets registration of any pet as put forth by the municipality of residence. Typically this is a $10 dog license and a rabies shot.

Personally, I make rent due on the 25th (payable in advance) and late on the 1st. On that day a 10% late fee is imposed. Disability benefits are paid on the 3rd of each month. When I send out pay or quit notices, the first step in collection in VA, I have a paragraph that explains that if they are receiving a majority of their income from any form of disability payment (SSDI, Disabled Veteran's Benefits) I will take a copy of the COLA (cost of living allowance) statement or benefit form letter and adjust the due date to accommodate the date monies are received.

A reasonable modification is a physical alteration to the property to better assist the tenant with access to and use of the facilities and property. A few examples include wheel chair ramps, visual smoke detectors, and doorbells. The modification can be big or small. If you need to modify a home to meet the accessibility needs of a wheel chair bound resident you may have to build ramps, lower light switches, sinks, and counters, widen doors, install grip bars in the bathrooms, and even increase the size of the restroom to meet ADA's turn radius standard.

Buildings built after March 13, 1991 with 4 or more units and an elevator are required to have common areas that are compliant with ADA guidelines as well as units which are wheelchair accessible. I am not going to go into all of the guidelines but please be sure to consult with an ADA specialist as the guidelines are very specific. This will include guidelines on how many handicap spots are required, how many sidewalk ramps are needed and the acceptable rise of a ramp added to a building (1:12 btw).

STATE LAWS

Additionally your state may have additional protected classes included in their Fair Housing Act.

Familial status is in some areas considered to only mean that you cannot deny the applicant with children. Other states wish it to be all inclusive to include marital status. Many states specifically list marital status as a protected class. This means you cannot make divorced, separated, widowed, married, or single a requirement or disqualifier.

Another protected class in at least DC is familial responsibilities. This can include anything from talking care of an aging parent to having child support payments due. These factors cannot be considered in the eligibility of the applicant.

Sexual orientation, affectional orientation, gender identity or expression are included in many states. Honestly, if you are in an investor mindset, the last thing you care about when it comes to solving the problem of vacancy is who your tenant kisses goodnight or who they see when they look in the mirror.

This is a hot topic right now though as many persons feel that being inclusive of this group may interfere with their rights to practice their religion as they see fit. The law in many areas disagrees with that. More and more legislation in this matter on state levels is occurring. I would not be surprised if this hits a national level soon. My best advice is this, if you are a person who feels that you are personally disrespecting your faith by being inclusive to the LGBT community, you might want to just hire a property management company or realtor to sell or lease your homes. I believe that you may find yourself on the news in a negative light if not.

Several states, including California, Connecticut, and Washing ton DC, include source of income as a protected class. Some differentiate between legal sources and just any source. Some do not. Since criminal history is not a protected class I think if someone applies for housing and states their source of income as "Street Pharmaceutical Sales" you can dig a little deeper. Otherwise, you cannot discern between an exotic dancer and neurosurgeon making the same amount of money based on income source. You will have to look at other factors.

Many states consider age as a protected class. This comes in several contexts. In states like Connecticut, Delaware, and DC age means and person alive over 18.

Pennsylvania has a requirement for persons 40 and over. On a personal level, Virginia holds elderliness as a protected class. So in Pennsylvania and Virginia you can set a minimum age but not a maximum age.

Hawaii and New Jersey both have made persons with HIV and AIDS a protected class. I dare to say that these same people are protected as a disabled person in all states.

Rhode Island has made victims involved in or previously involved in situations of domestic violence a protected class. How would a person who is being abused also be discriminated against?

I am showing a house to a lady named Ruby who tells me at first that she is an investor looking for a house that she can get with about $12,000 down no credit check. That's what I do so, cool. I am looking at this woman with a disheveled appearance, no make-up, and hair that is wiry and unkempt. She walks with great caution through the home. As an investor, I know what we look for and at. We will check the structural and mechanical components of the house not the living space.

She is continuously wringing her hands beneath the dirty sleeves of her tan Disney sweatshirt. The cuffs frayed and stained, I suspect from her continued nervous twitch. Her eyes dart nervously as she mouths her thoughts to herself. I am certain of two things. That she is not an investor and that she is in need of help.

I do not want to impose so rather I ask her a bit about the type of investing she does. After offering an answer off of an infomercial she stops for a second and looks me in the eyes. I can feel the connection of energy or empathy or something as she tells me with her eyes that something is bad. Really bad.

"*Ruby, do you need help*?" I ask.

I can immediately see a veil of relief wash over her. Her face suddenly looks 10 years younger, her posture corrects, and a twinge of a smile stirs across her lips for just a brief moment before she speaks. She shares with me how she and her son are living with her husband who is abusive to her and sometimes her son. She tells me that for the past decade she has not been allowed to work, how she and her son were forced to go on disability. She is allotted a certain amount of money for household necessities like groceries and utilities. She never sees the bank card or check book, only cash for which she has a strict budget. She is allowed access to transportation one day a week although they have two vehicles. On that day she has to complete the list of errands he requires and be home before her son arrives at 3:15. She has been hiding money for a decade longing to get away. Paralyzed by fear for years she has continued to save a dollar here, five dollars there up to what she believes is around $12,000.

Today she is scared but she is strong. She is going to leave and I am going to help her. She asks me to follow her to her house to get her money and her son. This is not the best idea as we know that we are already dealing with an unstable, violent man. I am no help if I am lying in a pool of blood beside her.

I want to point out that by now I have obviously matured past the girl who intentionally walked into a property that could have been the inspiration for House of a Thousand Corpses. I have begun, ever so slightly to have a sense of self-preservation but I am still a hungry investor.

Ruby lets me know that if she leaves without me she will not come back as she has never been able to follow through before. I agree to go.

I call my two male partners to let them know that I am going there. I also call my best guy friend who happens to be a cop and tell him my location. None of these men seem to have an ounce of concern for my safety. My partners are like "Good work. Get that money." And my friend is like "*K, are we going to do something Saturday?*"

We pull down a side street in a very affluent part of the county and drive down a tree lined road. The scene is picturesque, sprawling estates with stone or brick fences. Grass so green St. Patrick's Day would get jealous. The trees seem to bend in to greet each other, as if shaking hands along the way.

At the end of this street is one small, rundown, shack. The color escapes me as it all looked gray and decayed in my mind's eye today. The skeletal remains of cars long past scatter the large open lot peering through the overgrown weeds. She turns in the drive ahead of me stirring up an excessive amount of dust, enough for me to have to close my car windows.

I park my car beside an old barrel; the kind used as a burn barrel in the south. Inside is the murky blackish liquid of old motor oil and rain water. The remains of an animal float partially in the sludge. Maybe a squirrel, maybe a kitten. I am not sure. I was not about to investigate.

I follow Ruby in through the back door. Death metal music blares from down the hall. The stench of a bachelor pad fridge that has not been cleaned out in a couple of years smacks you dead in the face. It takes a moment for me to realize that I was in a kitchen for all of the piles of trash, dirty plates and rotten food. I see a refrigerator hiding amongst the debris. It is the only indication.

A shirtless kid with a striking resemblance to Harry Potter darts down the hall with a pentagram spray painted on the back of old Christmas wrap. Completely unaware of who I am, he tells me that he plans to sell his art online. I offer encouragement and follow his mother into her bedroom.

I am feeling very uneasy about this whole situation. My head is spinning with the realization that this psychotic husband could arrive at any moment and here I am in his home. He could kill me and probably have them trained enough to tell the authorities that I was attacking the kid or something.

In the bedroom, the obvious signs of hording continue to grow. The bed has only a comforter on the bed, no sheets. Ruby flings back the comforter and empty cans of Spaghettio's and Vienna Sausages fly off of the bed and ting against the dresser. Exposed is a large blood stain, more than can happen by accident, right there on the mattress. I am flooded with a barrage of emotion. Fear.

Is this a family that lures people back by pretending that they need help to kill them? Empathy. If they are not serial killers, this blood must be Ruby's. God, how can she live this way? Concern. What about this boy? What will he become? He needs to be away from this environment. Anxiety. What if this psycho comes home? Panic. I need to get out of here!!!

I manage to keep my composure and professionalism as Ruby digs through a pile of dirty laundry and trash to pull out a Crown Royal Bag. She stands up quickly looking very impressed with herself. "*Here it is!*" she says.

It is a bag of money. A Crown Royall bag of money. It is stuffed to the brim with ones and fives. She dumps it out on the bloody bed. She wants to count it there! Wtf???!!!

I say that we can count it at the new place. I even say that I will give her credit for the full $12,000 even if it is not. No. She insists on counting it there.

My heart is pounding, I am sweating, and the stench is overwhelming. I feel nauseous. I keep thinking that this is what they do. Bring a woman who is trying to help back to the house and count money until he gets home to kill me.

She counts it once. $8,848. She counts it again. $9873. She counts it a third time. $7417. I can't take it any longer!!! I have to go!!!! I think I have been there an hour. This maniac could be home at any second.

"Look Ruby, I have another appointment. I will give you credit for $10,000 which is more than any of the times you counted, give you keys, and let the bank count the money. If it is more than $10,000 I will take the difference off the payments if it is less than $10,000 I will eat the difference. Cool?"

She looks at me baffled as though the whole concept of my offer completely evades her. I want to help but I want to live. I have to get out of this hell house.

"*OK*" she finally replies.

Thank Gooooodddddd!!!!!!!!! Let's roll!

As part of our application process we offer considerable consideration to criminal history and a little to credit for our owner financed homes. I have to pull hers, due to Fair housing, even though I have decided that I am putting her in this house regardless.

Come to find out there have been many calls to the police for domestic disturbances and her credit was ruined when she was forced to quit her job and apply for disability. Additionally her husband opened numerous credit lines in her name and defaulted.

This is exactly why some states recognize domestic abuse victims as a protected class. Some other protected statuses are receipt of public assistance, matriculation, personal appearance, and political affiliation.

Best Practices

You now know the history, meaning, and consequences of Fair Housing and ADA, also known in the industry as compliance laws. We have touched on how to avoid violations. The way you conduct business EVERYDAY will be impacted by these laws. You want to be sure that you implement a written policy that is inclusive to all aspects of these guidelines. Below we will both review and touch on a few new concepts.

- Take a fair housing training class and require that anyone who will represent your company take one as well. Any person, employee or non-employee, that represents your company can cause issue for you in this regard.
- Be sure all persons are represented in all printed material. You should use a wide range of race, color, ethnicity, and age in your advertising. Never mention any religion in any printed material.
- Use the Fair Housing and ADA logos on everything! See below.

- Have a written policy on tenant acceptance and adhere to it strictly.
- Do not recognize any holidays through marketing or decorating.

- If you have a multifamily property built after 1991, be sure that the common areas meet ADA guidelines.
- Always allow service animals. Period!!
- Keep a record of who views your properties, who applies, and who is denied.
- Never give any opinion on how "good" a neighborhood is or is not.

I know this section seems a bit scary and menacing but once you have a full concept of the rules and guidelines of Fair Housing and ADA it just becomes second nature. Really. Piece of cake. Just cake, not German Chocolate Cake, a birthday cake, or lady fingers because that may violate fair housing.   Just kidding.

For more information regarding fair housing and ADA please see www.ada.gov, www.hud.gov, and www.justice.gov

Accounting

Being an investor means that you are a business owner, just like if you owned a McDonalds. You will need to make wise choices as to the financial aspect of each transaction. You will need to be able to prepare your budget and implement it. You will need to be able to track your income and debts. This is the only way to know which investments are assets or liabilities.

Once you decide to become an investor you will want to know how to evaluate a deal, understand what figures really mean for your bottom line, and budget reasonably to ensure that your experience runs as smoothly as possible.

When you are looking for property, a limited partner, venture capital, private funding, or an investor you will hear terms like *ROI, NOI*, and *IRR*. They will want to see your operating budget if you are looking for a significant amount. Some of you may have a solid grasp of what these terms mean, some may not. This is a numbers section. All math. This is a necessity of business.

I was working for a management company with two apartment complexes that I managed. I came in and rocked that place! It was a section 8 property that was transitioning from project base to housing choice vouchers. This means that in the past you could come there and if you were considered low income you could get an apartment with government subsidy for all or some of your rent payment. The transition meant that the tenants would now receive a voucher that they could take anywhere for the same subsidy. The owners were worried that the tenants would take the voucher and run. This was a layered property meaning that it was also operating under the guidelines for *LIHTC*, which we will discuss later.

Another issue was with keeping the residents willing to share their financial information even though it no longer impacted their rent. This would cause the property to fail the annual audits and lose funding at best.

The property was at 80% occupancy which is horrible for any property, especially one with section 8. The delinquency was through the roof as the *PHA* (public housing authority) owed thousands of dollars. The tenants were responsible for a small portion of rent based on their income. Many had never paid.

Anyway, I came in and increased the occupancy to 99.4% on average and decreased the delinquency to 3%. I collected the back payments from the PHA not only for my properties but a few others as well. I threw Recertification Parties to make people *want* to come recertify for LIHTC. I made improvements to the interior and exterior of the buildings and grounds, even doing the planting myself as I had no budget for labor. This is probably why I was not fired for my reckless accounting practices.

The company I had worked for in the past was a small company with one bi-polar dude and three apartment complexes. I managed them all with his lazy, crazy daughter as the leasing agent in one property and his 16 year old son as my maintenance supervisor. We had no real accounting practices. I gave the checks to the owner after marking them paid on the ledger and wrote what I bought on the receipts. That was it.

Fast forward to this 'real' company. I was responsible for the things a property manager should be responsible. I was always miscoding receipts and expenses, losing receipts, and taking too long to make deposits. #shouldabeenfired

Rents were entered in batches as they were collected. I would do a batch in the morning before I opened the office of everything that was in the drop box and another at the end of the day before I supposedly went to the bank; which often did not happen for a few days.

One fine day I entered my morning batch and afternoon batch, each with separate deposit tickets as per policy. I grabbed the batches from several days before, shoved them all in my purse and jetted for the bank. This was a Friday which happened to be a beautiful day. I could not wait to GTFO.

Commonsense tells you that you

1. Count the batches.
2. Re-add the amounts for each one.
3. Add all of the amounts together to be sure that you made a complete deposit.

Did I do this? Absolutely not!! I just went to the bank, pulled out the batches, handed them to the teller and jetted. Peace out biotches!!

I go to an outdoor concert series and drink some beer that night; I'm all pleased that I got out a little early. Went to a night club after. Still happy with myself. Probably went to an after-hours club. Who knows I was twenty something.

In my exciting endeavors of the weekend I find a Fossil purse at a trendy garage sale in the Fan. Going to work on Monday with a new purse. Woo hoo! My old one has a rip in the liner anyway and I kept losing my eyeliner in there so its double awesome.

It's the following Wednesday and the head from accounting calls me to say we are short about $3400 in deposits. Hmmmm… That's weird. We realize that a batch was not deposited. I tear up my office looking for the batch. Where is this money???!!! I do not have $3400 to pay this back.

Finally in a last ditch effort I went home to look in my old purse. There it is all tucked into the rip in the lining. Sitting in there all nice and cozy just looking at me.

I learned two lessons while signing my write up that day. Take the time to do things right the first time. This money shit is important. And, do not buy purses the same place you buy tampons. The liner will rip and you will think you are getting fired. *#blamethepurse*

ROI

ROI is Return On Investment and it is generally the starting point for determining the value of an investment. If you are planning to buy, lease, sell, or wholesale property you should also familiarize yourself with this calculation.

There are several ways to calculate ROI. The Cost Method is a more conservative way to calculate the return on investment. I recommend using the cost method when you are purchasing. The Equity Method shows a higher rate of return. This is most likely what the seller is using to show you the value. Finally, the Out of Pocket Method is used for financed properties.

You are looking at a property that cost $100,000 and needs about $10,000 in renovation. The ARV is $175,000. You are looking at $1000 for a cash closing versus $3000 for a financed close. The tax and insurance are roughly $200. The market rent is $1000.

The cost method would tell you that you will be in $111,000 if you pay cash. Your rent is $1000 but you know that you will have taxes and insurance on the property which works out to being about $200. Take the tax and insurance out of the monthly rent to equal $800 making an annual return of $9600. Divide the annual return by the initial investment to get the cash method ROI.

$$\$9600/111,000=.086 \quad ROI= 8.6\%$$

The Equity Method is best is you if are a wholesaler or dealing with a wholesaler. This also works for flipping. This measures projected equity against the cost. It looks like this.

$$\frac{After\ Repair\ Value- Out\ of\ Pocket\ Cost}{Out\ of\ Pocket\ Cost} = ROI$$

What that equates to here in a cash deal based on the same numbers as above looks like this.

$$\$175,000-111,000=65,000$$

$$65000/111000= .5855$$

$$ROI = 59\%$$

The Out of Pocket Method is used in determining ROI on a property that is being financed. If you are buying that same property with a loan through a bank you will be required to put 20% down and hope to be financed at a rate of 4% for a monthly payment of $381 on a 30 year amortization. Your tax and insurance escrows are still $200 per month and your rent is still $1000.

You will calculate the ROI based on two calculations. First is the rent. How much are we actually making in rent? We will add the monthly payment and the escrow to equal $581. We will deduct that from the rent for a profit of $419 per month. Multiply that by 12 months for an annual income of $5028.

Second you will need to calculate how much you are invested in cash. You put down 20% on $100,000, so that is $20,000. Closing cost equaled $3,000. You have put a total of $23,000 of cash in. Plus you had $10,000 in renovation. Now you are in $33,000.

You will calculate the ROI by dividing your annual income by the out of pocket costs. It looks like this.

Annual Projected Income

Out of Pocket Cost   = ROI

381+200=581 Mortgage + Escrow

1000-581=419 Rent Profit

419 x 12=5028 Annual Return

20,000+10,000+3,000=33,000 Out of Pocket Cost

5028/33,000= .1523

ROI = 15%

As you can see, the method for calculating ROI determines the outcome. When you are looking at ROI as presented to you by a seller it is best if you clarify the method and verify the numbers.

NOI / Proforma

NOI or Net Operating Income is your annual income after all sources are considered less the expenses. This is the same for single family as it is for multifamily.

NOI is positive if you earn more than the cost to maintain the property. NOI is negative if it cost more to maintain than is earned. Most of us will always want to have a positive NOI. However, sometimes in very complex and integrated portfolios one may wish to have a property with a negative NOI. This is often referred to as a dump property or offset property. We are going to focus on maintaining a positive NOI.

NOI is based on past performance whereas Proforma is based on projected numbers. Otherwise they are identical.

NOI =	Potential Rental Income
	-Vacancy and delinquency
	Effective Rental Income + Other Income = Gross
	Operating Income –Operating Expenses = **NOI**

Let's say that you are looking at a single family home as a rental with a rental income of $1,000 per month. You see that the home has an average of vacancy of 30 days a year, roughly 8%. You will pay a management company 10% to manage the property. You expect 10% in maintenance and repairs. The property has a billboard on the back that faces the highway that rents out for $350 per month on a long term lease. You cover electric since the sign is metered with the building which runs roughly $150 per month. We are now going to figure out the NOI for this property. First we need to understand what we are calculating.

Potential Rental Income is the sum of all rents if there was 100% occupancy for the year. You will use lease amounts plus planned increases for NOI and market rent for proforma. So for this property it is $12000.

$12000

–Vacancy and delinquency

Effective Rental Income + Other Income = GOI (Gross Operating Income)

Gross Operating Income –Operating Expenses = NOI

Vacancy and delinquency (or credit losses) are what is reasonable to expect to lose from the afore number based on past history for NOI or on market statistics for proforma. We said for this property it is 8%. $960.

$12000

–$960

Effective Rental Income +   Other Income = GOI

Gross Operating Income –Operating Expenses = NOI

Effective rental income is the potential rental income less the vacancy and delinquency.

$12000

-$960

$11,040 + Other Income = GOI −OE = NOI

Other income is any other income source that exist on the property. On this property it is the billboard in the back at a rate of $350 per month. Other income can include gym fees, parking, vending, laundry, and so on.

$12000

-$960

$11,040 + $4,200 = GOI −OE = NOI

Gross Operating Income is your effective rental income plus your other income.

$12000

-$960

$11,040 + $4,200 = $15,420 −OE = NOI

Operating expenses are what you spend to maintain the daily operations of the property. For this example you will use management cost at 10% of collected rents, maintenance and repair at 10% of potential rental income, plus the electric at $150 per month.

$11040

X   0.9

$1104

management fees

$12,000

X   .9

$1200

maintenance and repair

$150

X 12

$1800

electric

1104 + 1200 + 1800 = $4104

$12000

-$960

$11,040 +$4,200 = $15,420 -$4104 = **NOI**

NOI is calculated by deducting Operating Expense from the Gross Operating Income.

$12000

-$960

$11,040+$4,200 = $15,420-$4104 = $11,316

There are things that are not included in NOI but are included in the budget. The cost of your financing is not included as it is dependent upon the situation of the investor. Deprecation is not actual cash but rather an accounting entry. Income taxes are again dependent upon the situation of the investor(s). Tenant improvements, which are specific to commercial properties, are going to vary greatly as this is the alterations and renovations needed for a business to utilize the space for the needs of the business. If a restaurant is moving into a space where a hair salon once was the investor will probably be responsible for the rough in and structural necessary. Commissions and bonuses are also not considered as these are discretionary. Capital expenditures are not included however replacement reserves are optional. This makes no sense to me as the replacement reserves are to pay for capital expenditures.

Capital expenditures are big ticket items like a roof or HVAC. Replacement reserves are set-aside funds for said items.

NOI is a tool used in calculating the value of your investment for lenders, buyers and investors. It is a good idea to make this part of your annual accounting for each property. You can, and should, keep NOI records and proforma predictions on properties obtained through creative financing as well.

Here is an example of NOI and Proforma for a multi-family property. As you can see the actual numbers are used for several years (NOI) and the data from previous years are used to generate a reasonable estimate for future earnings (Proforma)

End of Year	1	2	3	4	5	6	7	8	9	10
	4/29/2013	4/29/2014	4/29/2015	4/29/2016	4/29/2017	4/29/2018	4/29/2019	4/29/2020	4/29/2021	4/29/2022
Bay 1	$57,500	$58,075	$58,656	$59,242	$62,493	$62,500	$62,500	$62,500	$62,500	$62,500
Bay 2	$116,250	$117,412	$118,587	$119,772	$120,970	$122,180	$123,402	$124,636	$125,882	$127,141
POTENTIAL RENTAL INCOME	$173,750	$175,488	$177,242	$179,015	$183,463	$184,680	$185,902	$187,136	$188,382	$189,641
General Vacancy	($12,162)	($12,284)	($12,407)	($12,531)	($12,842)	($12,928)	($13,013)	($13,100)	($13,187)	($13,275)
Turnover Vacancy	$0	$0	$0	$0	($10,417)	$0	$0	($10,417)	$0	$0
EFFECTIVE RENTAL INCOME	$161,588	$163,203	$164,835	$166,484	$160,204	$171,752	$172,889	$163,620	$175,195	$176,366
Property Taxes	($30,000)	($30,600)	($31,212)	($31,836)	($32,473)	($33,122)	($33,785)	($34,461)	($35,150)	($35,853)
Insurance	($5,000)	($5,000)	($5,000)	($5,000)	($5,000)	($5,050)	($5,050)	($5,050)	($5,050)	($5,050)
Maintenance	($20,000)	($20,200)	($20,402)	($20,606)	($20,812)	($21,020)	($21,230)	($21,443)	($21,657)	($21,874)
Total Expenses	($55,000)	($55,800)	($56,614)	($57,442)	($58,285)	($59,193)	($60,065)	($60,953)	($61,857)	($62,776)
NET OPERATING INCOME	$106,588	$107,403	$108,221	$109,042	$101,919	$112,560	$112,823	$102,666	$113,338	$113,590
Bank Loan	($55,436)	($55,436)	($55,436)	($55,436)	($55,436)	($55,436)	($55,436)	($55,436)	($55,436)	($490,987)
Leasing Commissions	$0	$0	$0	$0	($11,250)	$0	$0	($11,250)	$0	$0
Reversion	$0	$0	$0	$0	$0	$0	$0	$0	$0	$850,000
CASH FLOW BEFORE TAX	$51,151	$51,967	$52,785	$53,605	$35,233	$57,123	$57,387	$35,980	$57,902	$472,603

Cap Rate

Cap Rate or Capitalization Rate is used to determine the profitability of a rental property. This is the method widely used in buying, selling, marketing, and funding a property that is intended to be used exclusively as a rental. This is a simple calculation. It is widely accepted that a cap rate of 9% or above is a good investment.

Simply you divide the NOI by the cost. Using the example above, the NOI is $11,316. You paid $100,000.

11316/100000=.113 The Cap rate is 11.3%. This would be considered a good investment.

IRR

IRR or Internal Rate of Return is a profitability metric used in determining if a project will be profitable and how much so. This is rarely used as an investor, especially in single family. Every once in a while you may have a request for IRR when you are seeking venture capital, private money, or limited partnerships. You do not want to stand there like a deer in headlights. You want to at least be able to comment. Luckily there is an IRR function in excel so we do not have to learn how to calculate it. We just need be informed on it.

Pretend if you will that you are looking at an investment on a land development that requires $250,000 as an initial investment for land acquisition, surveying and plotting, road creation, bringing utilities to the lots, and so on. You are selling lots at $25,000 per. You know that once you begin the project you will be in a position to sell only 4 the first year. You are planning to be able to sell 2 more than the last for the next 5 years until all of the lots are sold. The first year you sell 4, the second year you sell 6, and so on.

DEVELOPMENT YEAR	SOLD	INCOME FROM SALES
1	4	$100,000
2	6	$150,000
3	8	$200, 000
4	10	$250,000
5	12	$300,000

You need an investor to back you on this deal. She wants to know the IRR. Here is how you calculate it using excel, as there is no reason to memorize this formula.

In A1 place the initial investment. This is a negative number. -250,000

In A2-A6 place the earnings for each year. These will be positive numbers. 100,000, 150,000….

A7, go to function. Under accounting, select IRR. Done. The IRR is 57%.

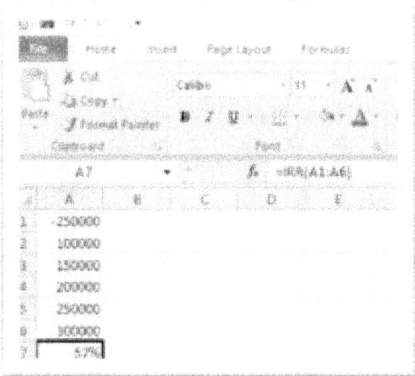

Budget

Having an operating budget on any property is a must. It matters not if this property is a single family, multi family, or mixed use. You need a budget for rentals, lease purchases, and owner financed properties in your portfolio.

A budget for your asset is no different than a budget for your home. You know you bring home X so you have to decide how much gets spent where.

If you bring home $2400 per month and your rent is $1000. You are left with $1400 for your other bills and so on. Below is a rough example of what this may look like except that you will want to be much more detailed.

ITEM	AMOUNT	BALANCE
PAYCHECK	+$2400	$2400
RENT	-$1000	$1400
UTILITIES	-$120	$1280
GROCERIES	-$240	$1040
GAS/TRANSPORTATION	-$100	$940
SAVINGS	-$240	$600

The budget for your asset is the same concept. You will know from this budget how much you can spend on marketing, repairs, renovations... You will also know what you actually stand to make.

A budget must be way more detailed than an NOI. You will be very specific in incoming and outgoing monies. I recommend using general ledger codes (gl codes) to assign a classification to all debts and incomes. This will assist you in tracking your budget as well as making tax time much easier.

You can get a list of gl codes online. I suggest you set up your accounting before you invest in anything.

General Budget

You will want to have a general operating budget. This is what it cost you to stay in business. Include your cell phone, landline (Millennials, some of us still have those ok?), wifi, marketing, and so on. You will know how much you need to pay your business for it to function.

If you are planning on having large multi-family properties I would suggest hiring a management company and letting them set these things up for you. There is a whole lot more involved with one 100 unit multifamily building than 100 single family homes in regard to maintenance and management.

The general budget for an investor is somewhat different than that of most other businesses. I utilize this really as a statement of outgoing expenses and a way to keep track of that.

The budget should be broken down into categories. You will have the option to tweak them as you deem necessary for your business. These will be the things required for basic functionality of your business. I use Office, Marketing, Legal, Professional Services, and Misc. This is very basic. For things that have a one-time occurrence you can either divide it by 12 to escrow or make it a one-time cost in the month it is due.

You will then determine the items in each section. Office should include space (if you have it), your cell phone(s), web based phone system, internet, any accounting, marketing, or rental software you buy, fees for running credit on applicants, web cost, office supplies, and gas and maintenance for your vehicle. You may have a few others as well.

Marketing includes buying list, yellow letters, yellow signs, having the signs written and placed if you chose not to do it, business cards, memberships to networking groups, budget for libations at networking mixers, charity events you attend to make connections, printed material, printed signs, and any other advertising or branding expense you incur regularly. This whole paragraph was one huge run-on sentence. ☺

The budget for Legal includes more than just what you pay your lawyer. This does not include the closing cost for property purchase or sales. That will be included in property specific budgets. We do want to include the cost of the creation and annual maintenance of any LLCs you own. You will probably have more than one or two although you may operate under one umbrella. Fair housing training for you and your staff can fall in here. Any business licenses you are required to purchase based on your locality should be included. General legal work to include if you are being sued or suing someone should be considered here.

Professional services include your accountant, continued education, marketing or branding consulting, and so on.

Miscellaneous is anything that does not fit in the other categories.

The general budget here is inclusive of the possibilities of the things you may want to add. Remember, if you are working from an almost zero budget, many of these things can wait. Don't panic.

General Budget

Office	Jan	Feb	March	April	May	June	July	Aug	Sept	Oct	Nov	Dec	Annual
Office Space	400	400	400	400	400	400	400	400	400	400	400	400	4800
Electric	120	120	110	65	80	100	120	120	80	75	75	110	1175
Internet/landline	150	150	150	150	150	150	150	150	150	150	150	150	1800
Ring Central	38	38	38	38	38	38	38	38	38	38	38	38	456
Cell Phones	338	338	338	338	338	338	338	338	338	338	338	338	4056
Domain Name	1.1	1.1	1.1	1.1	1.1	1.1	1.1	1.1	1.1	1.1	1.1	1.1	13.2
Web Hosting	30	30	30	30	30	30	30	30	30	30	30	30	360
Office Supplies	150	150	150	150	150	150	150	150	150	150	150	150	1800
Gas	120	120	120	120	120	120	120	120	120	120	120	120	1440
Vehicle Maintenance	160	160	160	160	160	160	160	160	160	160	160	160	1920
Total	1507.1	1507.1	1497.1	1452.1	1467.1	1487.1	1507.1	1507.1	1467.1	1462.1	1462.1	1497.1	17820

Marketing	Jan	Feb	March	April	May	June	July	August	Sept	Oct	Nov	Dec	Annual
List	150	150	150	150	150	150	150	150	150	150	150	150	1800
Yellow Lettrs	250	250	250	250	250	250	250	250	250	250	250	250	3000
Yellow Signs & Frames	16	16	16	16	16	16	16	16	16	16	16	16	192
Copy cat printing	24	24	24	24	24	24	24	24	24	24	24	24	288
WIRE Networking	8	8	8	8	8	8	8	8	8	8	8	8	96
RING Networking	8	8	8	8	8	8	8	8	8	8	8	8	96
Miser Misc	150	150	150	150	150	150	150	150	150	150	150	150	1800
Charitble donations	50	50	50	50	50	50	50	50	50	50	50	50	600
Print cost	25	25	25	25	25	25	25	25	25	25	25	25	300
Signs (printed)	10	10	10	10	10	10	10	10	10	10	10	10	120
Total	691	691	691	691	691	691	691	691	691	691	691	691	8292

Legal	Jan	Feb	March	April	May	June	July	August	Sept	Oct	Nov	Dec	Annual
New LLC Creation	750						750						1500
LLC Renewal	1200												1200
DPOR	150												150
General Retainer Legal	2500												2500
Total	4600	0	0	0	0	750	0	0	0	0	0	0	5350

Professional Services	Jan	Feb	March	April	May	June	July	August	Sept	Oct	Nov	Dec	Annual
Accounting	200	200	200	200	200	200	200	200	200	200	200	200	2400
Tax Preperation	350	350	1000										1700
Continued Education	100	100	100	100	100	100	100	100	100	100	100	100	1200
Total	650	650	1300	300	300	300	300	300	300	300	300	300	5300

Misc	Jan	Feb	March	April	May	June	July	August	Sept	Oct	Nov	Dec	Annual
Petty Cash	500	500	500	500	500	500	500	500	500	500	500	500	6000
Total	500	500	500	500	500	500	500	500	500	500	500	500	6000
													0
												Total exp	24942
													0

Flip Budget

When flipping a house you should already have a really good projection of the broad picture of cost and profitability. With the budget you will want to really break down the cost for each aspect of the flip. It is one thing to say "I am going to spend $40,000 on the rehab on this house" Ok. Great. On what? Where is the money actually going?

You have made the list of renovations you plan to make. Outline that with your projected prices, what you expect to pay for each item. Gather bids on completing those items and create your budget from there. Below is an example of one I used years ago.

Description of work	Estimate	Inspection price	A Notch Above	Jerry Pope	Tom Mount	Bee Jay Carpenter	Lowes	Peacock painting	accepted bid
Add Trim to Front Window	$125.00		$125.00						$125.00
Paint outside windows and doors	$525.00		$525.00						$525.00
Landscaping	$2,500.00				$1,000.00		$1,500.00		$2,300.00
Install vinyl fence	$2,000.00		$2,021.00						$2,021.00
Replace HVAC	$2,000.00				$2,000.00				$2,000.00
Stamped concrete pad	$1,800.00		$1,600.00						$1,600.00
demo plaster on back wall to expose brick	$500.00		$495.00						$495.00
light remod on half bath	$800.00		$625.00						$625.00
paint interior two color	$3,000.00		$3,250.00						$3,250.00
Custom kitchen with Granite	$12,000.00		$10,875.00						$10,875.00
reset banister	$50.00		$50.00						$50.00
repair 2 windows	$200.00		$225.00						$225.00
vynal in bathrooms	$700.00		$630.00						$630.00
Carpet	$1,200.00		$1,425.00						$1,425.00
Add french door to Bedroom	$500.00		$1,025.00						$1,025.00
upgrade light package	$900.00				$200.00		$500.00		$700.00
Add Bathroom and closet in 4th bedroom	$8,000.00		$7,996.00						$7,996.00
Add security system	$1,500.00		$1,150.00						$1,150.00
Stage	$2,000.00								$2,000.00
total	$40,300.00	$0.00	$32,017.00	$0.00	$3,200.00		$0.00	$2,000.00	$0.00	$39,217.00

As you can see, I thought I would be spending roughly
$40,000. I picked this budget at random but the rules of
flipping really apply here. In the flipping section you learn
that you always want to add 10% to what you believe your
costs will be. Allow me to show you why.

	A	B	C	D	E	F	G	H	I
	Date	Lowes	A Notch Above	Tom Mount	Jerry Pope	Inspections	Home Depot	Acquisition and Sales	Total
	06/01/12	$6,848.33	$34,895.00	$940.00	$0.00	$888.00	$0.00	$895.92	$44,467.25
	06/29/12							$472.40	
	07/07/12	$4,190.00							
	07/13/12	$400.13							
	07/14/12		$32,188.00						
	07/14/12	$155.76							
	07/16/12	$131.23							
	07/16/12	$229.24							
	07/17/12	$140.00							
	07/23/12	$1,601.97							
	07/30/12			$940.00					
	08/01/12					$888.00			
	08/06/12							$250.00	
	08/06/12							$50.00	
	08/07/12							$123.52	
	08/14/12		$865.00						
	07/25/13		$857.00						
	04/15/13		$985.00						

As you can see we went over by a little more than 10%.
Which brings me to, you will need to track your actual cost
as well. This can be a big problem for investors. You need
to see the difference in your projections and your actual
costs. Do not forget to include anything you put on your
credit card or use personal funds to purchase. You need
to pay yourself back.

Single Family Holding

When you have a single family home that you are holding as a rental, lease purchase or owner finance you will want to just track the incoming and plan for the outgoing.

Lease purchases and owner financed holds do not really require much in the way of planning. Upon acquisition you will need to account for any repairs, maintenance, upgrades, or cleaning you are planning for the initial sale of the property. You should also plan for marketing and vacancy cost as well.

The rule of thumb is that these buyers have a pretty good chance of defaulting after 24 months. You should take into consideration the vacancy and repair cost to get the next person in the home.

Standard rentals incur additional cost with maintenance throughout the term of the agreement. I recommend a home warranty to make budgeting easy but if you are handy or like to pay as you go that is fine too. I generally budget about $1000 per unit for multifamily and $1500 for single family per year for maintenance.

Multi-Family Budget

As I stated before, you do not want to jump into owning and managing an apartment building. You will be well advised to allow a seasoned property management company take care of that for you. I would also recommend that you take a CAM (Certified Apartment Manager) training even if you are not managing.

That said, when calculating the budget for a multiunit building it is imperative to consider all aspects of income and expense. You should include vending, laundromat profits, washer and dryer fees, pet fees, parking fees, gym fees, administrative fees, and so on in the income. There are all kinds of hidden income if you are doing it right. (By hidden I do not mean tax evasion. I mean that is not obvious.)

When calculating the expense for the property you need to consider salaries, taxes, parts, supplies, resident retention programs, vacancy, delinquency, grounds maintenance, and so much more.

I really do not want to get in depth here because if you acquire a sizable multiunit property and do not obtain professional assistance you have more dollars than sense.

I once worked for a man who bought an apartment building but had no idea what to do from there. He was a realtor and had been a property manager before but never really had his hands in the pot like he did at that point.

He purchased 80 units beside the VA hospital in, at the time, the most dangerous spot in the city. We began shuffling the tenants from their old, ramshackle apartments to the newly renovated we had just completed. To my shock there was much resistance to this move. Go figure.

When I get there I am trying to figure out who owes money, who is paid up, who is in what unit, who even lives there for that matter. I am asking about resident retention programs only to get a deer in headlights look. *Sigh

After many painstaking weeks I finally find out that the owner is owed a considerable amount of money. Also that they are not maximizing the earning potential of the property.

The owner had no accounting system in place really. He was drowning and had no idea that he just had to stand up.

We ended hiring a few consultants to come in and really get the books, budget, and federal program compliance in place so that we could focus on the day to day for managing the renovation and dealing with tenants. Without that assistance getting things set up the property would have failed. He would have lost everything he owned as he dumped it all in that one property.

Rent Roll

I'm bee-bopping along (I am using that kiddy term because I was 24, maybe 23. I think I bee-bopped back then) …I am bee-bopping along all proud of myself. I am a landlord; people are paying rent to me. Yea!!! I've got it going on!!!

My giant, Nokia, cell phone rings and it is one of my tenants, Jamie, saying "I am so sorry that we haven't gotten the rent to you. Are you going to put us out?"

Ummm… Yea. If I knew that you owed me rent!! In that moment I realized that I was just keeping track of who paid what in my head. I had not even thought about keeping track of who paid when on paper?

It gets better. As I am talking to this tenant she shares that they haven't paid in 3 months. I only had 8-10 properties so I assumed that I would notice if I was paying for you to live in my house. NOPE!! So after that I set up what is called rent roll but I did not know that. I just knew that I needed to be able to see who paid.

Rent roll is the term widely used in the industry for a way to track rents. You can be as simple or elaborate as you like. I find a simple format to be best. You need the address, tenant name, amount due, and amount paid. This should be done monthly and saved with your other items for that month.

It is very important that you keep up with the input of rents due and received so that you may know at just a glance who owes what. Sounds simple enough, right? I sure wish someone had told me that when I was still bee-bopping.

		Rent Roll May 2016			
Address	Tenant	Rent	Other Fees	Paid	Due
123 4th St	Smith, Mary	$775.00	$0.00	$775.00	$0.00
707 Adams St	Harvey, Andy	$1,800.00	$180.00	$0.00	$1,980.00
9999 Jefferson Ave	Neman, Neil	$1,200.00	$0.00	$1,200.00	$0.00
1515 Old Point Dr	Igloo, John	$1,550.00	$0.00	$1,550.00	$0.00
1897 Burn Lake Dr	Paterson, Pat	$1,250.00	$1,250.00	$600.00	$1,900.00
10830 Woodman Hills Dr	Williams, Bill	$900.00	$45.00	$450.00	$495.00

Tenant Ledger

I realize that Jamie's rent is not getting paid since she admits to being three months behind and has no real plan to catch up. Now I need to figure out how much she owes and take her to court to get possession of my house and collect my money. Guess what would have helped with that? A tenant ledger. Guess who didn't have one? This gal. I was able to get possession and judgment for one month. Eh. Better than nothing. I learned a valuable lesson that day, it seems that all of my lessons came at quite a cost.

A tenant ledger is just a real time list of monies due and monies paid. Period. This is a running total unlike rent roll.

Rent roll is a snap shot of the month. A ledger is the story of their history to current.

Below is an example of a Tenant Ledger. As you can see, the need for basic tracking practices are a necessity. With the things herein, a general ledger, and some commonsense you should have no problem tracking your growth, where you need to improve, and you'll have a pretty good idea come tax time where you stand with uncle Sam.

I only touched on the accounting you need that is specific to investing. You will need to track all incomes and expenses for your business.

Tenant/Buyer(s)		Down Payment Installment				
Address	12405 Graham Meadow Dr	Date		Monday, August 10, 2015	Sunday, November 01, 2015	Monday, February 01, 201
Phone 1		Amount		$4,000.00	$5,000.00	$5,000.0
Phone 2						
Email						

Date	Description	Payment Due	Payment Made	Balance
Thursday, May 38, 2015 EMD		$1,000.00	$1,000.00	$0.00
Wednesday, July 01, 2015 mortgage		$2,150.00		$2,150.00
Wednesday, July 01, 2015 Payment			$2,150.00	$0.00
Sunday, July 26, 2015 mortgage		$2,150.00		$2,150.00
Sunday, July 26, 2015 Payment			$2,150.00	$0.00
Saturday, August 01, 2015 Down Payment Installment		$4,000.00		$4,000.00
Saturday, August 01, 2015 Payment			$4,000.00	$0.00
Tuesday, August 25, 2015 Payment			$2,150.00	$2,150.00
Wednesday, August 26, 2015 mortgage		$2,150.00		$0.00
Saturday, September 26, 2015 mortgage		$2,150.00		$2,150.00
Saturday, September 26, 2015 Payment			$2,150.00	$0.00
Monday, October 26, 2015 mortgage		$2,150.00		$2,150.00
Sunday, November 01, 2015 Down Payment Installment		$5,000.00		$7,150.00
Sunday, November 01, 2015 Payment			$5,000.00	$2,150.00
Sunday, November 01, 2015 Payment			$2,150.00	$0.00
Thursday, November 26, 2015 mortgage		$2,150.00		$2,150.00
Thursday, November 26, 2015 Payment			$2,150.00	$0.00
Saturday, December 26, 2015 mortgage		$2,150.00		$2,150.00
Saturday, December 26, 2015 Payment			$2,150.00	$0.00
Tuesday, January 26, 2016 mortgage		$2,150.00		$2,150.00
Tuesday, January 26, 2016 Payment			$2,150.00	$0.00
Monday, February 01, 2016 Down Payment Installment		$5,000.00		$5,000.00
Tuesday, January 26, 2016 Down Payment Installment			$5,000.00	$0.00
Friday, February 26, 2016 mortgage		$2,150.00		$2,150.00
Friday, February 26, 2016 Payment			$2,150.00	$0.00

Flipping

We have all seen reality show after reality show about flipping houses. It looks so fun and easy that every Tom, Dick, and Harry are out there trying their hand at flipping. Most of the time Tom and Harry just end up looking like Dicks. Without proper training and knowledge people end up over paying and under profiting. Many people lose a lot of valuable time and money.

Don't be a Dick, or Tom, or Harry. I will walk you through each step to ensure that you are able to maximize profit by making the appropriate offer, utilizing your rehab budget most efficiently, and making top dollar on your sale. I will lead you to the money, knowledge, and resources you need to become a successful fix and flip investor.

Finding Property

The most tedious part of being a real estate investor in any capacity is finding a good deal. This is probably the most drawn out and frustrating part of investing. You are pumped and ready to apply all of your new knowledge only to have to wait......oh there's a bite....and nope...and wait...and so on. Be patient. Be persistent. Do not waiver from the formula I am going to teach you for making offers.

Many new investors make bids that are too high and end up getting burned and ultimately out of the real estate game. Remember this is a job and you should never make an emotional decision. Do not buy in an area because you had your first kiss on that corner or because the neighbor is super-hot. You buy the house because you are <u>going to make money</u>!

I have been writing blind offers, which we will talk about in a few, for quite a while. When an area seems to be in transition, meaning that the values seem to be increasing more quickly than in the past, I like to take a ride out and look at a few houses.

One such situation was in play in the north side of the city and I was elated to see the prices coming up. Ebony, my super classy realtor, and I hop in her car and take a quick drive to see what all of the excitement is about.

It takes some time to look at a property and write an offer so we only have 4 or 5 on the schedule for the day. We are at our last property; it is a huge, beautiful, expansive, brick home. I am in real estate lust with this home.

Right inside the front door is another door. I open it expecting to see a coat closet. Nope. Basement stairs in a house with no power. Obviously I want to go down there. My cell phone is acting as my flashlight and I am ready to explore. I'm thinking I'm thinking I'm Sacagawea, Ebony is thinking also something but it isn't nearly as pleasant.

Reluctantly, she follows me down, both of our stilettos thunking down the wooden stairs. As we are peaking around we see what appears to be a sleeping bag and the silhouette of feet peeking from around the corner.

"*Eb'nay*," because we have our own sassy language, "*is that feet?*"

"*I don't know Char'tay.*" She retorts, "*I do believe we have seen enough of this basement.*"

Casually we turn and klunk back up the stairs. At the top of the stairs I lock the basement door and continue to explore.

The kitchen is in need of a full gut job, the screened porch should be glassed in to make a sun room. The second floor is a bit confusing, almost like a maze... but exactly how horror movies start. The floors need refinishing, the bathrooms need refurbishing, the windows need..., wait, was that a chainsaw I heard INSIDE the house? Yes it is! We need to run right past the basement door where we locked the chainsaw wielding vagrant, if we can even find our way out!

We do. We made it down the stairs and past the basement door. Slamming the front door behind us, I run to the car expecting Ebony is unlocking the car door and ready to take off. Nope. That crazy woman is standing on the porch locking up the house.

This illustrates two reasons you should write blind offers.

1. You may accidentally lock the Northside Chainsaw Massacre in the basement.
2. We only wrote 5 offers that day, zero of which were accepted.

The most effective way to find property is writing blind offers through *your* realtor. A blind offer is an offer on a property that you have never seen and will not see unless you have an accepted offer. I know this seems both scary and crazy to a non-investor but once you are in the investor mindset it is the only way to do things.

Time is money. When most wannabe investors want to flip a house they call a realtor who may have sold 1,000,000 homes to end users (people whom buy the house to live there) and a couple of wish investors who got super excited watching a staged reality show, but never to a REAL investor like you will be. Mr. and Mrs. Wish hop into the car with Sally Realtor and look at 5 houses and go home to think about it, they go back and look again before making a highly uneducated, overpriced offer. This takes a lot of time. We will be writing roughly 25-100 offers before one is accepted. We have to write them sight unseen. Eventually, looking at a house you do not have under contract will seem like a silly idea.

You will need to select an area for which you would like to focus (to start out this is best). My local folks, an area would be West End, East End, South Chesterfield, Chester, and so on. You will put offers on homes with at least 3 bedrooms or the ability to turn it into a 3 bedroom. You will not put offers on anything other than single-family homes for the purpose of flipping. Properties with multiple units typically do not sell as quickly or at as high of a price per square foot as their single-family counterparts.

Your realtor will need to send a list of all properties that NEED to be sold for one reason or another. (S)He will also send the comparable sales for the area, comps. You will need to learn how to decipher a good comparison versus a non-qualifying one for the purpose of flipping but first let's talk about the type of listing you are going to want.

The most common is a *REO* or *Real Estate Owned property*. This is a foreclosure. You will also want estates, trusts, and released probate sales. This is the home of a person who has passed away. Homes on the market over 120 days, homes priced way below market value, and homes that have been listed several times are also good to look into.

The first time you get this list it is pretty extensive but after you make your initial batch of offers it will become way more manageable with only a few additions each week. I suggest working on this weekly without exception.

Direct mail is another method of finding homes that others may not be bidding therefore increasing your chance of an accepted offer. Direct mail is <u>exactly</u> what it sounds like. You are going to send correspondence on paper to potential sellers. What you say, to whom, and where the lists are acquired is somewhat a matter of taste while following a few guidelines.

First let's look at WHO. There is no need to blanket the entire area with letters when only a few meet the criteria to make a flip offer mutually agreeable. After all, if all parties aren't happy the deal will fall apart. You are looking for a person who wants to be rid of the property but either does not think anyone will buy it or does not know how to go about selling it.

The elderly man or woman who no longer resides in their home but still pays taxes, insurance, and upkeep are excellent candidates. We, as investors, are able to offer a better option than a reverse mortgage which makes one jump through hoops to possibly get a portion of the value of the home. Once they pass, the family is left with tons of debt from interest compounded from the time the contract was signed. In many situations the home is in need of renovation or repair that they cannot afford, so they cannot list it for sale. You are able to offer them cash quickly, no inspection fees, no repairs on the home, and no realtor fees. It's a real winner for all.

Homes with out of state owners prove effective in finding motivated sellers. It is difficult to manage a rental from another state and even worse if the home is just vacant. Is it making or losing money? How much time are they putting into this property? These key facts are perfect negotiation tools for you when talking to the owner.

Some others are unoccupied properties, absentee owners, and properties with code compliance issues (tall grass, broken windows).

List can be purchased from companies like Melissa Data and Info USA. You can narrow down to as large or small of a list as you like.

You may also target select neighborhoods and look for absentee owners by using public record. In Chesterfield, VA, for example you can go to http://www.chesterfield.gov/eServices/RealEstateAssessments/RealEstate.aspx?id=11063, select "Search Property Sales" and choose any subdivision by clicking on the name in the drop menu. Once you have selected the neighborhood begin at the first parcel number and select. You will then look for any parcel where the mailing address and the property address do not match. You have identified an absentee owner in the neighborhood of choice for absolutely free.

The content of your mailer needs to be attention grabbing. Exactly opposite of this section. (Zzzzzzzzzzzzzzzz. Wake up! You need to know this!) You want each recipient to

a) Open the envelope
b) Read the content
c) Become curious about it.

How do we meet this goal as effectively as possible?

Be tacky!!! Yep I said it!!

Be sure your envelope is hand written (or looks like it) with handwriting that is less than perfect. I used to have my father write these before he passed. He enjoyed helping me with work and I appreciated the response. People were asking "*Do you have kids help you with this?*"

That's what I'm talking about!!! I don't care what the question is; I got you on the phone! Pitch time!!!!

What you put in the envelope is a matter of taste with several styles and you should pick the one that you like the best, I honestly can't say which is better or worse as long as it is tacky and says the right things.

Say "*I want to buy your house*", "*Any condition*", "*As is*", "*Cash offer*", "*Quick Close*"!!

Many investors like to use a company called Yellow Letter. It literally looks like a hand written note on a piece of yellow paper. The yellow legal pad kind. Some investors also opt for coffee stains and such to be added. This gives the impression of an individual who saw your house and wants it. People love it!!! You can contract this out or do it yourself with a handwriting font and mail merge. The letter should basically read:

Dear (Homeowner name),

I am sorry if this is odd but I saw your home at (insert address) and I am interested in buying it. I would like to talk to you about paying cash for it in its current condition.

Please call me at (phone number) so that we can meet and talk about it.

Regards,

(Your Name)

Another option is to use a flyer that you would use as a professional but, *highlight key points,* circle your name and number, and write a message on the back saying "*I am looking forward to hearing from you.*" Of course, you can do all of this with a great copier and not have to write each one.

Sticking with the trend of tacky, signs. Big, plain, yellow or orange signs with a handwritten message. "I BUY HOUSES" Buy blank corrugated plastic in 18 x 24. Write your message and place your signs in areas where you want to buy a house.

One should always be on the lookout for a deal. When

I Buy Houses!!

804-555-1212

driving anywhere, the grocery store, doctor's office, to your hot date, be aware. When you see an abandoned home, get the address. A dilapidated home, get the address. A house for rent or sale by the owner, get the number. Use public record to look up the owner and send them the same type of note you would for your direct mailers.

Auctions and tax sales are also a good way to find property. You will be required to put down a sizable EMD, generally between $5,000 and a percentage of the winning bid. These are intended as cash deals so you must be able to close quickly.

You will need to pull the list from the courthouse docket in the jurisdiction of choice and research your maximum offer in advance. Once you arrived at the courthouse, expect that most houses will not be auctioned. The majority of distressed homeowners have filed bankruptcy, have a short sale pending, paid the past due, or entered into a loan modification with the bank by the time it gets to the courthouse stairs.

Calculating Your Offer

Knowing what to offer is the first step towards success versus becoming a huge failure crying on the floor because, yes, you won the bid but you lost your money and owe your lender on top of that. Avoid puffy eyes and smeared mascara and pay attention now. You can almost stumble your way through the rest of this but you WILL FAIL without this information.

I also want to stress that in this market that we are in currently, flips generally do not make $50,000 or $60,000. They generally make about $15,000 to $30,000.

Today my realtor Kevin sent a little gem that popped on the market and needs an offer ASAP. It's on Garland Ave and listed for $ 45,000 with 1700 sqft. The comps show the renovated homes in the area selling for an average of $174,256 with about 1844 sqft but the ones that fit most closely to the subject had a median price of $95.95 per sqft. Without looking at it I asked Kevin to make an offer of about $37,000. Why? I plan to make a profit of roughly $25,000. Where did that come from? Here is how you write an offer. The calculations apply for blind offers as well as traditional offers.

Once you have found a property....

1. Have your realtor run comps. Comps should be in the immediate area of your home and 90 days old if possible. Comparable sales should exclude properties in distress (bad shape, REO's, on the market for over 120 days).

2. Review the homes that are within 200 sqft of the subject home (your offer). Look at the price per sqft for these homes. Is one significantly higher than the rest? Exclude it. The remaining homes are comparable.

3. Calculate the average price per square foot.

4. Multiply the price per square foot by the square footage of the home. This is your ARV (After Repair Value). This is the basis you will use for calculating your offer. Now, take 5% to cover concessions, unplanned upgrades requested, and possibility of a lower offer.

$$1700 \times 95.95 = 163,115$$

$$163,115 \times .95 = 154,959.25 \text{ expected sales price}$$

5. You will need to calculate the cost of repair and renovation for the house. You will need to familiarize yourself with the costs of basic repairs and have a good contractor that you use regularly. If you are not writing blinds you can have your contractor give you a bid and use that number as well if you do not need to make an offer immediately.

When writing blinds you will have to estimate based on the pictures on the MLS. Realistically, if the home needs ONLY cosmetic repairs you will need to estimate at least $20,000-$30,000. It is better to over shoot than under.

This applies to a home that is in good shape but is not the new, wow, factor that sells a home.

If you are looking at upgrading HVAC, new roof, replacing siding, or mild structural or mechanical repairs you will need to calculate $30,000-40,000 for these items.

If a home appears to need a full rehab including electrical or plumbing and everything in between calculate $50,000 to $60,000 for a typical house. If the property is large or in a historic district you will need to go higher.

When a home offers nothing but most of the foundation and a few walls, this is a gut job. You will not get out of here for less than $100,000 to $125,000. This is a time when you should rely on your contractor for the bid and not try to estimate.

In the situation of the above home the repairs would be roughly $60,000.

6. Take your rehab budget and add 10%. This is your cushion and this is necessary.

60,000 x 1.1 = 66,000 Rehab budget

7. You will need to calculate the additional cost. ***This is how investors fail, forgetting the details.*** You should always calculate realtor fees, even if you are planning to sell the home without a realtor. Chances are that the buyer will have one.

A traditional listing agreement, listing your home with a realtor, charges 3% to you for both sides of the transaction. This is a total of 6%.

In the situation as listed above, I am going to use a flat fee listing which cost $595. That will come out of my marketing budget. We will need to calculate the 3% for the buyer's agent.

We will take the adjusted ARV (the ARV less 5%) and multiply that by .03.

$$154,959.25 \times .03 = 4,648.78$$

8. You will now need to calculate what you can expect to pay when the home is purchased and title changes hands, closing cost. This is typically equal to roughly 3% as well.

$$154,959.25 \times .03 = 4,648.78$$

9. You now need to come up with a budget for holding cost (utilities), marketing, and staging. I have found that $5,000 is very generous.

10. First lets calculate what a fair offer would be if the money was free. (Money is free to those with cash; hence they are at an advantage because they can make higher offers and get more offers accepted). This is calculated by taking the adjusted *ARV* (95% of the *After Repair Value*) less all of the expenses calculated previously.

154,959.25	Adjusted ARV
66,000	Rehab cost
4,648.78	Realtor fees
4,648.78	Closing costs
-5,000.00	Miscellaneous
$70,012.91	Less expenses

Use the new balance of the *AARV* less expenses and multiply that by .6. This is how we ensure there is a profit.

$$70,012.91 \times .6 = 42,007.75 \quad \text{Offer}$$

11. Most people are not going to use cash. I do not use cash even when it is available because (A) it ties up that capital for months and (B) I'd rather lose the house than

the cash if something goes horribly wrong. This of course is a highly unlikely scenario but I am sure it has happened at some point to someone.

These last several calculations give us the base for calculating (A) How much we are going to borrow? (B) How much is that money going to cost us?

We will begin by adding up all of our cost as we subtracted before. Obviously, we are going to just do this calculation once in practice but for the sake of learning we will do it again.

42,007.75	Cash Offer Value
66,000	Rehab cost
4,648.78	Realtor fees
4,648.78	Closing costs
+5,000.00	Miscellaneous
$122,305.31	Total Cost

This gives us a total expense of $122,305.31.

The following calculation changes based on HOW you are funding this deal and how long we expect it to take from the initial purchase until you are getting a check from your attorney.

We are going to discuss the different options for funding very soon.

Based on the repairs needed for this house you can look at a turn time of 7 weeks and based on comps you have determined that houses are under contract in an of average 22 days. It takes 21-40 days to close on average. We should assume that we will have these funds for roughly 4 months.

If you are using a private lender, your self-directed IRA (or someone else's), or a *HELOC* chances are you are paying just simple interest for the time you have the money. Simple interest is just the amount you borrowed plus the interest rate for 12 months. So if you borrow $100,000 for 12 months at 12% you pay $12,000 to borrow that money. However, if you only borrowed that money for 6 months you would only owe the lender $6,000.

Ok so let's say that you have talked your grandma Helen into lending you the money and she wants to make 6% on this investment. To figure out how much extra you will owe Grandma Helen you will take the total cost you calculate above ($122,305.31) and multiply that by .06. If you kept the money for a full year you would owe Grandma $7,338.32. You will only owe her $611.53 per month that you have the money. We are planning to keep it for roughly 4 months will cost you $2,446.11.

122,305.31 x .06= 7,338.32   Simple interest over 12 months

7,338.32/12= 611.53 Monthly interest

611.53 x 4= 2446.11 Interest for 4 months

Add this into your expenses before you calculate the offer.

154,959.25	Adjusted ARV
66,000	Rehab cost
4,648.78	Realtor fees
4,648.78	Closing costs
2446.11	interest due
-5,000.00	Miscellaneous
$67,566.80	Less expenses

Now calculate the offer the same way as before.

$$67,566.80 \times .6 = 40,540.08 \quad \textit{Offer}$$

If we are using hard money you should add an extra $5000.00 to your expenses for points and costs. Not all, but many hard money lenders charge points at opening and closing a loan as well as periodically. It is good to factor all of this in and include a cushion. A good estimate for all of the points and the simple interest is to just use 18% as the interest rate.

$$122,305.31 + 5,000 = 127,305$$

$$127,305.31 \times .18 = 22,914.90 \quad \textit{Simple interest over 12 months}$$

$$22,914.90 / 12 = 1909.58 \quad \textit{Monthly interest}$$

$$1909.58 \times 4 = 7,638.30 \quad \textit{Interest for 4 months}$$

Add this into your expenses before you calculate the offer.

154,959.25	Adjusted ARV
66,000	Rehab cost
4,648.78	Realtor fees
4,648.78	Closing costs
7,638.30	interest due
5,000.00	Hard Money
-5,000.00	Miscellaneous
$62,023.39	Less expenses

Now calculate the offer the same way as before.

$$62{,}023.39 \times .6 = \boxed{37{,}214.03} \quad Offer$$

That's great and all but how much will you make, right? To project earnings on a deal simply add the offer and the cost together and subtract from the AARV.

$$154{,}959.25 \quad \text{Adjusted ARV}$$
$$\underline{-130{,}149.89 \quad \text{expenses}}$$
$$\$24{,}809.36 \quad \text{Profit}$$

Finding Capital

Great! Let's flip a house! Wait! Yes of course, we need money.

We have all heard "*It takes money to make money*" but what if you don't have any? Or at least not as much as you need to buy a house and renovate it into the best home on the block. What do you do?

When we think of buying a home we think of going to the bank and getting a loan. There is one pretty big problem. Banks are not investor friendly. There are high interest rates, large down payments required, and a limit to how many loans they will give you.

Let's begin by looking at your own possible sources of capital that you may not think of immediately.

You've paid for your home for many years. Call that note and make it pay you back. **Turn your home into an income producing asset.** The equity in your home can be used as a Home Equity Line Of Credit (HELOC) to make money flipping. Most HELOC's are at low interest rates (2.75-3.5% typically). This money can be used as needed and when you are not using it, you do not pay for it.

No equity? <u>Convert your IRA into a Self-Directed IRA</u>. Shouldn't you be the one in control of your future? By converting your IRA into a Self-Directed IRA you have the option of investing in secure, profitable, markets. You can "lend" yourself the money at the interest rate of your choice. You replenish the money once you sell the home. You can save for your future while building your future. For information on Self Directed IRAs go to http://www.trustetc.com/real-estate-ira/real-estate-ira.html or www.broadfinancial.com/

You may not have equity or own a home at all. Maybe you do not have an IRA or a 401K. Maybe THIS is your retirement plan. What do you do?

OPM.

The answer is OPM. What is OPM, right?

Other People's Money. You should always be on the task of looking for Private Lenders. These are people who either have cash on hand or have access to cash in one of the ways mentioned above who want to make a high return rate on their secured investment, generally 8-12%. As a serious investor, you should always have a short intro to generate interest in being YOUR private lender.

Your private lender enjoys the benefit of high returns on a secure investment. The investment is secured by title. They are in first position on the title and have the same security as a bank if you default. They have the peace of mind knowing that you will never have over 75% of the renovated value tied up leaving at least 25% equity for the lender. The security continues as your attorney will draft a promissory note locking them into the interest rate and payment method as well as a mortgage document.

Obtaining a private lender is as wonderful as a unicorn who farts rainbows and almost as hard to find. In the meantime you can use hard money. It sounds worse than it is. Hard money comes from private lenders who understand the real estate market and capitalize on it by…well providing capital. AWESOME right? Of course it's awesome. What's the catch you ask?

Here is the catch… They know the market and are not afraid of it. They know that they can charge you points at acquisition, quarterly, and at closing. The interest rate is typically 10-15%.

When making offers it is important to consider the source of your funding and its per diem. This will be a huge factor in how offers are written.

Offers and Contracts

The different styles of marketing dictate HOW you make your offer. If you feel you are outgoing, a natural sales person, and do not fear rejection, you may love the offers that accompany non-conventional methods like mailers and signs. If you are not the best negotiator, are shy, fear rejection, or if you know you are a pushover, you should let your contractor and realtor do the talking with MLS offers.

MLS offers require nothing from you but a dollar amount and some signatures in the way of contract negotiation. Your realtor will deal directly with their realtor.

You will not need a contract of your own as realtors use the standard contract as provided by the realtor association in your area. You will need to provide evidence of EMD and Proof of Funds with each offer.

The EMD, or Ernest Money Deposit, is a "non-refundable" down payment that is to be held either by the real estate brokerage company (Keller Williams for example) or the closing attorney. Generally when one is buying a house to live in the EMD is about $250 and it is given to the realtor. Not for us. Investors do EVERYTHING differently. We will write one check for $1,000 to our attorney, scan a copy to our realtor, and done! The attorney will get the $1,000 when you deliver the closing package. The realtor will send a copy of the same check with all offers.

Why $1,000 rather than $250? This indicates a sincere interest in the property. It is sometimes considered by a seller as a deciding factor.

Your offer will also need to be accompanied by a proof of funds letter or bank statement. What you send should be determined by where your funding should come.

You will need to have your realtor make a CASH offer, even if you are using private or hard money. A typical closing is 45-60 days. You will close in 21 days from ratification. You may even choose to go with 14 days if you know that your attorney and your funding are fast and efficient.

Your agent will make your offer "AS IS."

These all give you an edge against other offers.

If you have been making blind offers and an offer gets accepted you will then go and look at the home ASAP. Do not delay. Take your contractor with you and find out if you bid close to the cost of repair. Hopefully you have overestimated the cost allowing for additional profit. If by chance you have under bid, you will want to recalculate the cost and determine if the home is still going to make money for you. If so, great! Sign the additional documents the seller's bank has sent and get the contract and EMD to the attorney.

In the event you get a counter offer, you can look into what the projected profit comes out to being and reevaluate. You may want to accept a counter or counter back yourself. Remember, it is a bad idea to allow your projected income to go below $10,000 because one major surprise (asbestos in the walls for example) will put you in a negative equity situation.

If the house is not going to make money once you have actually inspected it, simply, do not sign the additional documents and allow the contract to expire. No harm done. In conventional purchasing you are told that you will lose your EMD or will be sued for performance. This is untrue and ridiculous. The EMD stayed in you or your attorney's hands and if your offer doesn't go through there are 100 more waiting behind yours.

Direct mail, birddog or sign offers are a bit different. You will have to speak directly to the homeowner and negotiate an offer. But let's start from the beginning.

The owner will call you either off of a sign or a mailer. You need to be ready to pitch at any time as you never know which call it may be. Many people suggest the use of a script but I find that unless you are an actor you will sound like you have memorized a script. The initial call should go something like this…

> *Caller: Hello. This is Bob. I just got a letter from you saying you want to buy my house?*

You: Yes! Wonderful! I am so glad you called. Were you planning on selling the home already?

Caller: Not really. I have thought about it but it needs some work.

You: Oh, that fine what does it need?

Caller: Bla Bla Bla they go on about the house.

This next part is where you have to be on you're a game.

You: That's no problem. I like to purchase homes and fix them up.

There was no mention of being an investor or businesss. Why? People think of an investor like they think of the boogie man.

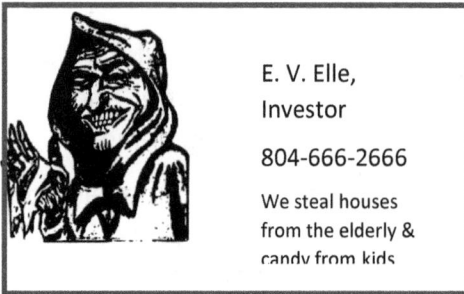

E. V. Elle,
Investor

804-666-2666

We steal houses
from the elderly &
candy from kids

How they see you   **Actual YOU**

Caller: Oh that's cool. Wait! Are you an investor? I am not giving my house away!

You: Of course you aren't. What are you doing with it right now?

> *Caller: Well, nothing but I don't want to be taken advantage of. I called one of those numbers and got a super low offer and I don't want to waste my time.*

If you are just a conventional flipper you probably will not have an offer that is much better. Guess what!? You are not!

> *You: Well, Bob, I don't want to waste time either but I am guessing that I have a few options that you have not considered before. I would love the opportunity to get together and talk about how we can both be happy. Can I meet you at the property tomorrow or is another day better?*

Now you might be wondering, "What is Charity talking about? I thought I was going to call my realtor, ask for comps, and use the formula we just learned to make an offer." That is accurate. But you will also have a whole myriad of arsenal to choose from if the cash offer is not a go.

Let's get to that. Now you learn that houses in Bob's neighborhood are selling for about $200,000. Based on what Bob said you guess that he needs about $30,000 in renovation to have a good solid flip. Based on those numbers you can offer about $76,000 and make about $50,000. So you know you can go higher if you want.

Another option is to have Bob become your private lender at 0% With this option you can make a significantly higher offer with very little risk. The calculation would look like this.

The ARV is $200,000.

The AARV is $190,000

Rehab cost is $30,000

Rehab cushion is $3,000

Realtor cost is $5,700

Closing Cost will actually be less but let's just stick with the $5,700

Staging and Holding is $5,000

Interest is only on $30,000 so it is $1,800 if you are using hard money. You shouldn't have points for such a small loan.

Because our risks are so much lower and we have the owner personally involved we are able to use a simpler and more generous amount.

We will add the cost, $51,200. Subtract the cost from the AARV, $168,800. Multiply that number by .7 to make an offer of $118,160. This is a total investment of $169,360 for a profit of $20,640.

So how do we convince Bob that it is a good idea to let us buy his property with no interest and no payments until it is renovated and sold?

You made the cash offer to Bob and he is not interested even after you break down the HUGE costs you will incur and raising the offer a few thousand. Next step is asking him to be a zero percent lender.

Bob: Well I didn't think it was possible but somehow your offer is worse than the last one.

You: Well Bob right now the house is just costing you money. I told you that I plan to put over $50,000 into the house and I need to make a few bucks for my time and work, wouldn't you agree?

Bob: I guess.

You: Great! If I can offer you $118,160 would that work?

Bob: Why didn't you just say that?

This is where it gets good.

You: This is what I can do. I can pay for all of the closing cost. I can close in two weeks. I can get you a little money back on the taxes you paid already for the property. Sound good?

Bob: Of course.

You: Here's the deal. I can't afford to give you cash today for the house. Instead, we will close on it with a promissory note and mortgage that puts you in first position

until I get the house fixed up and sold.
About 4-6 months. At that time you get
all of your money.

It can go a few ways here.

Scenario 1

> *Bob: What the %&^$!!!! Get your @$$ off my*
> *property!!!*

Scenario 2

> *Bob: That plan doesn't sound bad at all. I like*
> *it!!*

Scenario 3

> *Bob: I owe money on the house.*

What if Bob owes money? Does he owe $118,000 or less? In this situation you will want to first offer to enter into a lease purchase with Bob until the house is finished and sold. Your contract to him is for the offer amount. You will suggest having no payments for the term of the agreement. If the house is vacant and has been this option should not be too bad. If Bob wants payments you can make the house payment or whatever amount agreed upon. The payments will be deducted from the purchase price in the end.

Renovate to Sell

When renovating a home to flip you need to remember this is not your house!!! You need to make it look like the best house on the block based on current trends for the area and areas can be very specific. Is the home located in an urban, rural, suburban, or historic area? These all have different things for which buyers are looking.

It is a good idea when you get your first few offers accepted to go shop the comparable homes for sale in the area. You will want to get your realtor to take you into as many as you have time to look at. You will want to notice the difference between a home that is being sold by a person who lived there and the homes that are other flips.

When you are in the home look for kitchen and bathroom style, are the yards fenced and how, flooring, the colors that are being used on the interior and exterior, and so on. You want to stay within the same style of the community only better.

Immediately after having an accepted offer you will go with your contractor and realtor to inspect the home. (S)he will advise you on the mechanical and structural items that need attention. You will want to also tell the contractor what cosmetic things you need done at that time so that you are ready to roll as soon as the home closes and to be sure you are able to stay in budget.

All homes will need several non-cosmetic things to sell. I have learned the hard way more than once on almost all of these things.

- You must have central heat and

air. You may choose between gas and electric for heat. That is a non-issue. Generally all electric is less expensive and people love it. You do not need a dual zone system. All contractors will try to convince you that you do. You will not live there. It is fine with one heat pump!!

- You must have a new(ish) hot water tank. The year is not as much of a concern as the way it looks. If the tank looks old, in the eyes of the buyer it is old.
- Windows should be newer. If you cannot replace all of the windows be sure to do the front of the house. UNLESS you are in a highly historic district. Even if YOUR house is not historic but there is a heavy concentration of historic homes you do not need to replace them. People are used to seeing the old style of window for the area and it is not a turn-off.

- Significant structural work MUST be handled before attempting to sell. In older homes there are often leans in the floor. This can be repaired by having your contractor use floor jacks to raise the home at the part that is uneven and secure it either by replacing or "sistering" joist or adding support to the existing beams. You will need to have your contractor evaluate the benefits versus possible damage. A stucco exterior or plaster interior will most likely crack if you are lifting more than an inch or so.

- If the roof is in good shape leave it. It is an item that can be repaired rather than replaced as long as it is not an eyesore.
- The electrical must always be updated if it is not already. Fuses are a HUGE no. Be sure the panels are adequate for the home and the additions you might make.
- When you renovate the kitchen and bathrooms your interior plumbing beyond rough in will be new and shiny. Rough in is when the plumbing is brought to the house and to the point where you will place the fixture. This includes under the house and in the wall. You will need to be sure there are not any leaks inside the walls or under the house.

Once you have an idea for the trends for that area, you will want to get started on the esthetic side of flipping. Curb appeal is hugely important. The home must look good from the road. A first impression last forever. You will want to make sure the exterior is fresh and ready to be admired.

If the home is vinyl, brick, hardy plank, or stone, power wash the exterior. If it is Masonite or other siding that is in good shape and is not asbestos you may want to consider painting. The best colors are tans and light greys with white trim, black shutters, and a red door. This is a color scheme you can use for the exterior of all properties. The trim should always be painted to give the home a fresh appearance.

- The mailbox should be new unless your property is in a neighborhood where the community association owns the boxes.
- Flower beds and grass seed covered with hay should be added to each property. This gives the appearance of new. Everyone loves that!!

- Accent lighting is inexpensive but really adds a finished look to the home.
- Walkways are a great addition. These can be concrete, stamped concrete, or even rock.

Once inside you will spend the most money and energy on the Kitchen followed by the bathrooms. **Never** cut corners here. I have and I have regretted it every time.

- Kitchens should always have granite counters and the latest style appliances. Right now the dark steel is in but in 20 minutes it could be something else. If the kitchen is small, it is generally worth it to take out a wall. Flooring in the kitchen should be either wood or tile. Do not use linoleum!!

I literally did EVERYTHING wrong in this kitchen except take out a wall.

Custom Kitchens Sell!!!!

Unlike the mistake above, my flips include custom, handmade cabinets. Find a local cabinet maker who is willing to be affordable for volume.

You will need to pick the style of cabinet, color of granite, light package, and appliance package to meet the demand in the area.

This kitchen is in an upscale, progressive, urban, historic district. Note the clean lines and mismatched stains. This home sold in 7 days above asking price, unlike our unfortunate house above.

This is in an upscale suburban neighborhood. Note the added trim and attention to the backsplash.

Bathrooms are almost as important as the kitchen. People like for their home to appear fully custom. I like to use the same custom cabinets in the adjoining bathrooms in kitchen areas to give a feeling of continuity and flow in the home.

Roman showers are a bigger seller than jetted tubs. Roman Showers are stand up showers with multiple shower heads.

Use of tile is imperative in houses with a sales price putting them outside of the "starter home" category! In Richmond this home is above $175,000. The more tile the better these days. Ceramic wood grain and subway tiles are the current trend.

Ceramic Wood Grain Tile   Subway Tile

- Paint should be a natural color with a white trim. In most homes Right now light grey and greige (paint that looks kinda grey and kinda beige) with white trim is trending. It is important to stay up on the trends.
- If there is hardwood floors you will want to try to use as much of it as possible, especially in older homes. The weathering adds character as long as it is not damaged. Where you are adding all flooring, the most acceptable and cost effective method is to install wood downstairs and carpet the stairs and the upstairs rooms. When dealing with a rancher you will want to have wood in the living areas and carpet in the bedrooms. Tri-levels can be carpeted both down and upstairs with wood and tile in the main area.
- Lights should be the latest metal trend. Right now you can use brushed nickel, oiled bronze, and lightly oiled bronze. Brass is about to make a comeback. I am writing this in 2016. You can replace all dome lights with the same, cost effective, light sold at Lowes in packs of 6 for

roughly $40.00. I even have these in my own home.

You will need to put quality lights in high attention areas like the foyer, kitchens, and such.

The key things to remember are to stay natural and stay somewhat trendy. Do not skimp on the appearance of the home. This can cost thousands.

On the other hand, there is no need for heated floors, elevators, and expensive fixtures. The goal is to balance the look of luxury with an affordable budget.

You should establish a contractor relationship with a hardware store (Lowes, Home Depot, Ace) and select all of your materials prior to purchase. Ask them to get the best price for you. This typically saves between 10-25%.

Staging

When a buyer looks at a home they need to be able to visualize themselves in the home. Buying a home, the largest investment most people make, still ends up being an emotional decision for most people. When they walk in your house, versus the 99 other homes in the area, they need to feel at home. It needs to feel warm and cozy, new and fresh. You want them to envision waking up there, making meals there, entertaining friends there. You will do this by staging, furnishing and decorating, the home. You will want to touch as many senses as possible.

You should have plug in air fresheners throughout the house with a soft fragrance. I like a linen or cotton smell.

Each home has its own "feel" so it is my recommendation to rent the furniture from any furniture rental company rather than purchasing a set of furniture to reuse. I have negotiated with the store managers that the furniture is rented at half of the price as long as we leave the tags on them. This way they can still sell them as new items.

I have also invited local artist to display their canvas and sculpture in the home. This is a free way to decorate the home and to support the community. We will discuss this further down in marketing.

When selecting the furnishings for your home you will want to allow a budget of $500 to $1000 for extras like bed linens, throw pillows, and so on. You can reuse these many times but might want to keep a budget open for touches that are for each particular home.

You will want to make it look like a family lives in the home already. Not a regular family with dishes in the sink and at least one ill placed Lego for you to step on barefoot but like a super clean, minimalist family that everyone in the neighborhood talks about at the 'sac party.

Kitchens should have a few decorative pieces, dishtowels, a rug or something "soft", and evidence that there is nourishment in there. Use a couple of strategically placed coffee mugs (large and decorative is best), a picture with glass pebbles and some fake lemons to indicate lemonade, or bowl of fake fruit.

Pick a bright color as an accent. This is really a matter of taste. I like red because it is a power color. It is gender neutral. It is always popular. You may want to pick your own color.

Have a seating area in the kitchen so that they have the option to write an offer with the realtor right there.

Offer refreshments. I like to offer a sweet treat like individually wrapped cookies or candies. Buy cheap bottled water and remove the labels and replace them with labels you have printed on 3x5 labels with a small picture of the house and the address on it. Include a note that says "help yourself to refreshments."

Bathrooms should have shower curtains (when there is not a glass door), hand towels, rags, rugs, soap, and toilet paper! You do not want the memory of your home to be sending the wife back to the car for napkins out of the glovebox while the realtor pretends to be on the phone to avoid awkward eye contact.

When you have both a living room and a den, the living room should be tidy and trendy. The den should be comfortable and inviting. Use of fluffy throw pillows and a throw blanket brings this home. I picked up some antique books on how a woman should behave in 1877 at a yard sale. I sometimes put those out like someone has been reading it in a den. If you know me and read any portion of the books you will know that I haven't learned a thing from that literary experience. I often put a little basket of toys out for any children that might be present.

WARNING: Make sure the toys are not a choke hazard for any age. When there is only a living room you should base the feel of the room on the feel of the home. Toys should be in one of the smaller bedrooms if there is only one sitting room.

The bedrooms are pretty basic. You will need to be sure to demonstrate a master. Generally it is best to use a queen sized bed unless the room is extermely large. In the smaller bedrooms a queen, twin or even bunk beds can be placed. It is entirely at your discression. If the room is smaller go small on the bed. If there are low ceilings, avoid a bunk bed.

You have the option of renting matteresses for each of the rooms or buying blow up mattresses for the rooms. It is a cost effective option but it also proves a problem when people sit on the beds and pop them.

Once you have staged your home you should have a professional photographer photograph the home. This makes a huge difference in Marketing.

Selling the Home

Now that you have found a property, found a way to pay for it, figured out what renovations and repairs are needed and saw it to fruition, cleaned up sawdust for 8 days straight, and staged the property it is time to make your MOOLA!

You will need to have your realtor pull comps on your home again. In the short time that you have spent from the day you made the offer until now, things could have changed. Remember E. V. Elle, the other investor in your area. He could have flipped a house that sold $20,000 above market last week. That would make the one overpriced outlier a real comp bringing up your value.

There are three schools of thought on how to price a home.

One is to take the ARV and increase it by 5% because you are competing mainly with homes that have not been fully renovated. If you don't ask you will not receive. In my opinion this is a poor choice. You are prolonging the sales process increasing your holding cost and devaluing the home. Honestly, the longer a home sits on the market the more people wonder "What is wrong with this house?" After about 60 days you will actually need to pull your listing and relist it as a new one.

The next two are much better options if you ask me. First is to list right at the ARV. Your showings will be in line with the other homes in the neighborhood and you will have the best one. You should expect an offer before the rest.

The other option is to price the home 3-5% below ARV. You will have more showings and should get an offer fairly quickly. Many times it will be above asking price. When you are using expensive financing, this is the best option. Get the home sold!!! Make your money and move on!!!!

When you are calculating ARV the numbers generally come out to odd amounts. $246,580.21. This is not your list price. You will want to look at the list prices of the other homes in the area. You have only looked at the sales price before. Are there more other homes listed at $249,990 or is $245,999 more in line with other listings? That is your list price. You will want to list the home in line with the others. If you have decided to go with being the best priced, best house option you can be the $245,999.

When you are building your team, you will want to be sure that your realtor is willing to offer a flat fee listing for you. The standard is for a relator to make 3% for listing the home once it sells. If you get your asking price of

$249,999 that is a listing fee of $7,499.97. In a traditional system Mike and Sue Doe are selling their home to Joe and Jane Publique. Sally Realtor is going to put their house on the MLS and make some flyers. She will make a Postlets ad, put the house on Zillow, and put pics of it on her Facebook. When an offer comes in she will call Mr. and Mrs. Doe and explain the offer in "layman's terms" and advise them on what is next. Take the offer, counter the offer, sit and wait for another offer. Is that worth $7500? If you are a person who is uninformed about real estate and had difficulty understanding contracts then ABSOLUTELY!!!

You are not Mr. and Mrs. Doe. You are a real estate investor. Real estate is YOUR business. Why not save $7,000 and have your realtor list your home for a flat rate of $500? (S)He will put the home on the MLS. YOU will market your home outside of the MLS. You will receive, evaluate, and make decisions on the offers that come in. That's really not much work for $7,000.

The single most important person in selling your home is the buyer's agent. This is the person who will most likely influence the decision of if your house is the best value. It is a good idea to add an agent bonus into the MLS listing if there is a lot of renovation in that area. You can do this a couple of ways. First is you can simply say that rather than offering 3% you are offering 3.5%. That puts an extra $1250.00 in the realtors pocket. The problem is that the realtor may not do that math. You cannot give cash to a realtor according to DPOR. You can offer a $1,000 visa gift card to the buyer's agent. You can include that right in the listing. Get people in the door. Let the house do the work.

While discussing realtors, you can offer a Realtor Open House. You will invite all realtors to the house during the standard happy hour time of day for a tour of the home, wine and beer, light appetizers, drawings for gift cards, and some inexpensive entertainment. I find a one man acoustic show to be nice. Since we have opened the kitchen up this is usually a great spot to accent your best feature. If you have a great patio or back yard, use it. This applies to any room that you think best. Now you are an instant favorite among realtors. When their client describes anything even close to your house, you come to mind. Your realtor should be happy to assist you by sending notice to all the realtors with which (s)he deals.

Of course if you are able to find a buyer without an agent (this is rare like private money) you can put thousands back in your pocket. You will want to market your house to those who want to look without a realtor. There are a few out there. You will need to post your home on as many sites as possible. Zillow, Tulia, Craigslist, Postlets, and any that you can think of. You should be building a pretty good base in social media and have subscribed to all of those trash and treasure sites on Facebook. You will need to be sure to post your house on all of these sites. I generally post in about 85 locations for each house. You will need to take at least a half day to dedicate to web and social media presence.

You can host an open house for your home. You will use all of the sources above to advertise this open house. You will also pay some excited high school kids $10-15 per hour to put in head phones and become a human directional. A sign spinner. Get attention!!

Once you have guests at your property you will want to engage all senses. The house will look wonderful because you have spent a ton of time and money making that happen. (**Sight**)

Have music playing softly throughout the house. Wireless speakers are cheap these days. Depending on the audience you can select from classical, instrumental new age, jazz, or even light adult contemporary. (**Sound**)

I like to bake cookies scheduled to come out of the oven just as your open house begins. It is a great idea to also have coffee, tea, and water available. (**Taste and Smell**)

Be sure that the doors to the bathrooms and closets are shut. They should engage in opening them. (**Touch**)

Do not expect a large turnout. The number of people who actually attend an open house has dwindled over the past few years. I did sell one home that way a couple of years ago so I am going to keep at it.

Now, do you remember the local art you were going to put in the homes? Here is a great way to step up an open house and if you are not in Richmond I am pretty sure this has not been done in your area. You can have an "Open House Art Gallery." This will be done the same way that the Realtor Open House was done. Make sure you have non-alcoholic options in addition to the wine and beer offered. Lay out some light appetizers and some entertainment.

You will present this to the artist as a chance for them to showcase their art. Let them invite whomever they desire. Post this all over your social media sites. Put flyers out all over the area. The goal is not really to find a buyer that night, although it may happen. The idea is to generate some really inexpensive exposure.

Now, write a PSA to all media outlets. Written, web, print...everything!!! Spin it as a this kind real estate investor cares so much about the arts and local artist that they have opened their new home to host this even free of charge. **BOOM!!! Feel good story!! You are a local**

hero-celeb for the moment and your house is all over the news. Write in third person. A PSA about yourself is overlooked more times than not.

You are about to go to the opening exhibit gala at the art museum that you bought tickets for six months ago. You are looking all kinds of good. This, and moments like this, are exactly when the phone rings and you hear "This is Sally Realtor. My clients are about to write an offer. Will you be available to receive a fax in the next hour or two?" *Sigh. Of course you will. After all this is the moment you have been working towards for the past four months.

There are several points for which can be used to negotiate. You need to be sure to read the contract to ensure that you are not agreeing to make less than you think. You will soon learn where to look from experience. The contract varies from state to state.

Although most realtors are pretty awesome about the fact that you are representing yourself on the sale, I have seen a couple who have increased the amount of the commission. If you have it listed as the standard 3% they have the option to put a higher amount on the contract. I had one change the 3% to 6% and then justify it to me by saying that since I was unrepresented he will be forced to do the job for both sides.

NO!! Similarly, in a situation where I had not yet listed the home on the MLS through my broker, the agent tried to sneak in the contract for her to list the property hence doubling the commission. Again...*Absolutely not*!!

The most common requests are for closing cost. Generally between $2500 and $7500. You can always decline this or reduce the amount. If your home has been on the market for less than two weeks and has had activity for showings you can and should keep the $2500-$7500 that they want to take from you. Many times the buyer needs that assistance with closing cost. At that point you can counter the offer by saying that you will allow the closing cost but want that amount added to the price of the home.

Mr. and Mrs. Publique need $5000 towards closing. Fine. The purchase price becomes $254,999 rather than $249,999.

Since you are selling a rehabbed home you should not have this happen much but just in case…. Jane Publique dislikes the carpet you put upstairs. She wants a carpet allowance to replace it. She is asking for $5000. You have several options. One is to say no. It's unreasonable for a renovated home anyway.

You know you paid your carpet guy $2100 to put that first carpet in. Offer to allow her to replace it with the color of her choice within the same price point with your carpet guy.

Offer the $2100 you paid off of the price of the home.

Remember, it is entirely up to you to take an offer or not. You need to evaluate the level of interest, time on the market, time of the year, and how much are you paying in holding costs.

Once all parties have agreed on the contract you will need to order a termite inspection and the buyer will order the home inspection and send the ratified contract to your attorney.

Your house can be brand new, just out of the box, shiny and fresh, still had that new car smell; the inspection will find a TON of stuff and the buyer will ask for all of it to be done. Most of the items will be recommendations. Do not worry about "correcting" anything that is a recommendation. You will want to worry about any hazard that was missed by you and your contractor. Plan on doing those. Some things will just be simple like tightening a screw and so on. I just do that to look like we are super generous. "Look Mr. and Mrs. Publique we are doing everything on this list but I just cannot replace your roof and add a second heat pump"

Remember, when dealing with real estate contracts the expiration periods are very short. Time is of the essence. Do not drag your feet making a decision. You stand to lose the whole contract.

Expect the bank to have repair request in order to lend the money. I have seen everything from having the electrical lines buried to taking the security bars off of the window. Just do it! Seriously. It's not worth the battle. They don't care if this loan goes through or not. You do!!

Meanwhile your attorney had ordered title (or you ordered it through a title company) and has been lining up your title insurance. This is simply a guarantee that the person checking the title to be sure there are no loans, liens, or other encumbrances attached to the home did their job. It is required though so just roll with it.

You will also have a HUD statement to look at a couple of days prior to closing. This is like an itemized receipt of the breakdown of the monies received for the home. You will want to look it over carefully. Attorneys and paralegals make mistakes too. Once you see that all of the numbers are correct you will know the exact amount you are making.

When you "go to closing" you will swing by your attorney's office and sign your name a few times. You will then have the option of how you want your funds delivered.

Overnight, direct deposit, or mailed to the attorney for you to pick up. All but the later have a fee attached.

Congratulations!!! You just made your first money flipping a house.

You are a real estate investor!!!

Creative
Financing

Ladies and Gents, this is what separates the men from the boys. Real investor's vs amateurs. This is when others would throw their hands up and walk away; we have a solution!! We are not confined by the standard, run of the mill, real estate transaction. Yes, we can do this!

This is for the poor investor, the hungry investor, the investor who is not afraid to stand out! This is how you build wealth and increase income without having to have a lot of money. There is no hard money lender here. Just you and a fan-flipping-tastic option to a seller who didn't think he had any.

I am talking about *creative financing*. You will learn how to own a property without having to get a loan with very little money out of your pocket. Have virtually zero dollars? We can rock that too!

You will also learn how to make large chunks of cash and residual passive income with almost zero investment. You will learn how to landlord without having to follow the Residential Landlord Tenant Act in many states and never provide maintenance. Am I showing you how to be a slumlord? Absolutely not!

Your tenants will appreciate you for these options!

You will be able to help families who would not be able to purchase a home in a real ownership situation. You will be that guy who gives out second chances to people that deserve them (or don't).

Ok, so after you pull out your super hero cape and a classy pair of tights we can get started.

Lease Purchase, Owner Financing and Subject To

Armed with the information in this section you will be able to help people facing foreclosure, people in an upside-down mortgage, people who need passive income but cannot be a landlord, and people in many more scenarios. We will do this through lease purchases, owner financing, and purchases which are subject to the existing mortgage.

We are going to just jump right into this.

The first topic we will discuss is **Owner Financing**. The reason is because everything else will build from what you learn here. Owner financing is exactly what it sounds like. The owner of the property finances all or some of the purchase price. This is ideal when the home has no mortgage. This is called *free and clear* in the real estate investor world.

> Sarah owns a home with no mortgage. You agree on a price and make payments to Sarah. You are the owner. Sarah acts as the bank.

In this scenario you will need to agree on the *amount, length of time, amortization* (the payments based on a time frame that may not be the same as the loan), and the *interest rate*. You will record these decisions in your purchase agreement. Your attorney will draft a mortgage agreement and a promissory note. This transaction has a recorded deed. You are on deed as the owner and the former owner is the lender in either first or second position depending on how the deal is structured. I am going to go into a lot more detail on this later on.

Basically,

> Owner Financing = A purchase where the bank is replaced by an Individual or business.

Substitution of collateral is where you will use one person's money to finance multiple purchases.

> Nico owns a home and has agreed to owner financing for a period of 5 years but you plan to

> flip the home you are buying
> from him. When you sell the
> home you will use the capital
> from the sale to finance another
> purchase rather than pay Nico
> off right away.

You will hear someone say "3/2, 1500, ARV 180, 35k rehab, free and clear, 75 at zero on a 30 with a balloon at 5" As an informed investor you will know that this means ***"Today I bought a 3 bedroom 2 bathroom home that is 1500 sqft. The value of the home after I fix it up is $180,000. I will spend $35,000 on this renovation. I am purchasing it from the owner who is financing it to me for $75,000 with no interest for 5 years with payments based on a 30 year amortization schedule. After 5 years I will need to pay the balance."*** Is this sentence super relevant to owner financing? Not really. You just do not want to look like a deer in headlights when another investor tells you something like this. You're welcome.

The next creative financing method is to purchase *subject to* the existing mortgage. This is also very much like it sounds, as you will see once I explain it to you. This type of purchase is called **Sub To** by other investors.

A sub to purchase allows you to purchase the home while taking over their financing. For example, Henry Homeowner has been making the payments on his home but he has recently lost his job. He can be relieved of the payments and the home by assigning you homeownership on the title, and your ownership of the home is *'subject to'* the mortgage. You can assume ownership of the home and make the payments for Henry Homeowner.

> **Hint**: Do not confuse this with an *assumable mortgage*. They are almost unheard of these days with the rare exception of the VA loan. (VA loans are loans provided to military service members, this is not relevant to our topic.)

A sub to is a good idea in certain situations but not all as we will discuss later. You will draft a contract to reflect this and your attorney will close this with title changing hands.

> Sub to = buying a home by agreeing to pay off the mortgage they already have.

When you combine the last two financing styles you have a *Wraparound Mortgage*. For example, Bob owns a home that has become too much for him to keep up and he wants to move to a condo in the city. Bob still owes most of the purchase price on the mortgage he took out when he bought the house but not all. You will have him finance the difference.

> Wraparound Mortgage= Using owner financing and sub to for financing the purchase.

Our final tool in our superhero tool belt is a lease purchase. It is very similar to the owner financing arrangement without title. You will have all of the rights and responsibilities of the owner without title. Your rights are contractually governed because the home does not change hands in the eyes of public record. For this reason, you need to be sure your attorney has reviewed the agreement thoroughly. This is the least expensive way to begin building your real estate empire.

You will make payments to the owner and receive a credit towards the payoff. I like to use an amortized payment but many owners prefer a set amount.

> Lease purchase = possession of a property with the rights and responsibilities of the owner but not titled ownership.

Now that you have a basic understanding of each method, we can discuss how to obtain these leads and then enter in to the financing type that will best suit the situation we can begin from the beginning and ride it to the end. Hang on!

Looking for Leads

When your intention is to make a purchase with creative financing you will look for leads differently. The clientele is different so you will need to use marketing targeted at *that* seller. Utilization of the *MLS* is a futile waste of time and energy for both you and your realtor.

I convinced my realtor, Ebony, to send offers to every MLS listing that had a vacant home or was on the market for 6 months or more. In my mind, who wouldn't want to make money off a vacant property or want a full price offer on their home they have been listing for 6 months.

I thought I would end up with more houses than I could handle. I almost ended up with a realtor who became the proud owner of a few shiny new protective orders. Really but not really. *Close.*

I learned that realtors as a whole do not understand creative financing and are stuck in a box of conventional purchases. When they received the offer they were confused by it. They had no idea how to present it to the seller. A few called me for an explanation but most just grew angry at Ebony and I.

You will be looking for people who fit in a few select categories. People who are having financial trouble and are in fear of losing their home to foreclosure, those who are landlords to houses that are *not making them any money*, houses *that are for sale by owner and are not selling*, and the ones who just do not want to deal with the hassle of being a landlord. You will do most of your business with landlords. These are your bread and butter.

The easiest, best response rate, and cheapest (by cheap I mean free) way to solicit leads is through the internet. Obviously, right? Craigslist, FSBO sites, social media especially Facebook, military listing sites, and so on. In this list of sites there are two ways that we will market. One is getting people to come to you. The other is going to them.

Your social media will be the type where you bring people to you. I have found Facebook to be an extremely effective tool for marketing so that is really the main form of social media that I am going to focus on.

You need a personal profile. You will need to have a nice base of "friends" that are going to unknowingly help you. You should actively build your base to at least 2,000. Facebook only allows you 5,000 friends so you will have to get selective at around 3,500. Now how does one go about just magically gaining thousands of friends? Easy. Look for others who rely on networking for their career. Realtors are perfect. Send a Friend Request to them. They will add you, especially if you have "real estate Investor" listed in your about me section. People in local bands are good for growing your base. Once you create a base of local people others will follow and you will have to be selective eventually.

You will need to make your personal page a professional page. This can be an additional Facebook personality or adjust your current one to meet the specifications here.

Do not make every post about investing. Save that for your business site. You will want an average of 1 in 12 post to be about business. More than this will make you invisible to people as they will assume that all post are work related. Less will allow people to forget what you even do. I have been slacking and I was just asked if I still run an art gallery. Yep, time for a few work post.

When you are not spreading the word on investing you will need to be a positive, upbeat, but human person. Most things should fall into the category of a happy picture, an uplifting meme, a positive post about a good day or something. Pictures should be of you being happy, your friends or family being happy, your pets playing. Every once in a while you should have a post that is less happy. It cannot always be rainbows and sunshine. Sometimes it has to rain to be believable. Don't go all crazy with some rant about how your girl is hooking up with three other dudes or that you saw on your man's phone that he got a text from "side bae" and realized it was your text. Save that for another page.

You should appear as a complex person on the outside but not really give much specific information.

Do not post pictures of playing with guns. This is a best practice rule unless you are in law enforcement or the military but you will want to say something like "*practice with my service weapon*" or "*USMC standard issue, proud to have her by my side.*" Do not post pictures of you doing drugs. I do not care if you are in Jamaica at The World Cannabis Cup (I made that up by the way, don't get excited.) Do not post about being drunk. And please keep your clothes on! This is not the place to find a man. You can be half naked with your tongue stuck out on Tinder. Gym rats, I know it's hard, but please keep your shirt on for your flexed pics. Do not post anything that someone else can see as irresponsible or offensive. Which is pretty much everything these days. Remember, this is business. Being a real estate investor requires trust from your clients. If it is something you would not want to bring out at a job interview, do not make it public.

You should have no views on religion, politics, or other "hot" issues. Leave this to living room discussions.

Join as many "yard sale" type groups as you can. They come under many names like *Trash and Treasure, Consignment, ISO,* and so on. Be creative in your search. I think I am a member of about 80 of these. No kidding.

Once you have set this up you can make your post to target the client you want. Do not post all of these things at once. That is confusing and inundates your audience. Remember, over posting makes you seem uninteresting and people will either scan right over your post or delete you. Neither come even close to your objective.

Your post should similar to these. Add your own personality to your post. I am not a very interesting "poster" but I sure wish I could be more entertaining in looking for homes.

> *"I need help. Is there a house for sale by owner in your neighborhood? I am looking for one. Please inbox me. I will be glad to give you a finder's fee for the help."*

There are three things to notice here. First, you have asked for help. People love to be helpful for the most part. Second, you have requested that you receive a private message. This is because you will get little or even no response many times. You want it to look as though there may be others responding. You may want to even add to your comments "Thank you guys so much. Keep it coming" Even if there was no reply.

Finally, you offered moola. Of course you did. I give $500 to the person who brings me a lead if I actually get the house after I have made money.

> *"Are you tired of bad tenants? What if I told you that you could never have a late payment, vacancy loss, or have to make another repair. Message me for info. If you think you know someone who can benefit, please share."*

> *"Are you facing foreclosure? I can help. This is between us. Just IM me. If you think you know someone who can benefit, please share with them or on your page."*

You may or may not be able to post these on the "yard sale" sites but you can post it on your own page.

Facebook is far more helpful when it comes to finding the end user for your homes that you are going to offer. Do not expect a lot of action for this type of post.

Craigslist and other sites where people have homes listed as rentals or FSBO's (for sale by owner) are another free and more effective method of finding clients. You will simply contact the owner of the home and ask them if they would consider a lease purchase or owner finance on the home if you guarantee payments and they do not have to make a single repair for the entire term.

Many sites are email only or the preferred contact method is email. Your email should be simple and to the point.

> Hello.
>
> Would you consider a lease purchase or owner finance if you do not have to worry about payments or repairs for the term? Please feel free to email, call or text me at (804) 555-1234.
>
> Respectfully,
>
> Charity

When texting just use the bulk of the content without the pleasantries.

When calling you will just ask outright if they will consider a lease purchase or owner finance. I will get into the negotiation of the agreement later. This is simple lead generation.

You will stumble upon many homes that are represented for rent by a realtor or management company. You will want to get the address and find the owner's name and address. Be sure to note the month that you are seeing this. They will be a recipient of your direct mailers. I will explain further down.

Once you begin to acquire homes you will find yourself in court. This is just the nature of the beast and in fact part of your business model. We will get into that later as well. The relevance is here.

I like to sit on the edge of the row waiting to find a landlord who seems to really be struggling with the collecting his money. I am armed with my business cards and a note hand written on the card saying "*I can help. No cost to you. Wait for me outside or call*" My success rate is pretty high there.

I find bandit signs to be a wonderful way to reach pre foreclosure and unhappy landlord clients. The sign should be simple and direct. I have found a bright yellow, hand written sign to be the most effective. You can purchase precut 12"x18", coroplast signs with H frames fairly inexpensively. You will use a giant black marker to write on your signs.

Facing Foreclosure?

804-555-1234

Tired of bad tenants?

804-555-1234

You will place these signs in high traffic intersections in the areas that you want to target. Plan to drive the areas that you have signs weekly to replace the ones that are missing, faded, or damaged.

Direct mail is one of the methods that almost all investors I know use. Some only use this. I personally find it to be a good way to find homes but not the best. Direct mail is EXACTLY what it sounds like. You are going to send correspondence on paper to potential sellers. What you say, to whom, and where the lists are acquired is somewhat a matter of taste while following a few guidelines.

Mailers are expensive compared to the other options we discussed. You will want to be sure that you are reaching the right people with the right content.

The elderly man or woman who no longer resides in their home but still pays taxes, insurance, and upkeep are excellent candidates. We, as investors, are able to offer a better option than a reverse mortgage which makes one jump through hoops to possibly get a portion of the value of the home. Once they pass, the family is left with tons of debt from interest compounded from the time the contract was signed. In many situations the home is in need of renovation or repair that they cannot afford, so they cannot list it for sale. You are able to offer them cash quickly, no inspection fees, no repairs on the home, and no realtor fees. It's a real winner for all.

Homes with out of state owners prove effective in finding motivated sellers. It is difficult to manage a rental from another state and even worse if the home is just vacant. Is it making or losing money? How much time are they putting into this property? These key facts are perfect negotiation tools for you when talking to the owner.

People who are behind in their mortgage are excellent candidates. They will be open to at least hearing how they can salvage their dignity and credit.

Some others are unoccupied properties, absentee owners, and properties with code compliance (tall grass, broken windows).

List can be purchased from companies like Melissa Data and Info USA. You can narrow down to as large or small of a list as you like.

Foreclosures are required to be listed in the paper somewhere. What paper is not specified. You can see the attorney office that is handling the each foreclosure when the homes are listed at the courthouse for auction. Let's say that the office of Smith, Brown, and Jones are taking a lot of these cases. You can call their office and just ask what paper they are using for their public notices. You can either buy the paper or check to see if they are online. All of the information you need is there. The owner's names, address, property address, what is owed…everything. Remember, these people do have a home pending foreclosure fairly soon so unless you have a few thousand to get the home out of foreclosure this might be a waste of time.

You may also target select neighborhoods and look for absentee owners by using public record. In Chesterfield, VA, for example you can go to http://www.chesterfield.gov/eServices/RealEstateAssessments/RealEstate.aspx?id=11063, select "Search Property Sales" and choose any subdivision by clicking on the name in the drop menu. Once you have selected the neighborhood begin at the first parcel number and select. You will then look for any parcel where the mailing address and the property address do not match. You have identified an absentee owner in the neighborhood of choice for absolutely free.

The content of your mailer depends on what you are trying to achieve. Regardless it needs to be attention grabbing. You want each recipient to

    A. Open the envelope
    B. Read the content
    C. Become curious about it.

How do we meet this goal as effectively as possible?

Be tacky! Yep I said it!!

Be sure your envelope is hand written (or looks like it) with handwriting that is less than perfect. I used to have my father write these before he passed. People were asking "Do you have kids help you with this?" That's what I'm talking about!!! I don't care what the question is; I got you on the phone! Pitch time!!!!

When dealing with absentee owners and your focus is on creative financing, we assume that the home is occupied by tenants. In that case we are looking for a landlord who may have interest in a lease purchase or owner financing you may want to use a flyer that has something to the effect of: *"Who pays when your tenants aren't? If it is you, allow us to show you a better way."*

"What is your management company doing for you?" and follow **with** *"If they are not guaranteeing rent regardless of tenancy we can help"*

Highlight key points, circle your name and number, and write a message on the back saying "I am looking forward to hearing from you." Of course, you can do all of this with a great copier and not have to write each one.

You will want to include all of the really awesome reasons that you will make them rethink why they ever used a management company in the first place. I am going to tell you how awesome you are when making this offer in just a moment but for now include some things like this in your flyer.

- Payments guaranteed
- Never make a repair again
- Top dollar sales price
- No management fee
- No hassle
- Owe more than the value? That's Okay.
- We buy houses too.

Remember the list of homes that are represented by a management company or realtor? These are great!!! You know they are a landlord already. You are not guessing. You know that they are paying 8-12% of their gross rents to the management company. You know that when the house is vacant they do not get paid. You know that when the tenant does not pay it is actually costing them money. Put that cape on. You can fix all of that but first they have to call you.

When you find the names and addresses of the landlords in public record you will send them a flyer. But wait, they might be in a contract with the management company for 12 months. You log each of them as you send them. In 9 months you will send another and again at the 10 month mark. So if you find the house in January you will send them a flyer in September and October. Why you ask? Because their contracts generally expire in 12 months **or** the end of the lease. Most times you must give a 30-60 day notice to terminate the agreement. You are reminding them of the other options while there is still time to make a decision.

Pre foreclosure letters should be more professional than the others. You are going to offer to solve all of their problems, or so it seems. The biggest issue is that they generally want to stay in the home. You are going to help them to not have the neighborhood know they were foreclosed upon. You are going to keep a foreclosure off of their credit and even improve it. You are not going to help them stay in the house.

Dear Mr. and Mrs. Smith,

It has come to my attention that your family might be going through a tough time financially and I believe I might be able to help. I specialize in assisting families facing foreclosure to halt the auction, maintain the dignity of not having a public foreclosure, and regain your credit.

If you believe that you can benefit from my services please do not hesitate to contact me. You can find my contact information below.

Very Respectfully,

Charity Woods

When you pass a home that is for rent or for sale by owner get the number and call them. This is called birddogging. It surprises me how many people only advertise their homes with a sign in the yard. This is golden because the home will sit much longer with less advertising.

You now know HOW to generate leads for creative deals. You will next learn what to do with the leads once you have them. You will learn the benefits you can provide and the art of letting them know the level of awesome in front of them. People can't see the forest for the trees sometimes.

Finding Creative Solutions

Most people are stuck in the conventional mindset of real estate. You can only buy a house with cash or with a bank. You can only make money by either renting or flipping. Let's change their minds!

When you get calls on your signs, letters, and emails the person you are talking to probably knows less than you do right now. There is an occasional exception where someone will have an idea of what you are talking about but it is rare. You will need to understand the difficulties the other person faces and maximize your ability to extinguish the burden. Sometimes they do not know they even have a problem and you have to find it and point it out. Your prospect does not care how smart you are and how much you learned from this course, this is not your time to show off. Make sure you ask relevant questions and listen! Let them talk. Their life is on the line, their home is in trouble. You will build rapport by offering a sympathetic ear. Find out what is important to them, find their problem and make sure they know you can solve it.

Let's look at the types of marketing you will be doing and who your client will most likely be from each style. That helps us to know what the most likely hot buttons will be. I have said this before and do not wish to discourage anyone; creative negotiations are not for the faint of heart.

Anyone <u>can</u> do it but I can tell you that the shy investor will have to reach way out of her comfort zone and be able to overcome objection after objection. This is when you will be accused of being a scam artist, a swindler, and a crook. On the flip side this is also when you will get praise, accolades, gifts, and cards from those who were in a real bind.

Your leads from social media will generally come in the form of an IM, PM, DM, whatever that site is calling their messaging feature. (Hopefully not a BM. That just doesn't seem like a way I want to receive messages.) Anyway, these can come from a variety of sellers.

The most common are three follow.

(1) Folks who have a house with a really bad tenant.
(2) Those who have a house in awful shape and want to sell it but nobody wants it
(3) This one is a surprising one but believe it or not I get about 2 a year.

> Men who have made an arrangement similar to obtaining a mail order bride and he needs to go impress her family with money and gifts in order to obtain "permission" to marry the woman. Not kidding.

The good news here is that they lay their hot button out in the message they send you.

> "Hey Charity. I see that you can
> help people with bad tenants. I
> have a family that is living in my
> house and they have not paid
> me in two months. I sent them a

letter saying they had to leave in 30 days but they are still there. They are tearing the house apart. Are you able to help me?"

Heck yea I can and so can you. What is their hot button? Money!!!! This person has no Idea how to be a landlord. You will know exactly what to do with these tenants and with this property. Assume Judy, our IMer, messaged you.

You will respond with a little empathy and a pre offer.

You: Of course Judy. I am glad to help you out of that uncomfortable situation. I am really sorry you are going through that.

Judy: Oh thank you sooooo much. This has been a real money pit from day one. I don't know why I thought I wanted to be a landlord.

You: Would it be helpful to you if I get the bad tenants out of your house, while you are making the repairs I am lining up person to move in, and once I find that

> person I will guarantee all
> maintenance, repairs, and
> payments? What If I can even
> sell the house for you for the full
> market value in a few years?

How could Judy not love this offer?

Are you wondering how can you possibly make the offer work? I hope so. That shows me that you have a business mind and are thinking, "Charity is nuts!" NO!!! You will have a plan. Here it is.

You will get with Judy and find out if she is more attracted to a lease purchase or an owner finance. Basically you will want to know how _done_ she is with the property. The only difference is title. *If you do not have a budget for closing you will only offer a lease purchase.

You will include in your agreement that Judy does not receive a payment until you have found a new person to go in the home and the repairs are made. If Judy believes that this is not a great deal you will need to remind her that in her current situation she still will not get paid until the home is rent ready and there is a tenant in place. The difference here is that this is the last time she needs to worry about such things with you.

You will also look at the value of the home. You do not need to be as exact in this situation as you do for a flip. You can use free sites like Zillow and Trulia for an estimated value. That is your max offer. This negotiation should go something like this.

> You: Hey Judy, thank you for
> meeting with me. I am excited to

help you find some resolution to your tenant issues.

Judy: Thank you so much for coming. I feel better already.

You: I want to make you two offers and let you decide which you think works best for you. They are both similar but do have a few variables that are extremely important to understand. First let me ask you, do you remember when I offered to purchase the house? What do you think it is worth right now?

Judy: That's a good question. The one down the street, that is just like mine, sold for $189,900. So I guess about $190,000.

Everyone thinks a house down the street just sold for X amount and it is just like theirs. Typically, the amount was the asking price, the house sold months (or even years) ago, and they are not remotely similar. I typically just ignore the answer unless it is below what I am going to offer. In this simulated negotiation we found out on Zillow that the approximate value is $175,000. We will use that.

> You: I want to be fair in my offer but also I cannot put myself in a deficit either. I did my research and found the value to be closer to $175,000.

Judy is in a bad spot so she shouldn't get too upset here. If she does you can always tell her that if you both come to terms on all other aspects of the agreement you will be glad to have your realtor come and give her a market analysis and evaluate the sales price from there. This is really just a CMA (comparative market analysis) and takes 5 minutes. Judy's main goal is to get out of the hole in which she currently resides.

> You: I am offering to take your home on immediately. I will get the current tenants out of there as quickly as the law allows. You can then immediately begin doing the work to get the home back into rent ready shape, something you would have to do anyway. While you are having that work done I will be hard at work finding another tenant.

Once she moves in, I will give you the first pro ratta payment and guarantee every payment for the next five years. At that time we can give you the lump sum balance of the purchase price we agree upon today. Now, obviously, since I will be guaranteeing payments, regardless of vacancy or payment default by the tenants and I will be absorbing all of the repairs I have to have a way to make this worth my while. This is where I have two options for you.

In the first option I will purchase the home from you in two weeks but make the agreed payments to you each month. I will be paying down the value of the home just like any other mortgage. The second option is for you to stay in ownership but

contractually give me all of the
rights and responsibilities of the
owner so that I can make repairs
and improvements.

During this time I can make
payments paying down the
balance using an amortization
schedule just like a mortgage or I
can receive a set monthly credit.
The biggest difference here is
title. With the first option I have
title. With the second you do.
With the first option I am the
one who is legally responsible
for anything that happens on the
property. With the second I am
contractually responsible.

Our girl Judy goes with a lease purchase.

What about those tenants and how will you make money?
Your plan is this. After Judy signs the agreement you will
send a notice of management as well as a Notice to Pay
or Quit to the tenants. The latter is a requirement in most
states where you will give notice to the tenant(s) that
money is due and it is your plan to evict them. In Virginia
you must give a 5 day notice. On the sixth day you will go
to the courthouse for the municipality where the home is
located and complete the first step in the eviction process

through the courts known as an Unlawful Detainer. The entire process of eviction in most states takes roughly one to two months.

While you are waiting on the deadbeat tenants to leave you can begin to market the home to new folks where you will make money. We can go into that in a few. Remember you do not owe Judy a dime until you are making money on the home.

Now, Ned messages you about his house that has been vacant for a year needs a little work and you are going to go take a look. It is a super hideous disaster.

Ned opens the door to his home smiling as though his lips being stretched across his face have made the stench of mildew and cat disappear. It does not and it is only reinforced by the shrill screech of a feral cat as he runs past you. The décor of dangling drywall and wispy tufts of insulation scatter the floor make you long for the old couch and milk carton ash tray from the front porch…. You get the idea. Ned's house is a POS. (Urban dictionary POS if needed.)

Before going to Ned's you did your due diligence. This is a term investors like to use for not being a dumbass. You obviously want to know what you are offering so you ask your realtor to pull the comps in the area. Honestly, if you are not planning to wholesale or flip here you do not have a good option. You can only make a flip offer and ask for owner financing.

If Ned had a house that was bad but not falling in around you bad, you can make a lease purchase or owner finance offer. We will go down that road with Ned right now although the majority of the people who reach out because they cannot sell the home will have a house like first Ned.

You have negotiated the same way that you did with Judy except Ned has no money to fix the house up. That is why it has been vacant and costing him money. How can you make this work?

Ned is used to a vacant house. Any payment is helpful. Additionally, no payment is the norm. We will offer to make the repairs but will not make a payment to Ned until the value of the repairs have been paid.

You will not need to bring the house to Flip Condition but you will want a decent home. We will discuss this later as well.

Ned's house needs carpet, paint, and a really good cleaning. You call your contractor and get a bid of $1800 for carpet, $3600 for paint, and $500 for cleaning. That totals $5900. You have determined that you are paying Ned $1,000 per month for the house but will not make a payment for the first 6 months. I know that this is investing for the people who have not "*made it*" yet. You might not have $5900. That's ok. You can do most of that yourself. You can paint and clean for only the cost of materials, say $500. You probably will have to pay someone to do the carpet but $2300 is a lot more manageable.

If you are saying *"$2300 is not really manageable"* you do have the option of assigning the agreement to another investor who has the money. Charge him a couple thousand dollars as a finder's fee.

Chuck sends you this message.

"Hello. I don't know if you have seen on my page but I have met a beautiful Russian woman named Svetlana when I was in Europe for vacation last month. We are going to be married as soon as we can get her fiancé visa straight. She tells me it is very important to impress her family so I will be buying all of them cars. I am going there for 6 months. Also, she says my house is too small for all of the children we hope to have someday so we will be getting a new one once she is here with me. Can you help me show income for the house I have and also find a bigger one when I return?

Thanks,

Chuck

PS I had to quit my job to go there for 6 months so as much help as possible is appreciated."

Again, this happens about twice a year. They really do need to go "there" for several months, show as much income as possible for the duration, and generally "need" a bigger house upon return. I'm not saying she is a gold-digger, ya'll know the song…I'm sure they are all very much in love.

This client needs a quick fix, steady income, and to continue ownership of his property. Some insight, the department of immigration wants to be sure that the future husband is financially secure enough to support a new family. They do request the financial records of the applicant. They also want to see that he is stable and has assets. My typical client in this capacity is a retiree and does not *actually* have to quit his job but I have been asked for a letter of employment to show INS.

You will want to offer him a lease purchase with a fairly quick sale as he will probably need the equity from that home to purchase a new one. 12 months is generally my offer. I also refer them to a realtor to find the next house.

The good news is that they want to make moves fast. You can typically negotiate the monthly payment for below market rent and have a nice monthly return.

You will need to let them know that you are not able to offer the full value of the home for such a short period as a bank will only finance the actual value of the property. This leaves no room for you to negotiate the final sales price to your end user.

In situations where you are offering a 5 year term you are counting on two things to make the end sale work for you. First you are counting on the value of the home to increase. If the rate of growth for housing prices in the area has only increased 3% per year over the last few years you can assume the same to happen over the next

5 years. If you are making an offer of $200,000 on a house today you can assume the value will be $231,850 in 5 years. Second you will be paying down the balance over that period of time as well. We will use $200 per month here. That is another $12,000 off the price. You hope to be placing your buyer on your own so there will not be realtor fees. The buyer will pay closing cost. The bottom line is that you have approximately $40,000 coming to you at the end of the term. I like to call that projected equity.

Back to Chuck. Projected equity really doesn't exist in just one year. You will have to offer Chuck $180,000 on his $200,000 home to make any money on the back end.

When you have a buyer who is responding to an email or phone call from craigslist or the like you generally have a person who is already a landlord. A few will come from FSBO sellers but most of them will just break bad and call a realtor.

The landlord is typically ok with the issues of landlording. You will have to connect with them in a business minded capacity versus the emotional connection of the ones listed prior. The problems with being a landlord include tenants not paying, chasing rent, going to court to get your house back, repairs, vacancy, and turning the property after each tenant.

Turning is the landlord equivalent to flipping on a much smaller scale. When you turn the property you will clean or replace carpet, paint, clean, freshen up the yard, and fix anything that needs repair. This can include a leaky faucet, replacing light bulbs, a running toilet.

The best argument here is that you can eliminate the loss of revenue associated with the above things mentioned. If you are able to quantify the loss to the landlord you have taken a step in the right direction. Let's say her rent is

$1,000 and the average tenant stays for two years. The vacancy loss will be roughly $1000 per year as the typical turnaround time is 60 days. We can also assume that even if the carpet does not need replacement, the turn cost for paint, carpet cleaning, deep cleaning, and so on will cost about $2,000. That is a loss of $2,000 per year total. Over the course of 5 years you have made them $10,000.

When you are birddogging and find leads that way, you are calling a person who either wants to rent or sell their home. They are probably not using a realtor or a management company.

You will approach the rentals primarily with a lease purchase option and the sales with an owner finance option.

We have not discussed the owner finance option in depth so let's do that now. You have found a lovely 3 bedroom 2 bath in a desirable area and called the number. There are two schools of thought on how to proceed. The first is to do the majority of the leg work over the phone. The other is to make your offer in person. There is no wrong way. It is what is best for you. If saving time is very important to you I recommend trying to feel out the buyer over the phone. If you prefer a higher close rate and you are a good face to face closer I recommend the later.

Time savers your initial conversation should go like this after you have looked up the house on the real estate assessor's page and looked at the value of the other homes in the area.

> You: Hello. I am calling about the
> house you have for sale in Deer

> Run. Can you tell me about it
> please?

This is when they tell you all kinds of irrelevant stuff like when they bought it, how much they love it, and why they are moving. If they do not tell you the actual important items like price, square footage, and b/b (bedrooms and baths), ask. You should already know most of this from public record.

> You: That sounds like a lovely
> house. I am sure whoever buys it
> will be very lucky to have it. You
> said that you want $265,000 for
> the home. I see the other houses
> in your area with similar square
> footage are selling for $249,000.
> How important is the sales price
> being $265,000 to you?

This can go either way. Either it is important or it is not. Regardless they will try to tell you why it is better than the others.

Option 1.

> Them: You can make an offer
> and we can see what happens?

Option 2.

> Them: It is important to me. That is what I think my home is worth. I am not willing to just give it away.

Either way your answer is pretty much the same.

> You: I am sure that your home is lovely. I also believe that you have put a lot of extra work into your home to make it that way. The problem here is that a bank will not lend more than the perceived value of the home. That of course is based primarily on the sales of the other homes in the area.
>
> Now, I would like to buy your house very much but I do not have an extra $265,000. (*insert friendly laugh) What if I could offer you the full asking price but you had to wait for the equity? Would that work?

You just asked them to owner finance the home in a roundabout way. They of course will not understand the question fully but with that wording it doesn't sound half bad.

> Them: I am not sure what you mean. I want the full price for my house but wait how long?
>
> You: I am suggesting that I am able to make payments to you monthly until we are able to reach a dollar amount that the bank will finance. What amount do you need each month?

If they are receptive you will want to get as far as you can in a negotiation and set an appointment ASAP.

Ok, so you are a smooth talker, you have a cute smile, and people just trust your face…maybe you even have a trustworthy name like Charity. You know that face to face you have the best chance. Schedule an appointment and go.

They will take you on the tour of their home and point out <u>every</u> single thing they replaced down to a ten cent switch plate. Smile, nod, act excited.

> You: Thank you so much for showing me your lovely house. (hint: home is a feeling, house is an asset. When dealing with a seller they have a house. When

> dealing with a buyer, they are
> looking at a home.) I can see
> that you have put a lot of work
> into it.
>
> I know that you are asking
> $265,000, which seems very fair
> but based on the other houses
> that have sold in the area I do
> not think a bank would lend
> more than $249,000. How
> important is that extra $16,000
> to you?

This is when you break into the differed equity. Remember, this is your time to shine. Smile. Be sincere. Make them WANT you to have the home they love so dearly.

I absolutely love the people I find in court. Why? They are PISSED at the tenant. They are disheveled. They do not understand how the legal system works in relation to Landlord Tenant. You will treat this person just as you related to Judy. You will relieve this stress. You will have these people out of the house. You will be wearing a cape and tights to this landlord. Make sure the tights are control top. Nobody looks good in loose leggings.

Responses to signs will generally be upset landlords or folks facing foreclosure. You will deal with the landlord in the same way you did Judy or the folks in court.

Your pre foreclosure clients are generally emotionally attached to the home and this is why they haven't just walked away from it. Some may not have any interest in moving and will probably file bankruptcy. The ones who do want to work with you have accepted that they are in a bad situation and they will try to walk away as unscathed as possible.

Whether they are calling from a sign or a letter the negotiation should be the same. The phone call will probably go a bit like this.

> Mike: Hello. This is Mike Jones. I am calling because I received a letter from you.

Notice that the caller did not mention foreclosure. That is a good indicator that they are calling for that reason. A landlord or absentee owner will say why you sent the letter most of the time.

> **You**: Hello Mike. Are you calling because you are looking for foreclosure relief?

If that is not why they are calling they have no problem telling you. Do not make the conversation uncomfortable for Mike by making him say the word "foreclosure."

> Mike: Yes. You sent a letter.
>
> **You**: I am really glad you called. What is your address?
>
> Mike: 123 34th St. How are you able to help me?
>
> **You**: I cannot keep you in your home. I wish I could but I do not have that ability. I can, however make this transition as easy on you, your family, and your credit as possible. Can I get a little information from before we move on?

They may want to know the offer first. I find it better to discuss the offer in person if possible.

> **You**: How many payments have you missed?
>
> Mike: 3.
>
> **You**: What is the monthly payment?
>
> Mike: $1278.
>
> **You**: Has the bank sent you a foreclosure notice?
>
> Mike: Yes.
>
> **You**: Is there an auction date set?
>
> Mike: No.
>
> **You**: Excellent. On the notice the bank sent, what is the reinstatement amount? And when is the deadline for payment?

This is the amount needed to keep the home from foreclosure.

> Mike: $4,678 due in 10 days or it will go to the lawyer.
>
> **You**: How much do you owe on the house?
>
> Mike: I think I owe about $265,000.

At his point you will schedule a time to meet.

You should know the value of the home. You can determine if you want to work with a home that is under water based on your end goal. You should also research the market rent for comparable homes in that area. You can use craigslist for this. Have this prepared when you meet with them.

We are going to say that Mike's house is worth $250,000. Most investors would look at that and think, this is a bad deal. Not us and this is why.

You know the monthly rental amounts are roughly $1650 for the area and the house payment is $1278. There is monthly income and you are not having to use a tremendous amount of capital or credit to acquire it. Additionally you will keep the house way beyond the length of time where there is a disparity in value. Your rents and the value of the home will continue to rise and the balance due will continue to drop.

At the home you will explain to the homeowner(s) that you plan to purchase the home by paying off the debt to the bank and taking over their mortgage. This benefits them by allowing them to move from the home with only a few late payments on their credit. There was no foreclosure or bankruptcy. Their credit will continue to improve as you are making the payments on time each month.

The negatives are that they need to agree ASAP as you need to have this in place before the payment period has expired, 10 days from his call. You will want possession of the home quickly so they will have to move out immediately. Finally, almost all loans have a due on sale clause. This means that when one sells the house (the title changes hands) the lender expects to be paid in full the remaining balance. This of course should not be a tremendous issue for a seller in this situation as they are going to lose the house anyway.

I have never seen a single bank act on a due on sale clause. We do take precautions to avoid it nonetheless. We will write the contract as the buyer being the Jones Family Trust 34th St. You will acquire an LLC in that name to make the purchase. This looks as though the family just decided to place the property into a trust.

As you receive more and more calls from mailers, signs, whatever, you will realize that the nature of the calls generally fall into the scenarios as described in this section. You will soon be able to bounce back and forth between the styles of creative financing effortlessly.

Calculating the Offer

We touched on how you will make the offer to the client but we did not really talk about why you are making the said offer. Sure you can throw numbers out there but we need to know why so that we can make money. This style of real estate requires you to be willing to think of big pictures and long term gains as well as making money now. You must understand your client base on both sides and give them what they need in a way that gives you what you want, money.

Up until now you really have not known what you are going to do with these homes once you acquire them. We will get more in depth soon but for now I will give you a general idea.

To make money in real estate you can buy and sell or buy and hold. When you flip you are buying and selling. The offers on these homes are generally not going to have enough room for you to flip them. You will be holding these homes one way or another.

You can rent the house out like Judy but then you end up with the headaches Judy had. You will want to offer these homes as either a lease purchase or an owner finance. When doing that you will have the opportunity to make money upfront, monthly, and on the back end. Quickly, here is how.

When you have a home that you have acquired as a lease purchase you will in turn offer it as a lease purchase to your tenant/buyer. Your buyer will enjoy the rights and responsibilities of ownership in exchange for a non-refundable down payment equal to 5% of the purchase price, paying based on projected equity, and a slightly higher monthly payment.

If you have purchased a home using owner financing or sub to you can offer the home as an owner finance, recorded or non-recorded, or as a lease purchase. You already know the deal with the lease purchase. A non-recorded owner financed purchase, which is also called a contract for deed, is a sale to the new buyer where you are acting as the bank and they are buying the home with a title that is "held in escrow." This means that in the eyes of the public you own the home while their title is sitting in an attorney's office in a file. A recorded sale is where the sale is recorded in the city or county of the property. For these I require a minimum of 10% down and a high interest rate making payments above market. Right now it sounds like we traded our capes for evil villain cloaks. Not the case at all. We are offering an option to a client base that otherwise would be stuck as renters. Cape is back on.

When you are making an offer for owner financing you are offering to pay all or some of the purchase in the form of a loan to the seller. You may have a situation where you are taking a home sub to but the seller has equity and does not want to lose it. In this situation you will want to offer "terms" or payments to the seller for the balance financed over an agreed upon time. This is also called a Wraparound or Wrap Mortgage. Most people do not like you much if you start higher than 5 years. You will of course begin this calculation by looking into the factors influencing your cash flow.

You are buying a house from Jin. He owes $145,000. His payments are $900. The value is $225,000. Jin wants $225,000. Fair enough. I would not want to walk away from $80,000 either. The other houses in the area are renting for $1650. You know that you can get $1750 for the payment in any creative solution. You offer Jin payments on the $80,000 for 5 years but amortized over 30 years.

You will not offer any interest up front. This means that you will have a payment of $222.22 each month to Jin. This also means that you will owe Jin $66,666.80 in 5 years. Of course you have planned to sell the house at that point anyway. In the mean time you will make up to $25,000 up front and a monthly income of $627.87. So even if you make zilch on the back end you have the potential to make over $60,000 on that property over the 5 year term, or more if you have to foreclose. We will soon find out why bad buyers are part of our business model.

Jin likes the idea but wants interest on his money. Why wouldn't he? Start low. If you both agree on 3% you will owe Jin $71,125 in 5 years plus you will make $115 less each month. You lost roughly $12,000 with only 3% interest. Still not a bad deal.

When you calculated the deal with Jin you had to look at various factors to give you a full picture overview of the potential earnings.

We sometimes encounter sellers who have homes that are perfect for a flip but the seller is receptive to a long term payment. In this situation you have the unique ability to sell the home and continue to use the money. Remember, this money only existed in equity before the sale of the property.

You are meeting with Raul. He owns a property that is in pretty bad shape but is in an area where a flip would be fantastic. Raul inherited the property from his mother and father after they passed and it has really been vacant since then. Raul believes the house is worth about $100,000 in its current condition. You know that the comparable sales in the neighborhood put the ARV at around $220,000. Once you calculated in the repair cost you have to agree with Raul. You both are happy with $100,000 to purchase the home. When you addressed the terms with Raul you discovered that he is open to holding the note longer than the length of time to flip.

> **You**: I can offer you the full $100,000 you are asking but I will have to make payments to you. No matter what I do with the house you will still be receiving payments for the next 5 years. Can you work with that?

> **Raul**: Yes as long as I do not have to take care of this house any longer.

Done. He just agreed to a substitution of collateral. Now you will flip this house and as long as you have a home or multiple homes waiting on financing that value at least $100,000 you can finance it with Raul's loan. This can work for 5 years. You must have the substitution of collateral clause in the agreement and you must have property to transfer the note.

When dealing with investor to investor purchases or owner financed flips you may want to use the option of interest only payments. This is when you make a payment each month equal to the interest for the mortgage. This is calculated using simple interest. Assume that you are borrowing $100,000 at an interest rate of 6%. You will multiply the loan value by the interest rate and divide it by

12 for a payment of $500. You will need to remember that you still owe the full amount at the end of the term.

100,000 x .06=6,000

6,000/ 12= 500

When you are calculating the sub to or lease purchase offer the principals apply as do calculating your profit for an owner financed offer. You need to be able to make an offer other investors would not make because it seems to not make sense to a standard investor.

Going in to these offers you will need to know the value of the home and what is owed on it. You will need to know about the marketability of the area. Will it sit vacant between tenants? What is the rental rate for that neighborhood?

Armed with this information you will be able to make offers on homes that have negative equity and still make money.

Renee owes $215,000 but her payments are only $900. The homes in the area are selling for $150,000 but the average rent is $1500. Is this a good deal? Let's find out.

You know that the difference in payment versus the amount you will charge for rent is good. If you want to take the property as a sub to and hold it as a rental you could make some money there.

What if you do not have the money to close that loan right now? What if you do not want to hold it as a standard rental? You will need to find out if it is marketable as a lease purchase. You will need to be able to cover the loan amount with the purchase agreement from your tenant buyer at the end of the term. Here is how that is calculated.

Start with the value of the home. In this instance it is $150,000.

Next you will need to figure out the rate of growth in the area. Meaning what percent of increase, or decrease, has there been in the last few years in that neighborhood. You could have your realtor pull area comps for the same date for the last 5 years....or you could let a free app do it for you. Hello Zillow!!

If you type Zillow and the address in to the search bar on Google you will get a link to the specifics on any house. Scroll towards the bottom of the page and you will see a value projection chart. You can select 5 or 10 years. It will not tell you the percentage of change but you can calculate that by taking the price from 4 years ago and subtracting it from the price from 5 years ago. Divide the sum by the price 5 years ago then multiply that by 100. Repeat using 4 years and 3 years. Repeat using 3 years and 2. Repeat with 2 and 1. Add them together and divide by 4 to get the average increase.

YEAR 5	YEAR 4	YEAR 3	YEAR 2	NOW
134,000	138,000	141, 000	144,000	150,000
3%	2%	2%	4%	2.75% average

138,000-134,000=4,000

4,000/134,000=0.02985

0.02985x100=2.98 Roughly 3% for the first one

3+2+2+4=11

11/4=2.75

So now we want to know what the value of the home will be in 5 years. So we will take the value of the home today and multiply it by 1.0275 to total $154,125. You will take that new projected value and repeat for 5 years.

$$150,000 \times 1.0275 = 154,125 \text{ next year}$$

$$154,125 \times 1.0275 = 158,363 \text{ two years}$$

$$158,363 \times 1.0275 = 162,718 \text{ three years}$$

$$162,718 \times 1.0275 = 167,193 \text{ four years}$$

$$167,193 \times 1.0275 = 171,791 \text{ Fifth year}$$

The value will still not reach the amount due on the home in 5 years. You will want the projection amount less the amount for the down payment to be more than the amount due.

$$171,791 - 7,500 = 164,291$$

Using this logic the most you can pay for this home under a lease purchase is $164,291. So in this situation, unless you want to keep this home as just a rental, you are not going to be able to help Renee.

You might wonder why we are confined to this 5 year projection for a lease purchase. The reason is because you will be placing a person in the home who plans to buy the house at the end of their agreement. Unless you want to pay the difference, you cannot sell them the home. A bank will not finance it at that amount.

Maybe you are asking, what if I purchase it sub to and sell it to someone else under the same terms? Yes. You can technically and legally sell a house to a person for $275,000 after the down payment that is worth $150,000. Ethically it is obviously not good practice. Additionally, when the buyers learn that they paid almost twice the value for their home, I guarantee that you will receive some really bad publicity. Remember, everyone loves to hate an investor.

In investing, if all parties are not happy the deal will not work.

In order to calculate offers that are not using simple interest but an amortization schedule you will need to have access to an amortization schedule. There are apps for this but I find it helpful to have one made in excel. Here is how to do it.

1. Type "Principal:" in cell A1, "Interest Rate:" in cell A2, "Loan Term:" in cell A3 and "Monthly Payment:" in cell A4. Highlight cells A1 through A4, then click the right-align button on the formatting ribbon.
2. Enter the total loan amount in cell B1. Enter the interest rate in cell B2. Enter the loan term, expressed in months, in cell B3. To calculate the loan term in months, multiply the total number of years on the loan by 12.
3. Enter the formula "=PMT(B2/12/100,B3,B1)" in cell B4 to use Excel's monthly payment function, which takes into account the principal, interest and number of months to arrive at an ideal fixed monthly payment.
4. Type "Payment Number" in cell A5, "Starting Balance" in cell B5, "Monthly Interest" in cell C5, "Payment" in cell D5 and "Ending Balance" in cell E5.

5. Type "1" in cell A6. This represents your first payment period. Enter the formula "=A6+1" in cell A7 to begin the payment period iteration process.
6. Enter "=B1" in cell B6 to list the balance for the first period. Enter "=E6" in cell B7 to begin iterating the beginning balances.
7. Enter "=B6*($B$2/12)/100" in cell C6 to calculate the first period's interest payment. Enter "=B7*($B$2/12)/100" in cell C7 to begin iterating the interest payment.
8. Enter "=$B$4" in cells D6 and D7 to ensure that the previously calculated monthly payment remains the same throughout all payment periods.
9. Enter "=B6+C6+D6" in cell E6 to calculate the ending balance for the first period. Enter "=B7+C7+D7" in cell E7 to begin iterating the ending balance.
10. Highlight cells A7 through E7. Click and hold the small square at the bottom right of the selection, then drag it down according to the number of payment periods on the loan. Excel will alter each of the formulas to base the calculations on the previous row. You can tweak it to your specifications.

Interest Rate	7.60%			Balance Due	Tax	Insurance	Monthly escrow
Payment	Amount	Interest	Principal	$170,905.00	$1,512.00	$800.00	$192.67
1	$1,206.72	$1,082.40	$124.32	$170,780.68			
2	$1,206.72	$1,081.61	$125.11	$170,655.58			
3	$1,206.72	$1,080.82	$125.90	$170,529.68			
4	$1,206.72	$1,080.02	$126.70	$170,402.98			
5	$1,206.72	$1,079.22	$127.50	$170,275.48			
6	$1,206.72	$1,078.41	$128.31	$170,147.18			
7	$1,206.72	$1,077.60	$129.12	$170,018.06			
8	$1,206.72	$1,076.78	$129.94	$169,888.12			
9	$1,206.72	$1,075.96	$130.76	$169,757.36			
10	$1,206.72	$1,075.13	$131.59	$169,625.78			
11	$1,206.72	$1,074.30	$132.42	$169,493.36			
12	$1,206.72	$1,073.46	$133.26	$169,360.10			
13	$1,206.72	$1,072.61	$134.10	$169,225.99			
14	$1,206.72	$1,071.76	$134.95	$169,091.04			
15	$1,206.72	$1,070.91	$135.81	$168,955.23			
16	$1,206.72	$1,070.05	$136.67	$168,818.57			
17	$1,206.72	$1,069.18	$137.53	$168,681.04			
18	$1,206.72	$1,068.31	$138.40	$168,542.63			
19	$1,206.72	$1,067.44	$139.28	$168,403.35			
20	$1,206.72	$1,066.55	$140.16	$168,263.19			
21	$1,206.72	$1,065.67	$141.05	$168,122.14			
22	$1,206.72	$1,064.77	$141.94	$167,980.19			
23	$1,206.72	$1,063.87	$142.84	$167,837.35			
24	$1,206.72	$1,062.97	$143.75	$167,693.61			
25	$1,206.72	$1,062.06	$144.66	$167,548.95			
26	$1,206.72	$1,061.14	$145.57	$167,403.37			
27	$1,206.72	$1,060.22	$146.50	$167,256.88			
28	$1,206.72	$1,059.29	$147.42	$167,109.45			
29	$1,206.72	$1,058.36	$148.36	$166,961.10			
30	$1,206.72	$1,057.42	$149.30	$166,811.80			

Knowing Your Buyer

We are able to make offers that would not appeal to conventional investors because we have an unconventional client base. We are able to help the people who have been turned away by conventional lenders, lead to believe they are not good enough to be a homeowner. I told you in the beginning, this is all about being a super hero.

Banks are very particular about lending post housing bubble burst.

Back in the day, you could have a credit score of 525 and a stated income and get a loan. Banks were lending above the value of the home. You could refinance your house for 125% of the value. Banks often practiced ARM lending, which is an adjustable rate mortgage. Basically you can buy more house than you can afford today at a monthly payment you can afford but in a few years the interest rate will change and the home may not be in your budget any longer. People fell into this trap because real estate values were rising so quickly due to this false escalation that they were told that by the time the payment was higher they could just refinance and get a 20/80 loan based on the equity that would inevitably occur. People in the housing industry were making money hand over fist. This created a false economy with a glass ceiling that could not support itself and came crashing in. The foreclosure rate skyrocketed, banks lost money and people lost homes.

The result, it became much more difficult to purchase a home, as it should be. Banks should not in the business of real estate investing. But we are. We can take a chance because we do not mind taking the house back if the buyer does not meet his obligations. Our foreclosures and evictions do not crash the economy because we are able to solve the problem of a vacant house.

We will work with two groups of buyers really; those who are self-employed and those who have bad credit. Well, three if you count folks who are self-employed with bad credit. Hey, let me tell you, starting a business can cause some credit dings sometimes.

When I am looking for my buyer I advertise that I will not consider credit. I am quite alright with taking the house back if one defaults. In fact it is part of my business model. Remember, they are putting down a significant amount of money. In Virginia, and most states, it is fairly easy to get someone out of the house once they default. If you are in a state with strict pro-tenant laws, like New York and California, I recommend looking for housing debt on their credit. Look for evictions, foreclosures, and utility debt.

Your buyer will have great intentions. They will be excited and LOVE you. You are giving them a chance that nobody else would. In reality, unfortunately, most will default. The average time in a house is a little less than 2 years. So don't get too attached. The same person who loves you today will tell a judge in a second that you are a crook and a scam artist when they stop making payments. They can

go from  to  real fast.

> HINT: I call all of my clients buyers even if it is a lease purchase. This gives them a sense of ownership even before they have decided to sign the contract.

Marketing the Sale

Notice how everything is a sale rather than a lease. You are offering the opportunity of ownership in each of these creative transactions. You will want to make sure that you attract a person with a "buyer" mindset. This will mean that they expect a higher down payment. It will be understood that you are not providing the maintenance on the property.

When it comes to marketing, there are not as many methods for the sale as there are for the purchase. Knowing that some of you are starting this with a budget of $0, first I will touch on the free and most effective places to advertise your new home. Facebook, Craigslist, and Zillow.

We are going to jump right into Facebook. Remember you can post on all of you social media sites but I do not get the same response from the others.

Now that you have built up your friend list you have all of these people helping you to get the word out. People like to help.

You are either a "*this is my journey*" or an "act as if "social media poster. Meaning that if you have taken your fb family down this path with you from day one with post like "*I am taking this real estate investor class this week wish me luck*"; you are a journey poster. If you took the class and changed your profession to "**r**eal estate investor" and asked for leads; you are an act as if'er. The tone of your post should be reflected in the style which you share. Both are great.

That said; post a picture on your page with a description of the house and financing options. Here is an example from my own FB.

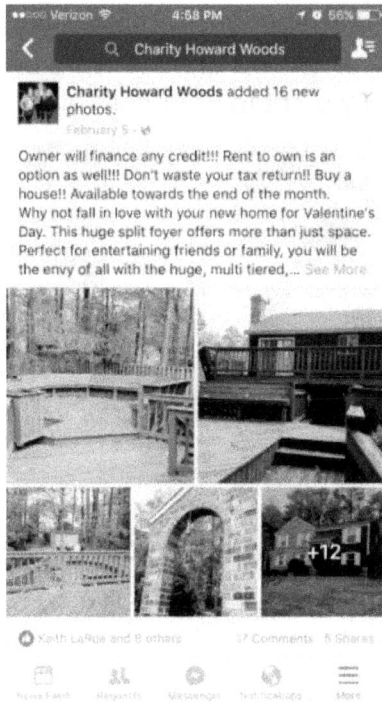

See how it was shared 5 times? That expands your network without you doing anything at all. That house was "sold" sight unseen. The new buyers moved in the same day that the old ones were evicted.

When you are posting you will want the focus to be first on the financing. You are tearing down their objections before they even get to think them. People are buying a dream of being a homeowner before the house.

Walk them through the emotions of owning that home. Describe it so that they can feel it. Make them embrace the way the floor feels in the morning or the smell of fall on a chilly evening.

Create an urgency to act now, a call to action. "This house won't last long." The more action the post gets the more urgent it appears. You may want to ask a few of your buddies to just go ahead and comment and share on your houses at first. This will be unnecessary before long as people will actually want to comment and share.

Owner will finance 90% or 95% lease purchase!!!

Any Credit!!! Self-employed ok!!!

Fall in love with this renovated Cape Cod on an acre in the heart of Chesterfield. Wake in the morning and sit in your screened sunroom. As you taste the first sip of your coffee a deer wonders from the tree line and prances gently around the yard. Life is good.

Do not miss the opportunity to enjoy owning this 3 bedroom 2 bath home. With inviting wood floors downstairs, large deck perfect for entertaining, screened porch, and so much more. With a sales price of only $189,900 and payments of $1495 per month this home will not last long.

After you have created your social media Mona Lisa you will copy it to all 80 yard sale type sites. Plan to make a day of responding to comments and messages. You will be super busy.

Do this when you have time to respond. A couple of haters can turn a seemingly innocent post into a real bash fest. You will need to shut that down immediately!

Luckily Craigslist is a bit faster. You do not have to repost it 80 times....only 2. You will post in the rental section and in real estate for sale by owner.

There are many scams on Craigslist where people are pretending to be an owner and either asking for a deposit or an application in an email. People are giving all of their credit information hence falling victim to identity theft. Some are sending the deposit and expecting keys to come in the mail. There are several tips to avoid being confused with that type of ad. Fortunately these are also just good business practices.

Post as many pics as possible.

You will want to make yourself available to your clients by phone, text and email. This is an option you have with craigslist now. Use it. If you don't text, begin.

You might be thinking, "Seriously, who doesn't text?" When I started one of my investment companies about 8 years ago one of my partners was a sharp, 27 year old man that plays in a band on the side. This guy didn't text!!! WTF??? You are friggin 27. Most 27 year olds I know act like they are unaware that you can actually call people with that same device.

So why is texting so important that I just went on a tangent about the only 27 year old to not text?

Simple, you are working with people who often have bad credit and many feel ashamed. They would rather talk to you via text than over the phone. Also, millennials are buying houses!! Except for my partner up there, millennials love to text. Honestly, I prefer it as well for responding to people about a house.

Your headline should be "*OWNER WILL FINANCE*!!"
You can use the same body as you used on your Facebook.   Just keep on copying and pasting. Easy peasy.
Zillow is becoming a more and more popular tool when people are looking for a home. Again free. Have at it. The same rules apply. It is difficult to distinguish that a home is ONLY available with owner financing or as a lease purchase with this site. That has been the biggest drawback.

There are tons of sites for all of these things. I am not going to talk about all of them. I went with the most popular of each.

Signs are tried and true. Although not free, a good value. An ugly sign with a good message gets attention. Remember our old yellow coroplast blanks. Yep they work here too. Keep the message simple.

House for Sale
Owner Will Finance
Any Credit!
Self-employed OK
804-555-1234

You should place signs at the intersections with heavy traffic near your home. If the home is in a rural area, put signs in the closest "town" as well as at the local gas stations and grocery stores, if there are any.

Rent to Own!!!

Any Credit!!

Must have down-payment!

804-555-1234

Hint: In areas where houses are well below the median sales price for the greater area using the wording "Rent to Own" rather than "Lease

Purchase" seems to be beneficial. In all other areas the buyer seems to prefer "Lease Purchase."

As you can see, the majority of marketing expense comes from acquisition. Sales are virtually free to advertise.

Prepping the House

After you have a ratified contract and are in possession of the house you will need to get it ready for people to fall in love with it. Knowing your buyer helps you to realize that you do not need to renovate the home as if you were flipping. A regular house is fine. Why?

When you are flipping a home you are competing against dozens of houses on the market. When you are offering a house as a lease purchase or an owner finance you have almost zero competition.

Imaging the house is a hot girl going to a speed dating event.

Now the first event she shows up and realizes it is a speed dating event for swimsuit models. Hot girl is now the norm. She needs to be the hottest girl to get date offers from the most eligible candidates. Her hair needs to be done without one piece out of place. Her eyebrows on fleek, eyes smoky, lips full and pouty. She needs to be in that little tight dress, worked out a couple of hours before so she still looks extra tone. This is the flip chic.

Her next event is a speed dating event that wasn't marketed well to the ladies but plenty of gents are there. When she shows up there is only a couple of other ladies. They are not dressed up and have not seen a makeup tutorial since 1987. All she has to do is show up. She, and the others, will have plenty of offers as long as they are average. This is your lease purchase life. Sweat pants and a messy bun, as long as you put on a little mascara and some gloss you are in the game.

When working with a creative sale you need to realize that the better the house looks the better, and faster, offers will come. You can get more down and will have more options for clients available. I have stated many times that this is a good option for the investor who is getting started because you *can* get a good profit with little or no investment. As your wealth continues to grow, you can put a little more into the houses.

When you look at the exterior of the home you will want to do the cheapest and most basic things first. You can add more if you have more in the budget. I will tell you that as an investor I do not recommend doing your own work once you are turning a profit. In the first few houses you may want to do what you can to save money.

Outside, look for any health or safety hazard. Handrails that need further attachment, broken glass, working locks, things that could get you in court you need to correct. This is a MUST in any financial situation.

Pick up any trash, limbs, sticks, and debris out of the yard. Cut the grass and pull weeds out of the beds. Trim down hedges if needed. For goodness sakes, haul away a rusted out shed! Do you have any idea how many people try to leave those? Everyone wants a rusty tetanus trap for small children and animals….good call.

It really adds a nice pop if you mulch the beds and add seasonal flowers. This is extremely inexpensive if you do it yourself. Only a few dollars.

If you have a higher budget and there is rotten wood or siding you may want to replace it and try to match the paint for touch up. If the exterior looks like real crap and you do not have the money or the cost is more than the reward you can discount the down payment.

Inside you will generally just make do with what is there especially if you are working on a small budget. The biggest thing is having a clean property inside. I would suggest that you buy an industrial carpet cleaner at some point in your career. You will use that more than any other tool. Carpets that smell like pets are a real turn off.

Here is a great example of the difference of expectations in a flip verses a creative sale. Remember my mistake kitchen from my flip section? That thing cost me thousands because I did not do enough.

Here is the kitchen of a home I have sold twice to the first people that looked at it. You really can't see how ugly it is in this pic. The painted trim on the cabinet doors are two different colors and the pulls on the cabinet doors are mismatched as are the appliances.

I am not suggesting that you do not improve the appearance of a home. This house happens to be pretty badass overall so a kitchen is not the biggest of issues.

Upgrades can make the difference between getting your full deposit up front and allowing them to break it up. You can also generally count on more consistent payments with a better quality house.

We will now look at some of the simple and inexpensive upgrades that are options you may choose to implement.

- Paint walls that appear dirty or dingy.
- Replace the lights with new, inexpensive brushed nickel. You can buy a 6 pack for about $40.00 at Lowes.

- Paint cabinets. I planned to paint the cabinets in the above picture both times it was vacant and it was under contract too fast. Here is an example of the difference some trendy paint makes. In fact this cost nothing because it is a color I used in my family room.

- Replace counters. The counters in a kitchen can make a huge difference in the appearance. New faux finish counters are not that expensive and make a huge impact.
- Carpet that is damaged or dirty where it cannot be fixed should be replaced. If you build a good report with a local flooring contractor you may be able to pay after you find your buyer.

Hint: Always repair missing or broken items. Do not offer a crappy product unless you want a crappy resident.

The art of mini model is one which all must master. This is how we inexpensively showcase the best things about the home while drawing the eye away from the worst.

Mini modeling is simply decorating but not furnishing the home. Place things where you want people to look or draw odd color schemes together with some art.

In the living room, family room, and den you will use pictures and knickknacks to accent the room, make it look bright and livable. You will do this the same way you would do this at your own house. Unless you are like my partner in this particular endeavor who is in his mid 30's and still has a bachelor pad. Then you will want to ask somebody.

If there is a fireplace place a picture on the mantle with a couple of decorations on either side. Draw the eye there. You may even want to put candles in the fireplace if you do not have a screen. Place tall vases on either side on the floor beside it. Make it pretty and desirable.

If there is no fireplace, decorate the wall. If the room is dark or small use a decoritive mirror to brighten and expand the room.

In the kitchen you will want to offer the illusion of being lived in but the unrealistic tidy look that really sells. Place a coffee mug or two out, put some fake fruit in a bowl, screw it put some real candy in a bowl (people love food), decorate that kitchen so that it pops.

In the bathrooms you will want to fully decorate. No half way job here. Typically the bathrooms in these are not the best as people renovate them last, so you want to go all out.   Get a shower curtain, cute curtain holder loop thingys, match the towels to the shower curtain, to the rug, and get decorations. DO NOT FORGET TOILER PAPER and soap. No matter how great your pitch and product, it is hard to get over having to use your own undies to wipe.

This is an example of how we used staging to make an ugly paint job less hideous.

You should have a welcome mat at the front door. This not only looks nice but helps keep your floors clean.

Remember, you are selling homeownership more than the home. You will want to be sure the property feels like a home.

Writing the Sale

Remember we are calling the transfer of possession "sale" regardless of if the ownership changes. A lease purchase is a "Sale" to the new resident. They are in the mindset of ownership if you have done your job correctly. By the time that you are negotiating the contract with your buyer you should have them completely excited and ramped up about owning a home.

When you determine the final sales price you will need to calculate it using this method.

Take the value of the home or your purchase price, whichever is higher, add the amount you want down. This is your minimum sales price. You may also calculate the projected equity into the sales price. Obviously, you want to make the most possible. That is why you are doing this. It is good practice to begin with the projected price and then work your way down if needed.

You will need to set the payment as well. For an actual purchase, recorded or non you will need to use a calculation based on amortization of the loan. For a lease purchase you have options. I find that I am able to get above market rent, the average rent in the area, if I use a PITI(MI) calculation versus a set amount with a standard monthly credit. Additionally, this leaves your buyer with a stronger sense of ownership. When they are paying down the house exactly like a mortgage, it feels like a mortgage.

PITI(MI) is *Principle Interest Tax Insurance* (Mortgage Insurance). I am going to break this down for you fully in a sec but first we can very quickly go over the standard method of rent credit for a lease purchase.

In the majority of the lease purchases of the world the tenant/buyer will pay a monthly amount, $1000 for example. Landlords will either offer a credit towards the purchase price in a set amount, say $200 or add an additional "fee" onto the payment that is offered as credit towards purchase. If the purchase does not happen the money is considered rent and not returned. Very simple. You can choose to use this method if you like.

When we use PITI(MI) we are able to adjust the payment to whatever we need or want it to be. This is also how we calculate the payment on all sales.

Principle is the part of the sales price that is paid down with each payment. This is based on the amount of the loan balance at commencement.

Interest in PITI(MI) is the portion of interest that is paid with the monthly payment. We know that we are going to give them a higher interest rate than ours but also higher than a conventional loan. Remember, they are a high risk buyer.

Tax refers to real estate tax. You will use public record to determine the real estate tax on the home. Divide it by 12. This becomes part of your monthly escrow.

Insurance is the amount you pay to insure the property. If you are unsure because you are paying on lease purchase you can estimate low. Generally a dwelling only policy is roughly $600-$800. Again, divide this by 12 and make it part of the escrow.

Mortgage Insurance is a standard in the lending industry. Basically it is an added fee to homes where a buyer has put less than 20% down. This number can be anything. I use this when I need to get the payment up because I might have a wrap mortgage or something that I am paying on. You should not use this when you have taken a down payment of 20% or more.

Working backwards from the $1000 payment, the market rent for homes with that payment are roughly $120,000. Give or take. The maximum rent you can get there is $1200 based on the rent plus lease purchase fee. The problem is that buyers will not take kindly to having a *fee* of $200 per month. The house will be vacant longer with this option and your buyers will act more like renters if you treat them as such.

Now if you charge 7.5% on $120,000 what is the payment? Use your amortization chart. Ok I will tell you. It is $839.06. If tax is $1512 and insurance is $800 you have an additional escrow of $192.67 each month for a total payment of $1031.72. Notice, this is right at market rent. You can set your MI where you need it within reason. Set it for $165.00. Your payment is $1196.72 which is about the same as the simple calculation but much more palatable to the buyer. Also rather than having a credit at the end of 5 years in the amount of $12,000 the credit will be $6459.08.

Hint: Payments that are not round numbers feel more like a mortgage than rent. If you want about $1000 calculate it to $998.76 or $1001.23. It does not have to be those exact numbers. The idea is to have a payment that feels like a mortgage.

When you place your buyer in the home you can determine the length of time they can stay under the arrangement you have set. The length of time is called the term. When the term expires for either form of financing the buyer will have to obtain his own financing. Typically this is through a conventional mortgage.

When calculating the months on the term you will want to first and foremost consider the amount of time you have with your underlying financing. If you are in a two year term, you cannot offer longer than that. This seems obvious but remember, you may buy a home with a 5 year term and move John and Jane in there immediately. After 9 months they have defaulted and you are looking for a new tenant. You only have 4 years and 3 months left. This is often overlooked as we are excited to get a new buyer in place.

You will want to make sure the term you offer your buyer is a few months less than the expiration of your agreement. Why? Chances are your buyer will not qualify for a mortgage at the end of the term. They probably did not work to build or repair their credit. In fact I used to pay for credit repair for my clients and was told by the company I was using that absolutely NONE of my buyers contacted them to get started. You will need the remaining time to get the house sold. If you are in a position where you have built enough equity to flip it, do that. If you are in a position of little or no equity you may want to renegotiate with the seller or just give the house back to them.

We also want to look at what our end goal really is for the property. Remember how we said that default is part of our business model? This is how. If you have acquired 12 properties and each is on a 54 month term you will get 12 down payments, assuming all buyers follow through. On the same concept, if you make the term 30 months, you have 24 down payments. You also have to turn the property and suffer vacancy loss. You need to weigh out the amount of the down payment, desirability of the area, and quality of the home.

When I have a home with a 12 month term I typically check credit and only offer it to people who will be able to qualify for a loan in 12 months if… The if can be many things. If they pay down some debt. If they raise their credit score 20 points. If the judgments fall off of their credit as planned. If they stay at the same job. Obviously, it is up to the buyer to make this happen. In this situation you really cannot sell the idea of a 9 month lease purchase nor is it fair to the buyer. You will have to offer the full 12.

Our typical buyer is not in as great of shape as the afore. I find that generally when you advertise for any credit you get the worst credit. I practice business in an ethical manner and that is what I would recommend to you as well. It is unfair to take a down payment and sign an agreement with a buyer with bad credit with less than two years to repair it. Period. I advise you to make terms at least two years.

Down payment is the topic of our next discussion. This is really a huge part of your income in this arena. We discussed that we use 5% and 10% but there are a few other factors you may want to consider.

In the situation of an owner financed home with a recorded deed you should have at least 10% down.

Period. You can easily require 20%. I caution you to not take less. It is a longer process to foreclose than evict.

As for lease purchases and non-recorded deeds, I never have a down payment less than $5,000. In areas where the sales price of the home is below $100,000 5% is less than $5,000. I have found that when a buyer puts down less than that the renter mentality is retained. I will allow my residents in low income areas to break the down payment up with $2,500 up front.

When you are looking at down payment amounts you may be inclined to take a lower amount especially when you are making payments on a vacant house. That is certainly up to you. Again, I would not fall below $5,000.

In this situation you may want to offer less than 5% to people with pretty good credit or offer an installment option. I find an installment plan is just as easy to sell as less down.

I generally offer installments to most of my buyers. I call it Down Payment Assistance. I require that I receive 2.5% upfront and we can work out a plan for the balance that is based on their financial situation and the amount of the balance. I generally offer the option of increased monthly payments or quarterly payments until it is paid.

In situations where the down payment is a large one, I use $20,000, I will allow the down payment be divided into 4 equal payments. First at possession and every 3 months thereafter.

When you live in an area with very strict landlord tenant law in favor of the tenant I advise getting a minimum of 5% or more upfront. It could take you months to evict. You want to be covered. You want to familiarize yourself with the landlord tenant act for your state.

The bottom line in all of this is that you need to be able to calculate income for yourself in all aspects of the agreement from acquisition to the final sale at the end of the term. You are now armed with the tools to make that a reality.

Closing the Creative Sale

When I closed my first creative deal in 1999 I was buying a house sub to. We did not have our attorney draft an agreement. There was no title check. No title insurance. We drafted a deed and took it to a bank where a bank teller notarized it and handed it back. I then took it to the courthouse for the county where I bought the house and gave it to the clerk with a check for filing fees. BAM!! I now owned this house.

I had <u>zero</u> security against the liens that were placed on the house for debts that were not even associated with the home before I even bought it. Guess what? During the 36 days it took the clerk to record the sale, I had two other liens attached. Well I sure wish someone told me the value of a title search and title insurance. I did not know any better.

In fact, at that time that is how investors did business. It was called a table top closing and it was dangerous. Can we still transfer ownership of real property with two people with no legal background and a bank teller? In most areas, yes. Should you? <u>Absolutely not</u>.

The value of a good attorney who is familiar with your contract and the method of purchase is priceless in this business.

When you sell a home to a buyer using creative financing, prepare your packet for the attorney just as you would when you are buying. Be sure to advise them that they can use any attorney they choose but cost for them will be less if you share an attorney.

When you have a lease purchase, this is the time you may want to walk in to your local bank and ask for a notary. Since the property is not actually changing hands you need not have title work or an actual closing. You are going to be getting a rather sizable down payment and many people do like to have record of that exchange recorded by a notary.

The notary is not actually recording the transaction but that you all are who you claim to be. You should have a short document that states the names of the parties, the address of the property, and the amount paid as a nonrefundable down payment.

CYA

I sometimes have this dream where I am at school and I am changing classes only to realize all my parts are showing because in my haste to get out of the door on time I forgot clothes. I grab my books and place them over my lady parts but my hind parts are still exposed. I try to look inconspicuous and sneak to my next class. Everyone starts to notice now. I sat there for two hours and no one noticed!! Not one friend, *frienemy*, or teacher. Not even the boy I have a high school crush on!! Now they all see my exposed hiney and apparently it is hilarious. Not one person saying, "OMG! Are you ok? Do you want my gym clothes?" Administration only sees that this is a clear violation of dress code. I am feeling helpless and ashamed when I wake up and realize that I am home and who cares what I have on. Shew! What is the moral of the story? Never leave your ass exposed….unless of course you are on a nude beach in the Caribbean. No wait, even then you can get burned.

If you haven't guessed, this little section is about **covering your *ass*(ets)**.

You were told in the intro that you need an LLC before you make a single offer. I will reiterate the importance of this. Real estate puts you in a position that is extremely vulnerable if you have not made sure that you have covered all of your bases. Having an LLC under which to limits the liability that you as an individual are subject.

Surprisingly, you will find fewer areas for "exposure" with a recorded purchase. This is primarily because your attorney has made sure of that by having you follow the same foundation of provided by a conventional purchase. Additionally, a sale is final and does not generally require further contact unless there is default. Default is less frequent because they have put more money down.

You want to be sure that you have verification of homeowners insurance if you are not holding it and putting it in escrow.

Write a clause for mediation into your contract. This is beneficial because many judges are not familiar with this type of purchase and may require you to go before circuit court for possession if you need to take the house for any reason besides non-payment. An example would be if you sell a house to Matt and Kathy with a 60 month term. At the end of the period they do not have the ability to obtain financing but they just keep paying and refuse to move.

This is a reason you would need possession even though they are paying.

I have my buyers sign a *Quitclaim Deed* at closing. This is a deed that reverts ownership back to my company if they default on the agreement. They will also sign an agreement saying that said deed will be held in escrow for the duration of the term and will be filed only if there is a breach in compliance with the mortgage or any other provisions in relation to the sale. Once the new deed is filed you can treat them not as a buyer but as a renter if you need to remove them from the property.

Lease Purchases are a little more risky because they teeter between renting and selling. Many judges are not sure how to rule. In Virginia, for example, being a lease purchase excludes you from the Landlord Tenant Act but there is no provision elsewhere to govern it. Also, attorneys typically do not "close" a lease purchase any longer so it is often a he said she said even though you have an agreement.

When you are acquiring a property using creative means you need to be sure that they add you to the insurance policy as additionally insured. Not doing this can cost you money and land you in court with a judge who is not sure if you should be paid back for the money you spent to repair damages to the property from the last big storm even though the owner is in possession of the insurance check.

I have always had that in the agreement but I never followed up until I found myself in that exact situation. Cost me thousands. You're welcome. I paid for this mistake so you do not have to.

When you are having your contracts drafted you will want to be sure that you have a clause that states that all payments are to be considered rent if they default on the agreement. Include also that no portion during any time of the agreement shall be due back to the tenant/buyer at any time.

Draft and include a CYA sheet. Of course it is not called that. It is addendum D. This will basically explain the contract in terms that anyone can understand. You will want to include the following items as well as any others you deem necessary. Have the buyers initial each line and sign at the end of the document.

- By initialing I am stating that I have read fully understand the section which I have chosen to initial.
- I am entering into the attached contract willfully and fully aware.
- I have taken the time I needed to make this decision based on my consideration and any counsel I chose to take.
- I understand that I am making a down payment that is not refundable under any circumstances.
- I understand that if I default in this agreement I am not entitled to any portion of my down payment or monthly payment to be returned to me.
- I understand that I am responsible for maintenance and upkeep of the property.
- I understand that (your company name) is not responsible for any maintenance or repairs to my house. In the event that maintenance or repair is required and performed by (your company name) I will be billed and expected to pay the amount billed.

When your tenants fall behind, as they all do, you can chose to be swift and take possession of the house immediately; serve the eviction and move on to the next one. I prefer to offer my clients the opportunity to catch up.

When you first become a landlord or investor you will probably be sensitive to the situations that make people fall behind. They will pull out all of the stops for this. Sickness, death, job loss, beaten, robbed… The list goes on and on. You may find it a bit entertaining eventually.

A favorite excuse of mine involves a single man living in a small home in the county right by the city border. We are in court because he has failed to pay rent for the month. Our judge reminds me of Judge Lynn Toler from Divorce Court. She is not listening to any sass or excuses. She even looks like her and she clearly wants to go to lunch as badly as I.

JUDGE LYNN TOLER

My tenant, we will call him Ray because that is his name, is standing before the judge when she asks *"Did you pay your rent or didn't you?"* His reply, *"Its not like that."* Her expression quickly turns to one of annoyance. *"Let me just tell you what happened?"* he pushes. She asks if he is saying that there are extenuating circumstances surrounding the rent and he agrees that there are indeed.

"You have two minutes to tell me why you think you should not be here today." she reluctantly offers.

"You see your honor, I was on craigslist after I got my check the first of the month and I met a lady..."

"Sir, I cannot imagine the relevance here. I just want to hear about the rent." By now she is getting very frustrated but he continues.

"I'm telling you" he countered. *"She came over later that night…"*

"SIR. Get to the rent!"

"Ok so anyway after umm…" he paused *"We fell asleep. I woke up and she done cleaned me out. My money. My liquor. My prescriptions. My smartphone. Everything"*

The judge was not amused. She looked like an angry pit bull sitting in wait for the order to attack from his owner. I am pretty sure she was salivating.

The judge ruled exactly as I suspected but her way in doing so really made maintaining professionalism difficult.

She said, *"Sir you just stood here and wasted the time of the court telling an irrelevant story that I am sure included you buying a prostitute off craigslist. Judgment and 10-day possession granted to the plaintiff"*

Poor old Ray was flabbergasted asking how he was supposed to pay if he was robbed never recognizing that he should have paid his rent before hiring a prostitute…or that admitting to picking up a hooker online in front of a judge was probably not the best of decisions.

The point here is that each tenant that is not paying thinks their reason is a good one. It is a good idea to have a policy in place prior to having to use it. That way you can refer to policy. "*I'm sorry Ray. It is unfortunate that you were burgled by a street walker but the policy does say that turning in rent on time is your responsibility*." The blame is off of you.

All payment arrangements should be governed by a Repayment Agreement. When accepting a payment arrangement determine an arrangement works for both of you. If you know there is no way they will be able to comply you are just wasting time. You will want to write in a "Good Faith" payment. This is basically all of the cash they have on hand. This is how you know they are serious. If they are not willing to give up all of their cash for their house you shouldn't be making a deal. Again you would be wasting your time.

In the agreement you need to include that you will continue with the eviction process and take possession of the property but not execute it. Meaning the judge grants the authority to evict but the eviction is not carried out if the terms of the repayment agreement are followed.

Also include that if they are late on a payment or any portion of a payment you have the right to execute the eviction without notice.

This section has not been designed to scare you but to make you aware and ultimately more successful. I have made the mistakes I am telling you not to make. I didn't die or go to jail. I lost some money, had a hit on my personal credit, and spent countless hours worrying about how to fix the mess I had created. Ultimately money, time, and legal counsel are the fix.

You now have all of your real estate investor super powers. Will you use them for good or let them go to waste? Many people know about flipping or being a landlord. Not too many know about being Super Investor armed with an unlimited supply of creativity and mad investing skills. More badass than Krav Maga.

So pull up your tights and straighten your cape and get out there and start building your empire!!!!!

Wholesaling

We have all heard the saying *it takes money to make money*. What if I told you that is not true? What if I told you that *you can make quick in and out cash in real estate without spending anything more than a small EMD*? Interested?

What is this magic beans of real estate of which I speak? I am speaking of what we call wholesaling. This is the practice of finding homes to flip or hold and selling them to other investors for a profit.

With this method you will use the skills that you have learned in other sections to make offers that will appeal to other investors who are in a different position than you. You may find a property while looking for a flip that you cannot use as you do not have cash and the interest on a hard money loan will cut into your profit. You may find a property that would make a great rental but you do not want to hold. You may find an owner finance that you feel does not have a wide enough spread. You can wholesale while doing all other aspects of real estate investing.

You may decide to just wholesale. You can use this option to build your capital or just make money in a fairly risk free manner. Whatever your goal, being able to make more deals work is never a bad idea.

I am going to show you how to practice the specific art of wholesaling. You can use this to move other contracts that you stumble upon through all other means you have and will learn.

Looking for Homes

When looking for a home that is marketable to other investors you will want to remember that most active investors want to flip. This will be our primary focus.

You will market for these properties much in the same way you marketed for your own. Signs are a great way to get a base of sellers who want to sell. This is important because the more motivated the seller, the better the deal.

We will use the coroplast, yellow, signs that we have used in the past. You will continue to handwrite your simple message. The message should convey that you are in the market for homes that others do not necessarily want. A quick simple message with a phone number is all that is required.

I have seen people who try to stand out with offers of fresh baked cookies, gift certificates, and so on. It has been my experience that gimmicks may get a couple more calls but they are generally not serious sellers. A plate of cookies is not going to get one to take an offer for a house that doesn't work for them.

Some other ways to stand out is just simply in the wording. Saying "I buy houses" is the message but saying "I buy any house" may send the message that you are able to make an offer on anything, and really you almost can if you are armed with all of the methods for investing that we cover in Wealth Warriors.

If you are primarily trying to wholesale you may want to target areas with a high percentage of homes in need of heavy repair or a lot of abandoned homes. You will need to be sure that there is a market for renovation though. For example if there are zero homes that have been flipped within a couple of miles, it will be difficult to A) find a true ARV and B) find an investor who is willing to be the first.

Good areas to target are the "next big thing" neighborhoods. If renovation is all around this district but not in it, that the one!!

Get your giant black sharpie and a blank yellow sign. Let's get to work.

I buy houses, any condition

Same day offer!!

804-555-1234

I will buy your house today!!!

Any condition!

804-555-1234

Make plenty. You need for the right person to see it at the right time. Remember, if you are targeting areas where there is an influx of vacancy the owners probably do not live in the neighborhood. You will want to be all over the area so that when they are driving to the house they own the will see your sign.

Since many of these homeowners no longer live at their homes, mailers are an extremely effective marketing tactic. Of course, as we have discussed

before this is not a free method. If your budget is beans and not yet the magic kind, you may want to wait on this or just neighborhood target and send letters entirely yourself. This means you are only paying for ink, paper, and stamps versus lists and a letter service.

I am speaking of direct mail of course. I need you pay attention here because some of this is repetitive from the other sections but not exactly. Some new content has slipped in. Also there are some things from other direct mailers that do not apply. I am being sure to be all inclusive because if you choose to focus on one style specifically I do not want you to miss critical information because there is more detail in another section.

 Direct mail is <u>exactly</u> what it sounds like. You are going to send correspondence on paper to potential sellers. What you say, to whom, and where the lists are acquired is somewhat a matter of taste while following a few guidelines.

First let's look at <u>who</u>. There is no need to blanket the entire area with letters when only a few meet the criteria to make an offer mutually agreeable. Keep in mind, if all parties aren't happy the deal will fall apart. You are looking for a person who wants to be rid of the property but either does not think anyone will buy it or does not know how to go about selling it.

The elderly man or woman who no longer resides in their home but still pays taxes, insurance, and upkeep are excellent candidates. Homes with out of state owners prove effective in finding motivated sellers. We already know that our primary focus here is unoccupied properties with absentee owners.

List can be purchased from companies like Melissa Data and Info USA. You can narrow down to as large or small of a list as you like.

You may also target select streets and look for absentee owners by using public record. In Richmond, VA, for example you can go to http://eservices.ci.richmond.va.us/applications/PropertySearch/Search.aspx, Enter the name of the street that you are searching. All properties on that street will appear. Once you have selected the street begin at the first address and select. You will then look for any parcel where the mailing address and the property address do not match. You have identified an absentee owner in the neighborhood of choice for absolutely free.

The content of your mailer needs to be attention grabbing. You want each recipient to (A) open the envelope (B) read the content (C) become curious about it. How do we meet this goal as effectively as possible?

Be tacky! Yep I said it!!

Be sure your envelope is hand written (or looks like it) with handwriting that is less than perfect. I used to have my father write these before he passed. People were asking "Do you have kids help you with this?" That's what I'm talking about!!! I don't care what the question is; I got you on the phone! Pitch time!!!!

What you put in the envelope is a matter of taste with several styles and you should pick the one that you like the best, I honestly can't say which is better or worse as long as it is tacky and says the right things.

Say "I want to buy your house", "Any condition", "As is", "Cash offer", "Quick Close"!

Many investors like to use a company called Yellow Letter. It literally looks like a hand written note on a piece of yellow paper. Some investors also opt for coffee stains and such to be added. This gives the impression of an individual who saw your house and wants it. People love it!!! You can contract this out or do it yourself with a handwriting font and mail merge.

The letter should basically read:

Dear (Homeowner name),

I am sorry if this is odd but I saw your home at (insert address) and I am interested in buying it. I would like to talk to you about paying cash for it in its current condition.

Please call me at (phone number) so that we can meet and talk about it.

Regards,

Charity

Another option is to use a flyer that you would use as a professional but, *__highlight key points__*, circle your name and number, and write a message on the back saying "I am looking forward to hearing from you." Of course, you can do all of this with a great copier and not have to write each one.

You can expect the same results for this mailer as the others and you can use the leads from your other mailers to wholesale.

If you are targeting an area you may want to spend a few hours driving the neighborhood. This is called birddogging. Look for homes that are clearly abandoned. Write down the address, look the owner up in public record, send a hand written note. Personally, I actually hand write them. I make a note about the house when I am getting the address and include it in the note to the owner. This distinguishes you from the other investors who are using a basic letter.

Dear Emily,

I was driving through Northside yesterday and saw your house on 3rd Ave at 2201. I love the renovations happening around there and I see a ton of potential with the bay window on the front of the house. I am REALLY interested in buying the home if you would consider selling it to me. I can pay cash and probably close in less than 2 months. Please give me a call. I am very excited to talk to you. 804-555-1234.

Regards,

Charity

Never miss an opportunity to solicit help from friends and strangers. Utilizing social media you can ask for help. Remember, people love to help. You can ask for help in exchange for a finder's fee or just ask for help.

If you are neighborhood targeting it is sometimes more effective to just ask outright for help. People will often assume that you want to live there and who wouldn't want you on their block?

> Facebook family, I want to buy a
> house in Northside. Please help!!
> If you see a house that is for sale
> by owner or is vacant please get
> the address to me. You can just
> message me. Thank you
> soooooo much!! <3

If you want leads wherever they come from you can word it a bit differently and I would suggest offering a finder's fee.

> Facebook friends, I am looking to
> buy a house to fix up. Please
> help. If you see a house that is
> abandoned or vacant please
> send the address to me. I will
> give you $500 if I buy it. Just
> message me. Thanks!!!!

Notice that the top is friendlier. The two styles are very similar but different enough to convey a slightly different message. You will see that the bottom message, although friendly, still has a sense of professionalism about it. Whereas the top message reaches out as a friend in need.

Craigslist has proven less and less effective as it appears that sellers are moving away from posting here. The majority of the distressed homes listed here are from other wholesalers. This doesn't mean there is not an occasional diamond in the rough. Should you find this, simply call or email the seller and inquire about the property. Set an appointment to go make an offer.

A unique opportunity craigslist offers is allowing you to find strangers to assist you in finding properties. How you ask? You can post ads in the "Jobs" and "Gigs" section looking for birddoggers. Basically they will ride around and get the addresses of homes that meet your criteria and send them to you with an address and picture. You send the notes. If you have a ratified contract, they make $500.00. Chances are your birddoggers are not going to last long. You can have multiple and plan to acquire more all of the time.

When you take the shotgun approach utilizing all of the options available to you for marketing you will have the best results. Of these only mailers and signs have a price tag attached to them. Unfortunately, those are also the most effective means to acquire new homes.

Calculating Your Offer

When leads come in you need to be quick to respond. Being able to answer your phone right then is best. The markets have been saturated with "investors" trying their hand at wholesaling. Remember Tom, Dick, and Harry. They are back. You have to stand out as an informed investor who is able to move quickly with a fair offer.

When speaking with the seller you need to be clear and concise that you plan to buy their house with cash immediately. This sets you apart from the ones who are looking for creative financing contracts. Which could also be you but right now we will assume that it is not.

I always say that I can make multiple offers. I will make a cash offer, a short term owner financed offer, and a long term owner financed offer (for this you will use a substitution of collateral clause in the offer.)

Lamar has called and he has a property 516 N. 29th St that is roughly 1700 square feet. He told you that it needs some work.

Before you go you will want to know a few things, the most important being the ARV. If you have MLS access or a good friend who is willing to pull comps for you, GREAT! Chances are that if you are focusing exclusively on wholesaling you will have a difficult time getting a realtor to want to pull comps for you unless you are dating him or something. He is literally getting nothing back in return. You are not going to list that property with him at any point.

That's ok. You can use other avenues to get there. The easiest is to take Zillow's word for it. I caution against this as you are going to be trying to sell to investors who probably do have MLS access. When you are asked from one professional to another, "How did you come up with this ARV?" You don't want to say "Off Zillow."

You can, however, use Zillow as a tool. If you go to the owner dashboard it will show a list of the other homes that have sold in the area that are similar to the one you are

123 N. 33rd St 3/15 $179,950 flip 1500sf

215 N. 29th st 3/12 $49,990 REO 950sf

307 N. 25th st 3/12 $249,900 homeowner 2100sf

505 N. 27th st 3/6 $89,900 REO 1850sf

900 N. 31st st 3/2 $199,850 flip 1700sf

616 N. 24th St 2/26 $101,000 estate 1660sqft

pricing. Take those addresses down and search them. You can then find the sales price and even look at expired listings with pictures to get a full view of your comparable sales.

Make a list of the square footage, sale dates, type of sale and prices.

Use the non-distressed properties to figure out an ARV based on the square footage of the subject property. The distressed properties above are the REOs and estate. Flips and homeowner properties are left to calculate the ARV.

We will have to divide the sales prices of the homes by the square footage to find the price per square foot.

179,950/1500=119.97

249,900/2100=119

$199,850/1700=117.56$

Add the price per square foot you calculated for each property together.

$119.97+119+117.56=356.53$

Divide the sum by the number of entries. In this situation there are three because there were three properties that sold as comparable sales.

$356.53/3=118.84$

Multiply the average price per square foot you just calculated with the square footage of Lamar's property.

$118.84x1700=202,028$

This is your ARV. This is a figure that *you* need to know. Lamar, not so much, not right now anyway. Maybe not ever.

For Lamar you have a few tools in your box so that you can best negotiate the offer. First let's look at what the price per square foot is for the distressed properties. Use the same method as above to calculate a possible offer based on price per square foot.

$49900/950=52.53$

$89900/1850=48.59$

$101000/1660=61.21$

$52.53+48.59+61.21=161.33$

$161.33/3=54.11$

$54.11x1700=91,987$

This is a figure that you will want to keep handy as well.

When you go to Lamar's home you will need to be WAY more detailed in documenting your rehab costs. You will want to have a check list that allows every aspect of the home to be chronicled. It is best if you have a contractor that is willing to go with you to offer a rough estimate on the spot until you are familiar with rehab pricing.

EXTERIOR	CONDITION	REPAIRS NEEDED	ESTIMATED COST
SIDING	Fair	Paint, replace 13 pc of siding	$6,200.00
BRICK	Good	Powerwash	$250
SOFFIT	Fair	Rot in 4 areas, replace as needed	$400
ROOF	Good	None	
WINDOWS	Good	None, replacement windows	
TRIM	Poor	Trim around exterior windows need to be wrapped	$1200
FOUNDATION	Good	None	
STRUCTURAL	Fair	Small area w termite damage to joist.	$500

CHIMNEY	Good	None	
FRONT DOOR	Poor	Needs replacement	$400
BACK DOOR	Good	Replacement suggested	$200

ROOM	CONDITION	REPAIRS NEEDED	ESTIMATED COST
FOYER	Fair	Cosmetic only	
LIVING	Fair	Cosmetic only	
KITCHEN	Poor	Needs replacement	$6,000
BATH 1	Poor	Needs replacement, cosmetic and mechanical	$3,000
BATH 2	Fair	Cosmetic replacement	$2,000
BED 1	Fair	Cosmetic Only	
BED 2	Fair	Cosmetic Only	
BED 3	Fair	Cosmetic Only	
		Interior Paint	$1900
		Carpet in bedrooms and stairs	$1150
		Refinish wood in living and foyer	$900
		Replace light	$500

package
Replace $50
switch
plates

Add the repair cost together. In this situation it is $24,650.00. You will calculate the offer a little more simply than you do for a flip offer. You will simply take the ARV, subtract the repair cost, and multiply it by .6.

$$202,028 - 24,650 = 177,378$$

$$177,378 \times 0.6 = 106,426.80$$

This is the maximum offer you can make on this and hope to make money. Of course you want to make the most money possible. You will begin by looking at which calculation, distressed sales or based on ARV and repairs, is the lowest.

$91,987 *Distressed sales*

$106,426.80 *ARV Calculations*

In this case the average price per square foot for distressed sales works out to being less than the ARV calculation. This should be starting point when negotiating with Lamar. Chances are, the distressed home were in worse condition than the one you are bidding on but that is not your concern. Your concern is to have three happy parties here. Lamar, your buyer, and you.

Seller Negotiations

When you go visit Lamar you will want to spend the time that he is showing you the house building rapport. Talk about his family, the weather, sports, anything the two of you connect on. Let him see you as a good, regular guy. Not a big shot real estate investor.

In a situation where you plan to wholesale you may want to even let him know that you are not the investor. That you work for investors who are looking for a good house in a good neighborhood.

Some people prefer to not disclose this information. This is also fine. The upside to that is that they know you are the final say on the price. The downside is that if you have trouble finding a buyer or if the buyer needs to negotiate further you will have to do a lot of back pedaling.

You want to ask Lamar what he thinks the house is worth and why? Make sure he understands that his house, although a sturdy solid home, needs quite a bit of work to be able to sell on the retail market. Ask him to give you ideas on his estimation of repair cost.

If your seller over shoots the repair cost or under shoots the value, go with it, everyone likes to be right. If his numbers do not work in your favor, show him your estimates.

> **You: Lamar, have you looked into what the houses around here are selling for? Any Ideas on the value of this one after its all fixed up?**

> **Lamar: Eh, not too much. I think the house is worth about $175,000 or $180,000 if I did all of the work to it.**

See how Lamar is of the opinion that his house is worth a little less than your calculation. He is probably basing it on the actual sales price of the homes in the area rather than the price per square foot.

You: Have you looked into fixing the house up? What do you think that will cost?

Lamar: I was thinking it would be around $10,000 or $15,000.

Now Lamar is way off in a way that is not going to work for you. You need to point out that your estimates are closer to $25,000 and explain how you got there.

You: I have a different number. Let's look at what I have and compare it to what you have. I have that we are going to have to paint the entire exterior and replace some siding. In my experience this should run about $6200. Does that seem right to you?

Lamar: I guess so. I didn't really price it out.

Go over each item until you agree, or at least come close. At this point it is time to let Lamar tell you what a great offer you are making him. Pull out a pen and start writing down figures.

You: If you are right about the sales price and it is $175,000 and I am right about the repair cost and they are about $25,000, we need to agree on what a good offer will be. If I am going to be able to get an investor to agree to the terms I am offering they need to be able to calculate all of the cost and still make a few bucks. I know that they will have holding and marketing cost of at least $5,000. They will *have to pay closing cost twice, so let's say $10,000? Sound about right to you? $5,000 each time? They have to pay the realtor 6% to list the property and sell it so that is $5250 right there. I know they use lenders that charge 18%. So even if they are financing only half of the sales price that's over $15,000. Ok. We can do this math together Lamar. You have a calculator on your phone?*

Lamar: Yea.

You: Ok. I will call the numbers out to you. $175000 sales price minus $25000 for repairs, minus $5000 for holding and marketing, minus two closings which is $10,000, $5200 to the agent, and $15000 in fees. What does that leave Lamar?

Lamar: $114,800

You: Ok. I know they want to make a profit. If you were spending all of that money and doing all of that work how much would you expect to make?

Lamar: I have no idea.

You: I can tell you that there is a lot of money and work involved here. If I make you an offer of $88,000 there is not a whole lot of profit in there for the investor after it is all said and *done. The average sales price for a property in your area based on square footage is about $91,000. My offer is right in line with that. If I can get you $88,000 in cash I your hands in 4-6 weeks would that work?*

You may convince Lamar that this is a great idea, and I hope that you do. If not remember that you should not go above $106.426.80. Once you have exceeded that calculation, you will surely have a difficult time getting any investor, no matter how novice, to bite.

A large part of what is going to get your buyer interested in working with you is the speed and ease of the agreement. You are going to offer a 45 day close. You are going to let them know that you are buying the house as is and there is no need for an inspection, termite inspection, or repairs to be made. The price you offer is the price without any hassle or haggle that is often associated with a conventional sale.

The Contract

When writing your contract you need to be sure to include several components to cover your legal butt and make sure this goes smoothly. Remember, when using your bag of magic beans it means that you may have to run from a few giants if you are not careful.

Assignment of contract is the verbiage that gives you the authority to allow another person or entity besides yourself to utilize the contract. This is done easily with just a few simple words in the first or second paragraph of your contract. Where the BUYER is described, you will add and/or his Assigns.

If your business is Jacks Magic Real Estate Service the vital sentence would look something like this.

> On this 15th day of May in the year of our Lord 2016 all parties as described herein agree to the terms and conditions of this Purchase Agreement, herein known as Agreement, between Lamar D. Giant, herein known as Seller and Jack's Magic Real Estate and/or his assigns, herein known as Buyer regarding the real property known as 123 Beans Way in the City of Makebelieve, and legally described as 353653456-213 Lot6, herein known as Property.

Legal documents are big fans of run-on sentences and too many words to convey an idea. This is why I am great at writing them. I also talk too much and over explain.

You will probably want to add another little blurp about your intention to assign the contract to another buyer. I do not believe this is really necessary but I would recommend it.

You need to offer and EMD, Ernest Money Deposit, as consideration. I offer $100. If the contract fails you are only out $100 and gas money. Some offer $10 or even $1. I find this to be a poor practice as it is difficult to take an offer seriously with only $1 ensuring their performance.

45 days is not a long time to line up a buyer and get them to the closing table. This is why you want to have a provision in the contract that if closing documents have been sent to the attorney or title company at the time of expiration there will be an automatic extension of 15 days. This is more than enough time for a cash or hard money closing.

We just discussed the logistics for wholesaling an assignment of contract. Simply put you made a cash offer and do not wish to actually purchase so you sell the contract to someone who does. You can also wholesale any other type of creative real estate contract that you do not wish to use. Acquisition is the same as you have always done it. You need to be sure that you have the assignment clause in all of your contracts if you plan to utilize this technique.

Most REO's are not assignable. If you do end up with an extra bank owned property you can assign it by buying the property under an LLC that has been established simply for the purchase of that property. So rather than Jacks Magic Real Estate Service the buyer can be JMRS LLC or JMRS1 LLC. You have the right to sell your business and its assets. The contract belongs to the LLC. This is Assignment of LLC versus Assignment of Contract.

Armed with this magic, many new investors make a little extra money before moving on to new things. Many seasoned investors look at wholesaling as an opportunity to make every deal work. You have many more options on the table when you are able to not only consider what works for your portfolio but also what can work for others.

So Jack, get your assets out there and make a comfortable life for yourself off those giants!!!

Prep for Sale

Once you have acquired a property you will need to quickly put together a hot sheet. A hot sheet is a marketing document that outlines the value of the property at a glance. This is going to be what you send out to all of the buyers I am about to tell you find. But first.

We are going to continue to use Lamar's property. Remember when we calculated the ARV. We used the standard investor calculation of average price per square foot multiplied by the square footage of the home. In this situation it was $202,028.

We are also going to use the repair estimation list we made. The repairs were valued at $24,650.

Using these two numbers we will need to calculate our asking price. Remember we determined that we would not offer more than $106,426.80 for the home. There was a method to our madness and I will share it with you now.

Most real estate investing books teach a calculation of ARV-Repairs x 0.7=Offer. We know that is not always the best bet so we take into consideration many other factors, such as interest, closing, realtor's fees, and so on.

Some investors do not have these considerations as they are working with cash, they own a renovation business so their cost are low on rehab, or they are a realtor. They are able to make higher offers based on their situation.

Let's calculate our asking price to the buyers we have on our list based on conventional wisdom in the investor world.

$$202,028 - 24,650 = 177,378$$

$$177,378 \times 0.7 = 124,164.60$$

We will begin by asking $124,165. This would mean quite a nice profit in your pocket for not doing anything. Over $17,000. That, my friends is the same day that you should play the lottery. A scenario like that is rare at best. On average you can expect to make $2,500-5,000 on a wholesale deal. That is still not bad.

Using the calculation above you will have plenty of room to make your buyer feel like you really gave in a ton and that you probably are not making a dime yourself.

When creating your Hot Sheet you will want to have the address of the property all big bold across. Note the area too if it is a desirable one.

Have pictures of the property on your Hot Sheet. This shows not only the property but that you are a full disclosure person.

List the ARV and how you came up with that number.

List the Asking price.

Tell them how much they will make. You do this by adding the sales price to the repair cost. Calculate the closing cost by multiplying the ARV by 0.3. Add that to the afore figure. Subtract the sum from the ARV.

$$124,165 + 24650 = 148,815$$

$$202,028 * .03 = 6,060.84$$

$$148,815 + 6,060.84 = 154,875.84$$

$$202,028 - 154,875.84 = 47,152.16$$

Add your contact information and viola, a Hot Sheet is born.

123 Beans Way Makebeleive, VA

Recently Sold

123 N. 33rd St 3/15 $179,950 1500sf

307 N. 25th st 3/12 $249,900 2100sf

900 N. 31st st 3/2 $199,850 1700sf

Price per square foot $118.84

Building your Buyer's List

When Jack traded that cow for some magic beans he was unaware that the beans were magical. He just knew that they were somehow more valuable to him than his current situation with an animal that had become a liability due to economic depression. When the beans sprouted into a spectacular bean stalk towering above his shack of a house he did not run. He did not hide. He did not cower.

He took action to make the most out of his situation. Many would look at this as a gardening nightmare. Not Jack!

This is how you can approach real estate deals that are unusable to you. Make the most of each one. In order to do so you will need to have a buyer. The best way to do that is to develop a list of investors who look for such things. How do we do that?

You will want to find those who are accustom to paying cash for property, are looking for a rental, or don't mind a little more risk. There are several way to do this. Some are free, some are not.

The obvious is to look for those who have already purchased property for which they do not occupy for cash. I have heard it said many times by other training classes that you can find this on public record. While this is true I find the statement to be misleading. There is not generally (or ever in my experience) a search for cash buyers in public record sites. This means that you will need to look at each land transaction. You will be looking for a cash purchase where the property address is different from the mailing address. Realistically, this will be way more time consuming than the value of the work. There are companies that do this for you and sell it to you. This is a value when you compare the amount of time it would take to look through public record. You can generally buy about 1000 leads for $300-400. You would be better served to take a part time job and earn an extra $400 and buy those leads than to try to find them yourself. You can buy these list from the same companies that sell the absentee owner list. I find InfoUSA to be the best.

Keep this list. This is going to be a constantly growing asset to you in your wholesaling endeavors. Let's keep adding on.

Networking events are perfect for finding a solid investor list. Most people there know what you are doing and are perfectly fine with it. You will find other wholesalers, flippers, and people in the industry in general.

When working with another wholesaler you each may give up some of your profit to make the deal work. That is better than nothing for sure.

When working with flippers they may have a more aggressive approach to working out numbers than the standard and you will have to come down a little. Again it is fine. You worked plenty of room into your offer.

You want to get the name and contact info of EVERYONE at the networking event, even the janitor, I don't care. Everyone knows someone and that someone may just be the someone you are looking for.

Put them on your Buyer's List.

Remember our good ole signs? Of course you do. You now are going to use the signs to build your buyers list.

It is good to have a list of folks who are ready to act as soon as you have a home. You only have a few days to get a buyer in place. How do we do this? We can put signs out for any deal, real or imagined, to generate interest. Be sure that it is a good one.

3/2 ARV $202,000

Under $25,000 in repair needed

Asking $124,165

804-555-1234

Done. An investor will recognize that there is profit potential in this property and call. Keep the signs up even after the property is sold. Simply let the caller know that you have sold that property but get homes like it all of the time and would be glad to let them know about it.

Add these callers to your list.

You can build your buyers list by posting similar information on craigslist and wait for the reply. Find out if they are interested in this specific property or property in general.

I have found a great way to create a buyers list is to simply tell your Facebook friends what you do. You would be surprised how many want to get good, quality leads on homes that are for sale with an awesome spread.

> Facebook Family, as you know I
> have been looking for homes
> that I can fix and flip or hold and
> offer as a rental or lease
> purchase. I think I might have
> found a few too many. If you are
> interested in taking one or two
> off my hands please send me a
> message. Thanks!!

As you acquire your list you will probably want the main form of communication to be email, saving a phone call for the best options.

If you are at a networking event and Tom, Sally, and Fae tell you that they plan to flip a house or two this year but have not been putting out blind offers. They are just casually looking, by all means, send them an email with your Hot Sheet.

If at the same meeting you meet Dave who is really excited to do as many flips as possible this year. He is writing blinds, has ads on Craigslist, and is standing up saying "If anyone has a deal they can't work, call me;" do it!! Call that guy!! He will be your best bet to get a deal done. Do not waste your time calling every Tom, Dick, and Harry (those three again…).

You should set your buyer list up to look like this.

NAME	ADDRESS	PHONE	EMAIL	SPECIFICS	NOTES
TOM DOE	12345 Sandy St	804-555-2265	td@aol.com	Flip only	Casual buyer
DICK JOHNSON	23265 Park Ave	804-555-5641	Dick@gmail.com	Flip and hold	Casual buyer
HARRY BUTTS	545 2nd St	804-555-4568	allofthebutts@yahoo.com	Hold only	Casual Buyer
DAVE DOESBUSINESS	1708 N. Leigh St	8004-555-6678	davedoingflips@msn.com`	Flip and hold	Active Buyer

The day you get a deal that you want to move the hot sheet should go out via email to EVERY person on your list.

> **Tom,**
>
> **I hope that you are well. The last we spoke you were telling me how you are looking for a house to flip. I have one that has a really good spread. Please see the attached info sheet. I am looking forward to showing the property to you. 804-555-1234**
>
> **Jack**

When you have isolated your serious buyers you can follow up with a call.

> **You: Hey Dave. It's Jack from the investor networking group. I know that the last time we talked you were looking pretty hard for a new property to flip or hold. I just sent you a great**

one that can work either way. Have you gotten it yet?

Dave: Yes, just before you called. I have a few questions though.

That is an interested buyer!!

Five Ways to Structure a Wholesale Deal

Jack was an entrepreneur...or maybe a thief... I don't really know. Had he been a Wealth Warrior he would have had many more options than to climb the stalk take stuff and run. He would have negotiated a deal with the giant so that they can have a continued relationship and turned this magic beanstalk into condos with a 20% Low Income Housing Tax Credit to fund the rehab. This is the difference between a person who watches a show about flipping and tries to do it and a person who is a fully informed investor.

In this section I will educate you on 5 ways to structure a wholesale deal where everyone is a winner. You should be able to make any situation profitable if you are able to come to an agreement on the numbers.

1. **Cash Assignment**. Cash Assignment or Assignment of Contract is the ability to sell a contract to another buyer. You do not actually own the property at this point, just the contract. The value of the contract is yours to sell to another for whatever sum agreed upon by both parties. This is

used when you have made a cash offer to a private seller.

For example, you offer to buy a property from Joe for $100,000 and he agrees. You have a contract between you and Joe. You do not own the property yet, just the contract granting you the right to own the property for $100,000. Sam wants to buy the contract from you. Sam pays you $5,000 for the rights to the contract. You have exercised your right t assign the contract to another seller. Sam now owns the contract.

2. **LLC Assignment**. An LLC Assignment or Entity Assignment is used when you have made an offer on a bank or corporate owned property. Remember you must plan for this in advance as you will be making offers in the name of an LLC that is not your primary. The purpose for this is that all REO's (foreclosures) are not assignable. I recommend this for an investor who is planning to write a ton of blinds and take what he wants with the intent to wholesale the rest. You avoid the problem of assignment by selling not the contract but the business.

For example, you and your realtor are going to put in offers on every distressed property on the market. You are pretty confident that you are going to get more than one offer accepted. You are writing the offers in variations of your business name that you use on a regular basis. When an offer gets accepted you decide that you do not want the property. According to the contract with the seller you cannot assign or transfer the contract to another. Instead, you sell the business as the only asset is the one contract. The buyer of the property is buying the rights to the house by buying the rights to the business.

3. **Owner Financing**. Assignment of Owner Financing can be done two ways. First and most simply, you will have the option for assignment placed into your agreement with the seller. You will simply notify him of your decision to utilize said option and assign the agreement to the new buyer. The second technically may not fall into the realm of wholesaling as this is an in and out business but I will mention it for the sake of information. You can wrap your owner financed assignment. This means that you will continue to make the payments to your seller while taking a higher payment from your buyer. This is an Owner Financed Wrap Assignment.

   For example, you are buying a house from Lily and she has agreed to sell it to you for $100,000. You are going to have the title in your name and make payments directly to her. Cassandra wants to buy the house from you. Cassandra can give you the agreed upon amount upfront and make payments directly to Lily. This is an Assignment of Owner Financing. If Cassandra has agreed to pay $200,000 for the house but only has $10,000 upfront, you can allow her to pay you an amount that covers her payment on $190,000. You will pay Lily for the $100,000 you agreed upon. This is an Owner Financed Wrap Assignment.

4. **Sub to**. A Sub to Assignment or an Assignment Subject to the Existing Mortgage is when you have a contract to buy a home from a seller for which you will be paying by taking over payments on the financing that is currently in place. When you

decide that you are not interested in buying this property and wish to sell it you will first need to be sure that there is an assignment clause in the agreement, there should be automatically. You will simply notify the seller that you have sold the agreement to another buyer.

For example, Harry bought his house a few years ago but has now fallen behind on his payments and wants to get out from under the property. You agree to buy the house by putting the title in your name and making payments directly to the mortgage company where he originally acquired his loan. Sue wants to buy this house from you. You sell her the option to buy your contract and the house goes in her name and she make the payments to the bank.

5. **Lease purchase**. A Lease Purchase is when you enter into an agreement under a lease with equitable interest (this is the ownership of equity without the ownership of the property) that allows the purchase of the property for a set amount. A Lease Purchase Assignment allows you to convey control of and equitable interest in the property to a third party.

For example, you offer to pay Jim $1,000 a month for 5 years with a $200 credit towards the purchase each month. At the end of the agreement you have the option to buy the home for $150,000 less the monthly credits. Fiona thinks that she can get $1400 per month for the house and sell it for $175,000 in 5 years so she would like to buy your contract. You sell it to her for $3,000. Fiona is now paying Jim. You are no longer involved.

As you can see, no matter the situation, there is a solution. The key when making offers is being mindful of the value of the offer. You want to offer a good solid deal to your end buyer especially if your end buyer is an investor. You can turn 1000 glasses or water to wine but turn one to shit and that's all anyone remembers.

Contracts

This section, AGAIN, emphasizes the staunch importance of a good legal team. One way is pretty straight forward but the other requires a closing attorney that is familiar with creative investing. You have a couple of ways to write your contract with a new buyer.

The easiest is to simply charge an assignment fee. This is typically between $1,000 and $5,000, depending on how great your deal and how much the investor is willing to pay you for all of your hard work.

This is done with a simple addendum to the original contract called Assignment Addendum. In this one page agreement the buyer agrees to pay you the agreed amount in lieu of the contract which you possess. The contract becomes his and you walk away.

The addendum simply states that ABC Properties agrees to assume the rights and responsibilities of the "attached" contract in exchange for the agreed upon fee.

He then takes this agreement to his closing attorney and begins the process of finalizing the purchase.

The other option is a little less straightforward.

Remember Lamar's property? There was a potential there for you to make over $17,000. Dave has agreed to give you your asking price because he is unaware of your purchase price. Do you think Dave would be happy to see that you are making that much on just an assignment? Probably not.

In this situation we write a brand new purchase agreement for Dave listing the agreed price. We need to schedule the closing date for the exact same day as your contract with Lamar. We then get both contracts to your attorney. This will be a simultaneous closing. Dave's money will simultaneously pay for your purchase from Lamar and Dave's purchase from you. This is a tricky close an you should be sure that you have an attorney that A) is familiar with this type of closing, B) is comfortable preforming them.

Pulling out your bag of magic beans has shown you many ways to make money in real estate when you have none... how to use contracts that you do not want... ways to make a win, win, win when others are not able to even make an offer.

The key to success in real estate is to be able to see the good in every offer.

Buyer Wholesaling

Literally yesterday I received a call from a woman looking for a home available with owner financing who was referred to me by a Facebook contact who has volunteered for the charity I started with my friend in honor of her son. I get this type of call all of the time and now, as I have become very involved in other things, I generally just offer them a number of another investor who has some inventory that matches their specifications. This call, however, was a little different. This woman, Eunice, is helping her daughter out of a bad marriage. Her daughter, Debbie, has until this weekend to find a new home. She wants a home in Chesterfield with at least 3 bedrooms and 2.5 baths. She really wants a garage and payments around $1000. There is nothing abnormal about this besides the strict specifications with such a short time period. I'm thinking "Beggars can't be choosers; I'm a real estate investor, not a miracle worker."

The part that made me want to help her with more than a phone number was the fact that between mom and dad, Debbie was able to put $72,000 down on a house. I am not letting that go!!! I told Eunice that I was going to do my best to find something for her and that I would let her know by the next day what I found.

I was supposed to be having dinner with the afore referenced friend, Kelley, but instead was texting, emailing, and messaging every other investor I know who offers owner financing. She asks me who am I texting. *"You have a crush on a boy or something? You're acting like a middle school girl...text, text, text."*

I explain to her what I am doing and that in this scenario everyone can win. Debbie, Eunice, the other investor, and of course ME. She says *"Why don't people just do this all of the time?"*

I had an epiphany. There was a time when I did this all of the time; especially when I did not have a great cash flow or reserve. What I did have was drive, determination, knowledge, and a network of other investors who may have gotten luckier or have more resources than I. I was able to make a decent living at times using *just this method* sometimes for months at a time. Why wouldn't some of you like to do this full time? Maybe at first, maybe forever.

At this moment, I have found a home that meets the criteria and looks great. The investor who is in possession of it is easy to work with and happy to make some versus none. We will have to restructure his deal with the seller (the owner of the home). All of this is doable. We are yet to see how this plays out but it did make me realize that this is a niche of investing that was not touched on previously by me, nor anyone else that I can find. I named it Buyer Wholesaling.

What is Buyer Wholesaling?

A quick refresher on wholesaling in general...you get a good price on a house then sell it to another investor for a few grand.

The concept behind Buyer Wholesaling is that you, as an investor, will invest in putting buyers and sellers together. Has this been done before? Of course it has. It is called networking. You will need to do it right and be consistent if you want to make money on a regular basis.

The benefit to this style of investing is plentiful. We will discuss that in just a second. I want to point out the downfall first. Residual income. You will be in and out like a flipper or wholesaler. This means that in order to make a good living you will have to ABC. Always Be Closing.

One benefit is that you will become all other investor's favorite person. They will be able to focus on obtaining new property while you bring the buyers to them. You want to be close to other investors. This is how your reputation is built but also your team. When you have a reach of investors that is larger than your grasp you never know where you may end up. And that is a good thing. These are the same people that can open doors for you if you decide to branch out into other areas of real estate investing. When you are done here you might think that you have found your niche. You never know where you will end up. When I was somehow avoiding getting a B&E charge in the worst parts of town I never thought I would be writing these words or teaching and coaching.

Here is a huge bonus!!! You will have ZERO liability. The buyer doesn't pay. Not your problem. There is an issue with the house. Sorry guys. Not your concern. There is an issue with the contract. You do not have to deal with that at all. You will have a consulting agreement with the buyer stating that you are not liable for the house or anything related to it. You will have an agreement in place with the investor saying that you offer no guarantee on this buyer. It is up to both to do their due diligence to ensure they are making a good choice.

You might be thinking, "Isn't this just a realtor?" No. You are specializing in homes with creative financing options. You will only look for persons who are interested in Rent to Own, Lease Purchase, and Owner Financing.

How Does Buyer Wholesaling Work?

Investors become full time investors when the time at a job outweighs the money they lose not being able to generate new real estate leads. This is across the board for all styles of investing. The time is money theory becomes a stark reality when you are up until 3am returning emails and have to be up for work at 6.

When you look at niche investing and the niche is creative financing you will spent about 60% of your time acquiring property and about 40% placing a tenant/buyer. How much is that 40% of their work time worth? Obviously, there is no point in buying property if you are not going to have a way for it to produce income so it is necessary to all investors.

This is where you come in. What if you could save them the 40% of time they spend finding the end user for the property finding more deals? That would increase their upfront cash with down-payments as well as their long term cash flow by having more properties. They could potentially almost double their earnings.

You will build a list of buyers using the same means you would as a creative financing investor but you will be able to dedicate all of your time to that list. You will have the investors you work with send you the inventory they have.

Creating Inventory

I was out of town in Beckley, WV for an outdoor event. I awoke to what looked very similar to a typhoon. Rain was blowing sideways!! This is a bad hair day for any woman but it's a full on disaster for a woman with naturally curly hair. I was really hoping for a cancelation. As I sit trying to eat the plastic tasting assortment of carbohydrates the hotel called a complimentary breakfast listening to two others in my group discuss how they were once on Jerry Springer the rain lets up enough to not cancel the event but not enough to not suck if I am wet and frizzy the rest of the day. I decide I am going to find a discount store and get a hat and some boots. I google the closest one and head over right after breakfast.

I walk in and immediately believe that this place is going out of business. There is a small assortment of pure crap. No one thing has another like it. If I found something suitable in one size, they didn't have it in mine. Granted, it was July and I was looking for boots. I thought I could find rain boots at least.

What I end up finding was a pair of bright purplesque-pinkish stiletto boots and a cowgirl style hat. With my capris jeans and tank top I look like a prostitute at a dude ranch.

What does me looking like an extra in a western Pretty Woman sequel have to do with real estate? Inventory. I am going to touch on two points here. First is that you need something to show your buyers before you bring them in. Had I walked in that store and someone said *"Oooo...We don't have any hats or boots now but if you wait a few moments I will be sure to bring you right to them once they arrive.*" I would have left and gone elsewhere.

The same goes for your buyer. If you are actively marketing for buyers, which you will be, you need to have established at least some resources to finding a home for her. It is best if you are able to offer a few that you know are available and then if that is not working begin a search.

The second point I want to make is that I was desperate to be dry because I had a long ride back to VA ahead of me and did not want to be in soggy shoes and frizzy headed. The same goes for the buyer of creative financed homes. The options are far less than when you have a realtor and can look at every home on the market because you qualify for a loan. You do not need to match them exactly with what they think they want. This buyer is very likely to be persuaded to buy what is available to them rather than what they have in mind.

You will need to create a network within the community of investors where you have an idea of their inventory, requirements, and if they are open to working with you on a regular basis.

By now you know that I am a huge advocate for networking events. You will want to get yourself invited to and attend every event you can. You should talk with investors about what they do. Ask them if they do much in the way of owner financing or lease purchases.

> You: It's great to meet you Jake.
>
> What type of investing do you

concentrate on? Much in the way of owner financing or RTO?

Jake: Likewise. I typically just see what the best option is for each lead. You?

You: I find lease purchases and owner finances to be my favorite. I do have a lot of residual buyers. I would hate to let all of that marketing go to waste by losing the lead. I would love to throw some your way if I have any looking or anything you have or will have coming up.

Jake: Sure that would be great.

You: If you like I don't mind posting your property on my site too.

Aren't you just the hero?

There is no need to discuss what you want in exchange at that time. Really the point is to get the contact info so that you can follow up with expressed interest in what he has going on the market. It is implied that you will be expecting a finder's fee.

You will want to make this type of connection with as many people as possible. The broader your network the more possibilities you will have. I find that there are generally only a small number of investors who consistently have creatively financed homes available.

You will also want to use social media as a source for finding investors in this niche. I have found Facebook to be the best social media avenue to target your investor. You will want to join as many investor groups on Facebook as possible.

These are groups where investors post deals they have, offer tips, or seek advice from other investors. You can create a simple post asking if anyone has a need for your roll over buyers for lease purchases and owner financed homes. Of course they do!!!!

Let them come to you and ask them for an email address, phone number, and list of what they have available. Make a hot sheet, a list of the homes and their requirements.

Also, make a spread sheet of all of you investors. You will want to stay in contact with them to see what they have and what has been sold since you last spoke. I would recommend touching base every 3 to 4 weeks. Do not be annoying.

You will want to reach out to them the way they first reached out to you or told you to reach them for follow up. If Jake says, "*Yea, man. That's great. Ill text you my info now.*" Jake is a texter. Follow up via text. If Jake says "*My email address is on my card, reach out to me.*" Email Jake every time….unless you have an actual buyer. Call or text then.

Your follow up should be short and sweet.

"Hey Jake. Did you get a buyer for that house on 7th? I'm keeping my eyes open. Any new properties?"

When you make a deal happen, it is great to brag about the other investor to your network. A post on social media or a group email goes a long way. The other investor is happy because you gave him some street cred in the investor arena. Everyone else who has not used you is thinking that you might have had a lead for their house if you had known about it. Also, you will find this is a community. People like a team player.

Your props propaganda should look similar to this;

"Congratulations to Jake on the lease purchase of his house on 456 7th St. Only 3 days on the market. Way to be awesome!!"

Tag Jake or say his full name. Hopefully Jake will respond saying that he couldn't have done it without you.

The list of available properties will be the ones you offer to your buyers. Your buyer list will always be longer than your property list. That is fine. That means you are doing the next part right.

When you have a really good buyer, like Eunice, call, text, email, snapchat, tweet, DM, IM, post, and Flip (is that what you call a post on Flipogram?) about it. Get attention. Do not make them wait!!! They will go elsewhere.

How to Find Buyers

Guess what? This will keep you very busy. Everyone wants to buy a house with crappy credit. You will need to dig through the poop to get to the truffle. And this will be the black hole time warp for which you will find yourself with a large part of your day. This is also exactly why you are valuable to other investors.

You will use the same techniques as you would with a specific house offered with owner financing except you will be vague. HUH?

Ok here goes.

You will use hand written, 12" x 18", yellow, corrugated plastic, signs strategically positioned throughout the area which you wish to work. You will want to put them in high traffic areas, preferably at intersections where people will be stopping. Keep the message simple. Just a few words go a long way. Here are some examples.

Owner financing any credit

Must have 5% down

Self employed OK

804-555-1234

Rent to Own Home

Any Credit OK

Self employed Ok

804-555-1234

Plan to replace some of these signs weekly as they get removed, damaged, and just plain ugly. I recommend driving the route late on a Friday night with a few extras in your car so the sign is less likely to be taken down by a management company or business until Monday at least. (By late I mean after 6. I know you have some serious networking to do Friday nights.) I also suggest changing the location of the signs monthly. If any advertising sits in the same spot for too long those who pass it regularly will stop noticing it. It will start to blend in with the scenery. If you remove it for a month or two and replace it, it is new. So just rotate routes monthly.

You will want to post on social media saying that you have financing options for people with any credit situation and/or self-employed. You will get a TON of calls and messages from people who want to pick their own home and use you like a bank. If you do not mind the time spent, you can turn some of these people into a buyer. If you do not have the time or patience for a bunch of calls that you might not be able to use you will want to specify that you can only provide this service on specific homes in your inventory.

Your post should look like this:

> Want to buy a home with bad or no credit? Did the bank turn you down because you are self-employed? I will finance you. You must have a minimum of $5000 or 5% (whichever is greater) to put down.

If you do not want to field the extra calls you can add:

> Please note, I can only finance the properties in my inventory. I cannot provide financing on any other home.

If you have any investors who are happy about you marketing their property, you can make specific social media and craigslist post utilizing their home. Use the extra leads to build your list or for other properties.

Once you have calls coming in you will want to have a spread sheet with the criteria for each buyer at your fingertips. You will need to know where, what they can afford, how much they have down, and so on. The typical call looks like this;

> Caller: I am interested in your house with owner financing?

> You: Ok Great. Do you know which house you were interested in?

They generally say that they want to hear a list of all of the homes that you have to offer or they will give you the location where they saw the sign. I like to divert this into getting the info I need.

> You: Let me just get a little information from you so I can see which house or houses best fits your needs. First, do you mind if I get your name?

Get the basics. Name, cell number, email, address if you want. Now let's get to the qualifying questions. You want to determine the minimums and maximums you have to work with for each person. It is all in the question.

> You: Thank you for that Ms. Smith. When we look at our inventory, what parts of town would you consider? (List options if needed, Southside, Northside, East End, West End)

> You: If we had a home in the areas you prefer, what is the minimum number of bedrooms you would consider?

> You: If we found the perfect home for you, with how much of a payment would you be comfortable? If it was a little more would you still consider the home?

> You: When we find your new home, how much do you have on hand to put towards the purchase of your new home?

You will need to keep this list updated. If you do not have a house for Ms. Smith this month, you should check back with her next month to see if she found anything. Also, if you have a person who has a down payment below the minimums set by the investors with which you work but is close; follow up with them to see how they are doing reaching their goal.

When you get a home to show, email blast everyone on the list to let them know that an option is available. Offer a $100 referral bonus if they send a buyer. Match the people on the list who are a potential fit. Pick up the phone and give them a call, send them a text. Make contact with the ones who are most likely to buy the house.

Easy enough, right? But how do you get paid?

Making Moola

As I mentioned earlier, I started a charity with my BFF. I work my ass off and the only pay I get is knowing that families with really sick kids have at least one really fantastic day. (Insert shameless plug here.. MasonsToyBox.org & Facebook.com/MasonsToyBox). This is the only work I care to do for free. Trust and believe. If I am putting my time in I have come up with a plan to get paid. Of course this is real estate investing. Investing by its very nature means that we do not always get paid for everything we do. Deals fall apart or never materialize in the first place. That's ok. We do not trade time for money.

So obviously there is a plan for making money here.

First, most investors are happy to kick you some cash for bringing a buyer. We will give you a pat on the back and a visa gift card for $250 if you let us. That is not worth the time you are spending. You need to set the tone by letting them know what your buyer is worth. You need to predetermine what your expectations will be and lay it out.

If you are bringing a lease purchase tenant buyer with $5,000 to put down it is not unreasonable to ask for $1000 or even half. Now do not fall in this half of profit from the down payment trap.

Let me tell you....

I had my own properties at this time. I had a buyer who called me with $8,000 looking for a lease purchase in the southern part of the area I was covering at the time. I do not have anything that he loved but I knew who did. I could have talked him into one of my properties but I looked at it like this. I could win thrice. 1. My customer is happy. 2. I make a few Benjies on a house that is not mine and still have my house to sell to another buyer. 3. I'm a good gal bringing a referral to another investor. Win. Win. Win.

Just as I knew he would the buyer falls in love with the house. I call the investor and let him know that it is a go. My plan is to split the down-payment. $4,000 each for 2 hours of my life. I'm ok with that.

I know this investor and I know that he is a smooth talker. Not some fast talking sales guy from Long Island. Not some sugar and spice fella who hunny-darlins you in to feeling secure from Dallas. Just a smooth talker that you never see coming. I really still admire this about him.

Somehow I end up agreeing to half of the down payment PROFIT. Had no idea what he considered "marketing cost." After taking out for REHAB to the property I received a shiny new check in the amount of $133. Really? I have never brought him another deal.

The point I am making is to be clear and specific about the exact amount you want.

When you are bringing an actual buyer with at least 10% to put down on a home it is perfectly acceptable to ask for 25% of the down payment with a minimum of $1,000. So if it is a $200,000 home and your buyer has $20,000 you can expect a minimum of $5,000. This also works out to being 2.5% of the purchase price which leaves a much better taste in the mouth of the investor than 25% of the down payment.

So being careful and specific in your verbiage is important. Let's talk to our old buddy Jake about the house on 7th.

You: Hey Jake. I think I have a buyer for your house on 7th. It is exactly what they are looking for.

Jake: Awesome. What do you have?

You: They have $10,000 to put down. I upped the price buy 5k since you were just asking for 5. They both have good, garnishable jobs. Bankruptcy a year ago when the husband got laid off. He is back to work with more pay. If they like it I will just keep $2500 and get $7500 to you.

Tell them what you expect. Do not ask or you will end up with the Ace Hardware gift card they won at last month's networking event.

In some situations, like Eunice, there is an extra-large amount of down payment. In this situation you want to evaluate the deal and tell the investor what you expect. Do not be afraid to ask. This particular investor is far newer than I and needed help with restructuring the deal to make it work for all parties. Below is the actual email sent. I added the entire email for two reasons. First is obviously so that you can see that you let your investor know what you need to make this work but secondly because this is a complicated restructure and it is good for you to get an idea of how creative you can get with financing.

Charity Woods ████████████████   6:47 AM (10 hours ago)

to ████████████

I am working with the mom, the one with the money.
The daughter says the price is too high. So this is the option I propose. See what your seller thinks.

First look at what if they sold conventionally now.

Assuming your comps are accurate a sales price of $227,000 less 6% to realtor fees, 3% to closing, inspections, and standard repair, and $3000 to concessions they end up with a takeaway of $203,000.

Option 1
Offer the seller $40,000 in cash in 90 days. (the mother is pulling from her 401k and that generally takes 45 days) A new sales price of $215,000 (still more than the takeaway on a conventional sale) and the rest of the equity in 3 years with you paying only the mortgage pmt amount. $200 monthly credit towards the purchase. He gets $35,000 in 3 years.

We sell to the buyer at $235,000. She puts $20,000 down now (cash on hand) which we split. She takes immediate possession. Within 90 days she pays the remaining. It goes to closing at that time. At that time $40,000 goes to the seller and $7200 goes to you. She is looking for a price of $1000 per month. She has an IO payment for the balance at 6% of $844 plus tax and insurance bringing it to right at $1000. You "escrow" the $7200 to make up for the $200 per month you are losing but of course you have access to the lump sum of cash for other endeavors, like cash on hand for other flips. Everyone wins a little.

Option 2
Offer the seller $40,000 in cash in 90 days with new sales price of $215,000 and the rest of the equity in 2 years with you paying $1400 per month. $200 monthly credit towards the purchase. He gets $35,000 in 3 years plus what ever gets payed down on the mortgage.

Everything with the buyer stays the same except it is a two year versus a 3 and we require a little more down as your escrow will be $9600 vs $7200.

Either way you are making $10,000 now versus a maybe later. The seller is getting a really large chunk of change now and later. Also, during the time when you are paying down the mortgage, that $35,000 is increasing.

Basically, the existing contract says the only thing he is GUARANTEED is $21,000 in positive cash flow over a 5 year period. $350 per month. He may end up with the house back and who knows what the value will be in Chester. The average growth for that area is between 2-3%. The sales price will probably be too high to close on. Pitch it so that the cash seems like an obvious option.

What do you think?

What you charge is ultimately between you and your investor. I am saying tell them what you expect but do not be a bully or a butthole. If you pitch the investor at a certain amount and they counter, that is fine. Open a dialogue and try to come to terms.

CYA

When I was a little girl, 9 maybe, I decided to "open a store." In reality it was a thrift store/yard sale. I told all of my friends that I wanted to make a store for them to come shop in but first can I have their old toys and clothes that they didn't want any longer. I went around all week collecting my friend's "junk" and hauling it back to the house. I made tags and priced each item. I handmade circulars with crayons and markers to hand out to my friends as this was before computers were popular for home use. I set my alarm and woke extra early on Saturday morning. I turned my back yard into an outdoor shopping experience. I had cookies and Kool Aid for them just to say thanks for coming. I even used my sister's toy cash register that day.

I was extremely pleased by the turnout. Almost all of the kids in the neighborhood came. I was beaming with pride as they rummaged through the neatly organized displays. The first person found an item she wanted. A Strawberry Shortcake vanity set I had priced at $3. Really good deal in retrospect.

Mandy was walking up to the "register" when Shelly yells, "*THAT'S MINE*!!!!"

"*No its not!!! You gave it to me*!!!" I retort as the word "donated" was not yet in my vocabulary.

"*Well I am taking it back*!!!"

Soon this erupted into a backyard brawl where I was the bad guy and was not backing down. Soon my parents rushed to the rescue. My mother, the sweet appeaser, decides that everyone can just trade their old stuff for the new stuff they want. My father and I were not happy but mom ruled the house with a quiet force so we were SOL.

What about all of my work? This was a sad day for me.

In kid world, how quickly we forget. A few months later I was at it again. This time I had saved up for a Polaroid camera selling Merlite Jewelry.

I collected the goods. Took a pic and hand made the ugliest catalogue you have ever seen. I took that bitch door to door and sold my friends stuff to each other. BAM!!!

Lesson: Do not let your buyers and suppliers mix. You will be cut out of the deal.

When you find a potential buyer call the investor and say that you have a buyer and let them know that you are going to show the property. This should not be an issue for most. In fact I know I LOVE to stay doing whatever I am doing rather than rushing to show a property.

> You: Ok, Jake I'm glad that down payment works for you. Do you have a contractor lockbox on the property so I can show it?

Bam! That easy.

You will also want to have the aforementioned consulting agreement. This should be part of the signed contract that you give to the investor. You want to include several important things.

1. The amount you are either keeping or receiving in exchange for your services.
2. What you are doing in exchange for the afore fee. Are you running credit and verifying employment or just bringing the client?
3. State that you are acting as a consultant and the final decision is ultimately theirs.
4. You offer no guarantees and it is up to them to take the steps to verify information.
5. You have no liability or guarantee in regard to the actions of the tenant/buyer you place. You are not responsible for payments, the condition of the house, or any other aspect of the agreement with the tenant/buyer.
6. You are not a realtor!!!! This is very important (unless you are then check with the RA in your area)
7. You are being paid for MARKETING AND CONSULTING SERVICES. You are not acting as a realtor.

You will want to have a signed agreement with buyer before you show them the house. They do not mind sneaking behind your back and cutting you out. Their agreement should have different points than the other.

1. You are not a realtor!!! This is very important (unless you are then check with the RA in your area)
2. You do not guarantee the condition of the home. It is their responsibility to have any inspection they deem necessary.
3. You do not guarantee the value of the price of the home. Again they must do their own research.

4. You are acting as a consultant and any advice you offer is only advice and the final decision is theirs.
5. You are a consultant hired by the investor to market and consult.

Ladies and Gents, you now know the least expensive way I can think of to be a real estate investor. I do want to caution you that you should check with your local Realtor's Association and the Department of Professional and Occupational Regulation to ensure that you are not infringing on the guidelines they use to define a realtor for your area. Referring a client between investors is not a violation but only referring clients might be in your specific area

Landlording

First, I know someone here wants to challenge the word "Landlording." Yes. I made it up but believe me, being a landlord is worthy of a verb of its own. Trust me on this.

When you thought of being a real estate investor before you started down this journey you probably thought of two things.

1. Flipping
2. Renting.

These are the two most common and comprehended styles of investing. Do not confuse comprehension with the ability to do it well. I am referring to the fact that if you say you own rentals no one is asking "*What the heck is that*?"

I am going to talk to you about single family, multi family, and mixed use property. I am going to focus primarily on single family and just touch on the day to day involved with other forms of landlording and property management. Single family includes homes that have one dwelling. It can also be used to include duplexes with two properties. Multi family is a property that has two or more units. It can be 2 units or 999,999,999,999 units and is still multi family. Mixed use is a property that has residential and business units under the same complex or building. This can be a store front with an apartment over head or a huge development with restaurants, stores, condos, and apartments. I will not touch too much on commercial or development. If it is your plan to get into this type of investing it is recommended that you build a good team to assist you.

Keeping rental properties is an excellent way to secure your future or add to your current income. You can keep one or all of your rentals in a self-directed IRA for your retirement or just use the residual income to continue to improve your lifestyle knowing that when you are ready to retire they will be right there waiting for you. Holding rentals is also an excellent way to ride out declines in the housing wave in your area. Maybe you want to buy some rentals now while an area is still inexpensive, hold them as cash producers for 8-10 years; sink a little money into renovation and sell when the neighborhood has improved. Having rentals in your portfolio is always a plus.

Landlording, or the act of being a landlord, is universal in many ways whether you have a single family portfolio or a multi-family portfolio but not in every way. Some things in this section will be geared towards one or the other. I will identify the differences.

One thing that is the same is that you will have many wonderful stories to tell later. Remember, most wonderful stories do not start out feeling wonderful.

In 2000 I purchased a duplex in Richmond in an area called Jackson Ward. This is an area full of historic buildings and quaint cafes and shops….now. At the time it was a transition area complete with beautifully renovated homes scattered throughout a healthy mix of dilapidation and housing rented to the less affluent college students of VCU and VUU.

My house was a beautiful white colonial with a picket fence out front. We moved the fence in the back yard up 10 feet to accommodate parking for several cars, which is a real commodity in that area. The old home had paint peeling and a few broken windows when I bought it. The house was in pretty decent shape for the most part considering that my plan was to rent it to college students and have their parents guarantee the lease.

By the way, guarantee the lease means co-sign. It is a less imposing term. You say "*Ms. Jones, your son has no credit. I'm sure you wouldn't mind vouching for him by guaranteeing this lease, right*?" I use a separate guarantee agreement so they feel more comfortable.

Back to the fantastic story of a bunch of college coeds in a duplex.

I rent the upstairs unit to four boys aged 19-22. I rent the bottom to three girls all 21 years old. Yes this is asking for trouble but I had no idea.

I had several calls from neighbors about the number of people living in the home and a few about pets. They had, of course, all moved in girlfriends, boyfriends, friends, a couple of dogs, and a homeless guy that sold weed.

A wonderful couple, Frank and Paul, lived in the adjacent home. Their house was BEAUTIFUL! They had a lovely roof top terrace that had a very clear view of the back yard.

One summer evening I am enjoying a float around my above ground pool in the back yard of my home when the phone rings. I answer to the frantic voice of Paul. He is really a drama king so I am not all that concerned when he tells me that there is a huge party at the house. I only become alarmed when Frank, the level headed one of the two, says "*Stop all that talking and tell her about the tub.*" The tub?

By the end of the conversation I am completely befuddled and have no idea what is going on there except that both

Frank and Paul believe my attention is necessary. I throw on some clothes and drive over.

I should have really known the gravity of the situation when I could not find parking for about four blocks but I did not. I finally get to the house and walk around the back yard where a party is in full force!!! No body questions my presence as I am only 24 at the time so I fit right in.

I am sure that I clearly look pissed and concerned. My nostrils had to be all kinds of flared up at this point. I am a walking Nostrilla. No matter, I am hit on, offered drinks, and confirm that the homeless guy sells weed by default. After rejecting all of these fine offers I make my way through the crowd to find my antique, claw foot tub sitting in the yard filled with purple passion. That thing weighs 1000 lbs, is attached to plumbing, and I am fairly sure has a dangerously high concentration of lead. There they are just dipping their solo cups in a concoction of any alcohol that they could get their hands on mixed with a few grape soda two liters. All I can think is "Lawsuit. Waiting. To. Happen." UGH!!!

I am trying to find the tenants, any of them. I am asking *"Who's house is this*?" *"Do you know* _____?" Nobody has a dang clue.

I end up having to call the cops on my own house. They get there and want to question me because I own the house.

"Ma'am, didn't you say you OWN this house?"

"Yea! But I called you!" Here I am 24 in cut off jean shorts and a damp tank top as I still have my swimsuit on, pink faced from being on my raft in the pool looking like I am flushed from drinking at my own house party.

Eventually we clear up the confusion and I go home too pissed to check out the damage. The next day I come back, the yard and house are trashed. I go in the girls unit to see how much damage was done by removing the tub. Their tub is there.

No way!! The boys didn't carry that thousand pound tub down the stairs did they? Well, yes they did. For a split second they became a bit more attractive to me knowing that they obviously workout rather hard to accomplish that feat. (Hey! I was 24, no judging.)

Anyway, the good news is that they did turn the water off before disconnecting the pipes. The bad news is because it is so old it cannot be put back together utilizing the existing plumbing. Not hot anymore guys; not hot!! You are messing with my $$$!

All is well that ends well. The parents paid and I evicted the whole house. I am left with a great story which at the time was not so pleasant. I am sure they are all married with great jobs laughing about how they got evicted from their first apartment.

The Right House for Renting

If that last story did not scare you off and you still want to be a landlord I will tell you how. You will need to know how to make an offer that will yield a profitable return. For this you will need to know your market and do a little research.

You will need to know what other homes are renting at in the area. I really thank the internet for making being an investor so much easier. We used to have to look in the paper, call and ask for the address, get a map book out and find it, see if it is a viable comparison, and repeat.

Now we have craigslist and Zillow at our fingertips. You can search a certain area and see what things are renting at. Bam! Done.

When considering rent you will need to know if you will want to utilize housing choice vouchers in your decision to purchase. A housing choice voucher is a promise to pay a certain amount of money to a landlord from the government for a particular tenant. We will get into more detail on that at a later time.

When you are calculating the value of a home you are going to flip you will calculate the after repair value by dissecting the purchase price of other homes in the area and coming to an exact price based on price per square foot. Here we are going to look at a snap shot of the rental amounts in the area. The main factors will be the number of bedrooms rather than the actual price.

The price of the home should allow for a cap rate of 9% or better. Remember, a cap rate is the NOI divided by the purchase price. So at a glance you know that if you plan to pay $100,000 for a property the NOI must be $9000 or higher for a cap rate of 9% or better.

Keep in mind that the NOI is the net operating income, not just the rent.

Typically, the higher the price point for rent the better condition your property is kept. This is not always true but as a general rule there is a huge difference in the way I get a property back after having a rent of $600 and a rent of $2600. That is a factor you may want to consider in deciding what homes you wish to make a rental and which you do not.

If you are specifically looking for a property to turn into a rental the best option is to look for a three bedroom 1.5

bath home in the lower end of midrange pricing. These are typically the easiest to rent. I do not go looking for rental property so I have had 1 bedroom 1 bath and 5 bedroom 5 bath homes. The key is really, do the numbers work?

What's a Rental Without Tenants?

When I was working for the larger management company that employed me I was quickly promoted to assistant divisional manager and compliance officer for Virginia, Maryland, and DC. All of my properties that I oversaw were considered "affordable" as they had as a minimum LIHTC (we will get to that later), and were often layered with federal bonds and section 8. They were also across the board suffering from vacancy and low rents. Obviously they wanted me to fix this.

In the heart of Richmond, right on the James River Canal, stands a basic, boring, brick, building. This is an apartment building. No sign, nothing. It was hard to determine the use of the building. In fact, it kind of just blended right into the surroundings. The area is an industrial historic area so the only permissible signs are a restored version of the ones on the building from its original purpose. There are condos called Nolde Bakery, apartments called Cold Storage, and an upscale restaurant with a trendy night club downstairs called Tobacco Company.

I have to figure out how to get people aware of the fact that there are apartments in that building without the use of signs. GOT IT!!! Human directionals. What is this you ask? A person dressed up with a sign. I buy a chicken and an ape suit and have two signs made. "Egg-traordinary Apartments" on one side with "Egg-traordinary Value" on the other and a sign shaped like a banana with "You'll go bananas for our apartments" on one side and "A-PEELing Prices" on the other.

My plan, stick one of our maintenance guys in there on a Saturday for 4 hours and get some traffic to the leasing office. Maintenance was not having it!!! They pointed out that their job was to fix and maintain stuff not dress like dancing monkey. Well this could be a problem.

I do what any good leader does, I start bribing them. I say for every hour worked I will give them two hours off with pay. I tell them that I will pay them time and a half in addition to the free vacation day. I remind them that NO BODY KNOWS IT IS YOU!!! This part is important. Remember it.

Finally I say that I will have business cards made that say "director of outside marketing" on the card. "When you go to the club you can throw that card at the ladies and swish... that's the sound of panties dropping" Finally Chad thinks the offer is sweet enough. Chad is an attractive fast talking 26 year old who aspires well beyond the reach of his actions. He had no problem hitting on his direct boss (the manager at his property) and his boss's boss (me) in the same room at the same time. Everyone took him with a grain of salt...and a lime...just like a shot of cheap tequila. Not so palatable but for some reason everyone still likes it.

We get our fella, Chad, in a chicken suit on Friday as a test run. We get a bunch of balloons and tie them to his wing, give him the sign, and send him out to cluck for our bucks. I take a picture of course.

The next day I have a hair appointment and we are discussing driving traffic and I tell the story of how we got Chad in a chicken suit. Next thing I know this adorable blonde comes flying over saying "I think I know that guy!! Let me see that picture!" Well it's a guy in a chicken suit..so..K.

"*Is his name Chad*?"

I am looking like a deer in headlights at this moment.

"*It is. I already know! I recognize that short @#$% stick anywhere.*"

Girlfriend is on point and should work for homeland security. She positively identified this guy while he is dressed entirely in a chicken suit.

He had told her that he had been promoted and she was pissed!

The point here was not Chad, although I never find that story to get old, but that marketing needs to be creative, innovative, and never allow an obstacle prevent you from getting it done.

You already probably know that you need to use craigslist, postlets, Zillow, and your social media to market. You probably know by now that I am going to tell you to put yellow signs out to advertise your rental. Let us take a moment to look at some of the other ways you can market for your new tenant(s) to really get attention and not break the bank.

If you have a front porch or even two upstairs windows you can hang GIANT banners on the house. You can have them made or you can make them yourself. You can go to any party store and buy banner making kits. They are tacky but BOY, do they get attention.

Building a network of businesses that work together to prop up and support one another is an excellent indirect way to find renters. It doesn't matter what the other businesses do. You can help one another. Is there a locally owned hair salon near your properties? Great. Ladies chat while they are getting their hair done. Where is the first place most people go when they come to a new town? Probably the local pub. Wouldn't it be great if the owner there knew you had properties available?

Further, if you own or manage a sizable portfolio or are working with a multi family property, I recommend partnering with the businesses in the area by offering a move in packet with coupons and gift cards to local establishments.

You will always want to offer referral bonuses to your clients. Allow their fantastic renting experience with you translate to a fantastic experience for their friends.

Keeping your options open to less conventional marketing methods will assist you to stand out but do not forget the tried and true. You should budget a day to spend entirely to marketing a property as it is available. Be persistent on craigslist, social media, and putting out signs. These three will bring in the highest yield.

What's it Worth to You?

We touched on what to charge for rents but we will take a closer look in this section. Telling you to take a look at a snapshot of the rents in the area is not really much direction.

There are several free tools that you can use to calculate the market rent for a single family home. First Zillow is a wonderful tool for an investor. If you put in the address of a home it will give you a rent estimate. I am going to use this tool right now for a rental I have very close to my house. It is located on Graham Meadows Dr. It is a 5 bedroom 3.5 bath home in one of the pricier areas in Central Virginia. I have been charging $2150 for the past year. Let's see if it is worth it. According to Zillow the rent should be $2250.

Let's look a little deeper. Still on Zillow, go to the rental tab and houses for rent in that zip code. I then get a list of homes that are listed as rentals on Zillow in the area. I then need to gather the information from the ones which are similar to the house I am researching. Not just in bedrooms, but also in size and appearance. Take notes.

I get two hits on Zillow that are at least 4 bedroom and 2,000 sqft as mine is 3,000 sqft but that is tough to find in a rental.

| 5 bed 3 bath | 2960 sqft | $2300 |
| 4 bed 3 bath | 2392 sqft | $2200 |

We cannot draw a good conclusion from two comps. So we go to Rentometer.com. Guess what they say? My house is worth $2625. WOW! Never believe one source. This site does not discern between single family, multi family, and condos. We have a really high end condo community in the area pushing the rents up. We will keep digging and see who is closer though.

On to Craigslist. We are going to select "house" in housing type and enter the name of the area. In this case it is "Short Pump." I narrow the search to at least 4 bedrooms and a minimum of 2000 sqft. I get 4 results now.

4 bed 3.5 bath   3150 sqft

     $2100

5 bed 3.5 bath   3276 sqft

     $2450

5 beds 3.5 bath   3836 sqft $2700

4 beds 2.5 bath   2100 sqft $2275

So let's look at the overview of all of those numbers together.

5 bed 3 bath   2960sqft $2300

4 bed 3 bath   2392 sqft $2200

4 bed 3.5 bath   3150 sqft $2100

5 bed 3.5 bath   3276 sqft $2450

5 bed 3.5 bath   3836 sqft $2700

4 bed 2.5 bath   2100 sqft $2275

We have one that is bigger and more expensive so that one can be eliminated.

5 bed 3 bath   2960sqft $2300

4 bed 3 bath   2392 sqft $2200

4 bed 3.5 bath   3150 sqft $2100

5 bed 3.5 bath   3276 sqft $2450

5 bed 3.5 bath 3836 sqft $2700

4 bed 2.5 bath   2100 sqft $2275

We can now get the average price on the other homes.

2300+2200+2100+2450+2275=11,325

11,325/5=2,265

This, kids, is the market rent for your property.

If you are working with multi-family properties you should use rents on apartment rental sites like forrent.com and apartments.com. The rest of the equation is the same.

Hint: For multi-family properties that are not operating under max rent restriction, if you are consistently leased under 95% your prices are too high or your product is not good enough to compete. If you are consistently over 97% you are not charging enough. Make the maximum you can or someone else will.

Maximizing Your Assets

I woke up at 4 AM, like most days. I slept in yesterday until 5:45 so I ended up at the gym late at night and then came home and passed out. I woke up this morning looking ROUGH!!! Seriously, bad. Bags under my eyes, hair everywhere with kinks from my sweaty braids, breath to kill a horse, and leftover make up smeared about my face. We all wake up similar to this. Most people know that we cannot compete in a job market or even maintain a decent social life if we just rolled out of the house that way. Imagine the kind of job or friends I would have.

My gym will open in an hour and I will go get sweaty and gross but after.... I will take the time to be the best version of me possible.

If you are offering a product that is like the 4 AM me, you will attract people who will think that is acceptable. If you offer a product that is substandard, your tenant will be as well.

Your home should have curb appeal. When someone sees a pic online or pull up out front they need to be impressed!!

What does this mean? Really? The exterior needs to be kept up by means of faded paint, wood rot, weeds, and trash need to be eliminated. I also recommend a nice bright front door. Red has been tried and true throughout time but you can go with a cute trendy color if you feel the area will support it. Plant flowers in the yard and put down mulch.

Inside you will want as much bang for your buck as possible. The more modern and well-kept the house the better. The better the house equals a better tenant, better retention, and better rents. Here are some tips to modernize your home as inexpensively as possible.

Paint. Paint goes a long way. A light gray or a taupe with white trim are very popular right now. Color continuity throughout the home is a good way to make the house pop. This is the least expensive way to add value to the house.

Flooring is also very important. I was looking at a rental owned by Wayne, a neighbor who could not understand why he kept getting tenants that disrespected his home. It seemed that every tenant lacked concern for the house no matter how much Wayne emphasized that caring for the home is the most important thing to him. He would rather you be late on your rent each month than to damage the house. As I walk in Wayne is giving me a tour there is plastic on the floors (I assume while painting) and work is under way. The walls are painted, the kitchen is updated, beautiful screened porch on the back…nice place. This is confusing.

As I am leaving the last bedroom I stumble on the plastic and the carpet is revealed. Just a small spot. There were little dark spots all over the floor like the carpet was wearing polka dots. "Wayne, what happened here?" I go through the house pulling back the plastic with Wayne running along behind fussing at me because he was not done painting.

The floors were horrible!! There was a blackish line around the edge of the cream colored carpet where it had been neglected for so long that dust had just taken up residence there. Between the kitchen and living room there was what I am assuming is a large Kool-Aid mishap as it looked like a Manson murder house right there.

I explained to Wayne that he was setting the tone for nasty tenants by giving them a nasty house. All of the other upgrades and renovations were completely negated by not replacing the carpet. Only a person who doesn't care about cleanliness would agree to live in that house.

I am not sure if Wayne replaced the carpet and has had better luck or left it and decided to not tell me about the continued parade of hoarders and families living like a bunch of teen boys in there. But that was the last I heard from Wayne.

Paint and carpet are two things that you really cannot skimp on. It has to be done. Use a darker, neutral, builder grade carpet. I do recommend getting a carpet to match the color of the paint. For example, if you put gray on the wall do not put tan on the floor.

For wood floors you can usually just mop them with a quality product designed to shine a hardwood floor. This might take a few tries. If not you can get a buff and polish from a flooring company. If you have pet damage you will have to either cover it with carpet or have the floors sanded and stained with a dark stain.

We go through cycles of the finish of hardware that is popular. Right now we are transitioning out of brushed nickel, which is a dull stainless steel look, to an oiled bronze, which is pretty much black with a touch of bronze showing through. Right now either is desirable. This bronze trend will progress to less and less black and more bronze I am sure. What is out is brass and white. You can give your house a real facelift by replacing the light package with a trending finish. Remember you can get a 6 pack of dome lights for $40. A modern dome light is better than an old ceiling fan any day of the week.

Kitchens are expensive to upgrade. You need not put a whole new kitchen in a rental. You can paint the cabinets if they are an out dated look. Counters can be refinished for about $600. Replacing the hardware on the cabinets goes a long way in updating your space. Go to Wal-Mart and buy the 6 or 12 packs of knobs. It is much cheaper than going to a hardware store and getting them individually or even in a pack.

Having a quality home attracts a quality prospect. Just like if I walked around like my 4 AM self all day I would attract different people in my life. I doubt any of you would take me seriously nor would I be in a position to even talk about investing as I would not have attracted the business contacts necessary for me to grow a successful business.

It's Cheaper to Keep 'er

I have said it before, you can market your way into a new customer but you cannot bullshit your way into keeping one. What does this really mean? You need to offer the product your client expects and deserves to keep them. Further, in rentals, people do not tend to stay long. You want a good tenant to stay FOREVER. You have to make it happen.

When I started as a property manager for two retirement communities in the heart of Richmond I saw a lot of vacancy and underpriced rents. Even though the buildings had maximum rents we were not meeting them. I began doing monthly breakfasts for the residents, monthly movie night, thank you gifts with lease renewal cards rather than letters, monthly bingo night, and began making common areas a place they want to use. We had an event each week. We partnered with churches and volunteer programs as well to provide activities and entertainment at random times throughout the year. Bottom line my tenants WANTED to be there even though the rent increased.

Later as I acquired the entire "affordable" portfolio I spread the same type of ideology to all properties. Obviously a property made up of young professionals does not have the same desires as a retirement community so we tailored the programs to the community. We added a WIFI café and fancy coffee machine to one building. We had pre made breakfast and coffee prepared between 6-9 once a month in a bag ready to roll out of the door with each tenant on their way to work.

We ended up with waiting list for the properties which suffered from vacancy in the past. All of our rents were at max. All we did is act like we care. A few upgrades to the vacant units and a bagel once a month goes a long way.

You can do this with your single family portfolio as well. I am not suggesting that you show up at their house with a bagel at 6 AM but I do recommend a few simple things.

First and foremost, have your maintenance on point. Do not let them suffer in the heat for days before you get the AC fixed.

Acknowledge holidays without violating fair housing. Thanksgiving is not a holiday that violates fair housing. It is also a wonderful time to reach out to your tenants. Send a thank you card letting them know that you are thankful for them. If you have only a few tenants try to make it personal.

Bob and Sarah,

I hope you are doing well. Isn't it about time for you all to have a new addition? When she finally makes her appearance I would love to get some pictures.

Best,

Charity

You can also host a holiday party if you have enough tenants to make that a good idea.

If you have any tenants in the military or are veterans send a little note thanking them for their service for Memorial, Armed Forces, and Veterans Day. This can just be an email or text.

Send a card as well as a little gift for renewals. I literally go the dollar store and get cookies for a dollar.

Making a tenant feel as though they are important to you has the same effect as it does in any relationship. Do you have that one friend that only hits you up when stuff sucks and now she needs advice or worse, money? Or the one who only wants to talk if it is about making plans to go get ripped at a bar? This is probably not your "best" friend and in fact you may find this person replaceable. But no one can replace the friends who want to see you succeed, has your back when things are tough, and notices when you are not yourself. You do not have to be your tenant's BFF but they should know that it is important to you that they are your tenant.

Why are we so focused on keeping a tenant rather than getting a new one? Cost my friend. When a tenant moves out you incur vacancy loss (the rent you are not getting), holding cost (the mortgage you pay and utilities), and turn cost (the cost to get the place ready for the next guy). Now we are going to break down what that really cost you.

You receive $1,100 in rent. Your mortgage is $600. Paint is $2500. Carpet cleaning is $600. Cleaning service is $400. Even if you lose only one month you will have lost the difference in rent to mortgage plus the mortgage so the full $1100 plus the cost to total $4600. The equivalent to over four months of rent or 9.2 months of profit. Not all turns will require a full paint job, many times you will be able to get away with just touch ups. You may want to clean the house on your own. Either way, it's cheaper to keep 'er.

HELP!!!

You know what most successful people I know say? *"If you want something done right, delegate it to someone who does it better."*

There is no shame in having people assist you. Take this whole program and book for example. One of my best friends for years is the most motivating guy you will ever meet. He has motivated me to really get into health and fitness and he motivated me to take the plunge with Wealth Warriors. Guess what? That friend is going to motivate you as well as a contributor to this book and a speaker in the classes. My girl is great at brand development. That's right the brand that you are seeing now, she was a big contributor to that. I found out one of my friends is an amazing writer. Guess who is revising and editing this book for me? That guy. My sister is very meticulous and has a keen eye for detail. She is doing a second round of editing, so if you see a mistake blame her. Seriously though, they are better than I at the things they are doing for me hence making this experience better for you.

If you plan on having a sizable portfolio I do recommend either hiring a management company, which I have not had much luck in finding a good one; or hiring a staff once your portfolio supports such things. I do not think that you should hire even a part time staff if you are not

     a. making bank and

b. struggling to quantify the time you spend versus what you would be able to make working in other areas of investing, like portfolio expansion.

I want to talk about a management company as a possibility for you first. The management company will act in your stead to lease and manage the property. First, what will they do for you? Second, how much will it cost?

A management company is supposed to market and lease your home(s) utilizing the rental guidelines you establish for credit, income, and criminal acceptance. They should provide maintenance support as needed allowing you the option of using their staff or hiring your own contractors. This is how it is supposed to work. In my experience, unless you have a large portfolio, you do not get much attention. This is not to say that is how all management companies work but the ones I have used have been that way. Do your research.

The average cost to contract a management company to take care of your property is roughly 10% of the gross rent and 50-100% of the first month to place a tenant. Maintenance fees are generally a little high so you may want to have a handyman or contractor that you rely upon.

If you plan to keep 100+ properties or to manage others properties I do suggest creating a management company of your own that you pay separately from the investments. Your staffing needs will be based on your level of involvement and number of properties.

Most likely your first hire will be a manager. (S)he should be familiar with property management as well as dealing with people on every level. (S)he will need to be able to tell the nastiest tenant to go suck a dog dodo in a way that is so sweet they have to make an appointment with a dentist when they leave. She should also be good at leasing (which is sales), accounting, and able to lead. I suggest bonusing your manager based on resident retention.

The person to step up after she becomes too busy is going to be the leaser. This person is a sales person, period. No if's ands or buts. This person needs to be able to convince the client that they are wasting time by going to look at another home. I suggest bonusing your leaser based new leases.

A maintenance supervisor can fix it all and if they can't they have the hook up to do so. My brother-in- law is this dude. Before I even finish telling him what is going on he has a solution or a phone number for me. This person MUST be able to delegate and lead. (S)he will keep your cost down hence why I suggest that his bonuses are based on staying under budget.

> Hint: When your managers and staff get the budget from you they tend to want to spend exactly what is in there because most companies will give you less money the next year if you are under budget. Let them know that you encourage them to offer the highest quality for as little as possible and their bonuses will reflect this decision.

A maintenance tech is good at maintenance but not to the capacity of the supervisor. He should be running more complicated tickets like HVAC and plumbing. If you chose to offer him bonuses it should be based on review from the manager and the maintenance supervisor.

A porter will work on grounds and turns and such. This person will take care of the manual things that the maintenance tech and maintenance supervisor are paid too much to quantify spending time on.

Having the right people in place will allow you to develop and grow an extensive and expansive portfolio.

Using Uncle Sam's Money

We have learned how to calculate market rent. If you have a home in a low income area with market rents for a four bedroom around $950 would you be interested in finding out how you could get a guaranteed $1386? Of course you would.

What if I told you that you could also get money back on the acquisition and renovation of the property? How does that sound? Too good to be true? Well it is not. What it is though, is a huge commitment to meticulous record keeping.

So at 23 and I apply for a job for which I have about zero qualifications but I was a good bullshitter and I needed to make some money. Seemingly by means of a piping hot concoction of magic and fate I land the job. This is on a property under renovation with Housing Development Bonds, LIHTC, and Project Based Section 8. If you are confused right now imagine my first day. I have no idea what this stuff is nor what is expected of me. Awesome first day.

I am somehow hired as an assistant property manager but soon find that there is no ACTUAL manager on or off site but since it was only 80 units the property did not "qualify for having a manager" according to corporate budget so I am a standalone assistant manager. I found out three things that first day. 1. I got screwed into a lower salary by corporate America. 2. My plan for riding on the direction of a solid manager was shot. 3. I was pretty much screwed.

I had until after the end of the renovation to get the files perfect so that was good news. Now this property is not an easy one. It is located in a really, really, really bad area. I had been there only a couple of weeks when I was walking 20 renovated units that were ready except for the certificate of occupancy. I enter the first one and something looks weird but I cannot place it. The same goes for the next few. Finally about 5 units in it hits me. THE APPLIANCES ARE GONE!!!!!

Frantically I run from unit to unit. Yep they are all gone. I CAN'T BELIEVE THIS!!!! SOMEONE STOLE ALL OF THE APPLIANCES FROM 20 UNITS!!! WTF!!!

I call my boss who obviously tells me to call the police…this is how green I was. I really feel like this is HUGE. The second precinct in the city of Richmond did not agree. This was not worthy of dusting for prints, asking to see video from the surrounding businesses, or even a trip to the property. They just gave me a report number for my insurance company.

At that moment it struck me. They are too busy dealing bigger crimes than 60 missing appliances! Not the best spot.

Anyway, I do not consider failure as an option so I just hunker down in the midst of an urban war zone and make due. I realize a few things really help. Be too nice to people who are up to no good. I see a car parked and some dudes walking up all sketch I put on my biggest smile and most southern charm. Waving at them like I know them I yell, "Hey y'all. You lookin for an apartment?" Generally they just leave. The other really important thing was to build a good relationship with a glass company. Bullet holes do not rent apartments and the tenants don't like it much either.

So I spend much of my day holed up in my office researching wtf I was supposed to be doing with all that bond, LIHTC, section 8 stuff. I find that each thing wants the same information but calculated differently and on different forms. Soon enough I had it down and 3 years later was actually in charge of compliance for these programs for a large company throughout three states. (Well two and DC)

I learned some other things as well. This was brilliant! Utilizing the affordable housing act to make money and get paid back for your investment is an amazing concept.

Here comes my disclaimer, I am sure my attorney, Sean, will be very pleased. I am not going to 1. Teach you compliance on any of these programs 2. Suggest that you should attempt to put together a deal this complicated without some serious legal direction 3. Give you enough knowledge to even try.

We are going to discuss Section 8 of the Housing Act of 1937 and Section 42 of the Tax Reform Act of 1986.

Section 8 is a program that was designed to allow extremely low income families, the elderly, and disabled to obtain suitable housing with guarantee of payment from the government to a private owner. Housing choice vouchers can be used at any property where the owner is willing to accept. Project based section 8 is where an owner has a contract with the housing authority to reserve a property or a portion of a property for section 8.

A tenant with a housing choice voucher can go anywhere. The landlord has no responsibility to the verification of the tenant meeting the qualifications; that is handled by the PHA (public housing authority) that issued the voucher. In most areas there is a long waiting list which is generally closed. This means that the people with the vouchers keep them and others are waiting and hoping to get them. The average length of time on Section 8 according to HUDuser.gov is 8.5 years. So the ones on the list are waiting a long time but if you happen to snag a section 8 tenant and can keep them happy you could have a long term tenant. That is great news.

The catch here is that you do have to allow an annual inspection from the PHA each year. You can be sited for things that are not your fault, like the cleanliness of the home. This is clearly a tenant issue but the PHA will withhold payment until it is cleaned up. I suggest doing an inspection on all section 8 properties quarterly. This thwarts any unforeseen issues when inspection time rolls around.

You will also want to know the origination of the voucher. If you are offering a 4 bedroom in an area that yields $1200 per month for market rent a voucher from LA would be worth $3098 before the utility allowance and from NYC would have a pre UA of $2122. This means that if the tenant comes to you in any other part of the country, as long as you can justify the higher payment you are entitled to it. On the flip side if their voucher cones from McPherson, SD you are only entitled to $892 before they deduct for the utility allowance. Be careful.

Most of the time the voucher will originate from the PHA in the area they are looking. I have found that it is not uncommon for renters to head to less expensive areas with a voucher where they can get more bang for the buck. I have not really see much the other way around.

Before taking a voucher you should research the max rent and UA for the area where it was issued. This will maximize your return.

If you plan on taking advantage of the Project Based Section 8 program you might as well layer it with Low Income Housing Tax Credits or LIHTC as it is commonly known. These two programs are not mutually exclusive; either can stand alone.

LIHTC is a dollar for dollar tax credit offered for "affordable housing investments" offering incentives for use of private equity. You receive a tax credit equal to the amount you spend for renovation and acquisition. In exchange you have agreed to 21 years of rent and income restriction (there is a maximum income allowed for the tenants at move in) and a ton of paperwork.

Private equity simply describes funding from a private source; a company that is not publically traded. This funding generally comes in the form of a private equity firm, venture capital firm, or what is known as an Angel Investor. The end result is the same but the approach is a little different for each one.

A private equity firm acts as a "partner investor" standing beside the limited partnership that was developed to create the entity that will or does own the property that will be converted into an LIHTC property. Generally the private equity firm specializes in seeking out funding from multiple sources. The developer (who would be you if you wanted to own a property under LIHTC) will offer this investor part ownership or an amortized payment like any other loan.

Venture capital firms trade money for ownership interest in the company. Think of Shark Tank. They are venture capitalist.

An angel investor is generally a private person who will lend money to the developer in exchange for convertible debt, a percentage of equity, or simply interest. Convertible debt is a bond that the holder can convert into a specific number of common stock or into cash of an equal amount.

The average developer will not earn enough to be able to use these tax credits so they partner with another company who then silently owns 99.9% of the development. They pay you, the developer, roughly 75% of the value of the tax credits. So if you spent $1,000,000 you could get $750,000 back almost immediately. This leaves you with a property valued at 1M and cash producing as a 1M property but with only $250,000 in debt. You, of course, only own .01% for a term of 21 years as this is when your commitment to HUD is satisfied. Then your new General Partner will give you full ownership back. During the 21 year period you are entitled to all rents, debts, and so on. You are responsible for the record keeping required under LIHTC. As long as you do your part, the majority owner remains silent.

This program was introduced as part of the Tax Reform Act of 1986 (TRA86). Under this act Affordable Housing was determined to be rents that are restricted at 60%, 50%, 40% or 30% of the median income based on the theory that there is roughly 1.5 persons per bedroom. The lower you are willing to go the more likely you are to "win" the bid for tax credits but also the less you will earn each month. The max rents are determined based on 30% of the target monthly income. For example, if the median income is $100,000 for three people you would be allowed to charge $1500 at 60%, $1250 at 50%, $1000 at 40%, and $750 at 30% for a two bedroom. You can see why bidding into deeply skewered rents can present an issue for making money in the long run. Unless...of course there is an unless...your tenant receives Section 8. Now, you can get as much as the max rent for section 8 allows as long as your tenant does not pay out of pocket more than the max rent allowable by LIHTC. Bam!!! That is why you layer programs.

A Few Things I Learned Along the Way

Do not get caught with your pants down so to speak. You should have at least $1000 per unit in a reserve account to cover large repairs. If you have 20 homes you should have at least $20,000 in reserve. When you replace a roof or HVAC unit the money is there for you to use. You need to immediately begin building it right back up.

I recommend getting home warranties on your rentals. They run between $500 and $750 per house per year. This eliminates a lot of surprise costs that may be incurred from standard maintenance issues. You know that you will pay a set fee for all things covered, even old appliances.

Tenants will be late on their rent. They will have fantastic excuses as to why they are late paying. DO NOT LISTEN!!! Do not fall prey to excuse city. As soon as the tenant is late begin the process that is required by your state for eviction. If they pay up, wonderful. Do not believe that they are paying tomorrow or Saturday. Just get the process started.

Which brings me to, look up the Landlord Tenant Act for your state. Read it. Read it all. Know it cover to cover.

This is a landlord's bible. Mistakes can be costly. Do not make them if you do not have to. Of course, when in doubt, ask your attorney.

Happy Landlording!!!

Now What?

We have now reached the end of our lessons and there you are with a wealth of new knowledge. Now what are you going to do with it? I would like to be able to tell you that you are going to walk out of here and begin on the journey of building your empire. Unfortunately, that is not statically likely to happen.

I know that all of this information can seem overwhelming and even confusing when trying to absorb it all at once. This is one of those times when looking at the big picture can be too much to take in.

You do not have to quit your job and delve into full time investing. You only need to take a step. Maybe tomorrow you can set up your LLC and order business cards. That is a small but necessary step. If you are a little more motivated you can also order those yellow signs and H frames. Next week attend a networking event. Take small steps if you need that.

If you want to jump right in, by all means, do it!! Get right in there and go down the entire checklist I have put at the end here.

If you are the guy (or gal) who is saying "*I spent my extra cash on this but I really want to get started.*" That's fine too. Start going to networking events and building a team. When you can form an LLC, do that. When you can buy business cards, do it. You will get there.

If you take just one hour a day to dedicate to real estate investing at first you will soon realize that you have accomplished a lot in small steps.

I know there are always things going on to create a distraction. Work, family, friends. My brother is getting married, my sister is having a baby, my son is graduating, my daughter is starting school, my dog is horrible and I can't leave him alone for long. Whatever the excuse, you need to identify it as just that, an excuse. Every day that you procrastinate is another day that you are not building wealth and income. How much longer can you really afford to do that?

Taking action today can quickly grow your portfolio into a money making machine that will consistently pay you and allow you to fully enjoy the lifestyle you have created.

Some of you will be able to wake up and say "I am a real estate investor" in a very short period of time. Will you be one of those? When you take that first step you become a wealth warrior, a real estate investor. You are a real estate investor. Say it. "I am a real estate investor."

My partner, John Dixon, is going to take over the next few pages to let you know some ways that you can mold your mindset to be one of the people who walk out of here and begin your new adventure.

Think Like a Spartan Wealth Warrior

You come first. Be selfish.

Don't confuse this for revolving the entire planet around yourself, but you have to come first. Someone will argue, but I have kids, they come first. I will disagree, I know your children will be the most important thing in your life but if you can't work or make a living because your health is so bad, how will you support them. If you have expensive china on a table, what will happen if one of the legs gives out? It obviously becomes less stable and you run the risk of having a shattered mess on the floor. The expensive china is important but you have to do whatever it takes to keep the legs up or else. If that's your mission, you have to take care of yourself so you can do right by other people. Placing yourself at the top of the list of priorities will start the process. If your health deteriorates immensely, or other areas of your life become a major catastrophe the emphasis will be put on you sooner or later. There is a reason why flight attendants tell passengers to put the oxygen masks on themselves first. This is so you have the ability to assist others by remaining conscious. So neglecting the key essentials in your life will eventually lead to placing yourself first. Be preventively selfish. Preventish. Awesome word. That is just selfish enough to keep the legs up and the table from falling. Stop the catastrophes by being preventive. This will invoke change when you realize you are the most important factor to increase your quality of life and for the people immediately around you.

Ownership

You are the captain of your ship. The captain has a crew, a boat and sails to keep it moving. The wind is constantly blowing, so you can raise the sails and steer in a purposeful direction or drop an anchor. Most people will hit a point in their life and then drop the anchor. They stop growing because they docked at "getting by" island. You were growing until you get by. That's when we feel stuck and the longer we're at getting by island the harder it is to get out. The growth you had before getting to the island was such an auspicious time. Such high hopes, but you dropped the anchor and it's been so long you might have a few leaks and repairs to get the boat moving. You lost the momentum.

As you can see I hate boats. However, stop blaming others or circumstances for your misfortunes. Slap the excuses right out of your mouth and put some stank on it. Have some time to sit down and think about all the things in your life that contribute to your stagnation. Once you know what they are, put a stop to it. If your friends are a bad influence, cut some off, keep some distance or even just surround yourself with some new friends that are where you want to be, and are a more positive influence.

Everything that happens in your life good or bad is your fault. At least 99%. If you take a flight and the plane goes down, what could you done differently? You could have investigated the airline for some time, interviewed, drug tested, and confirmed the credentials of the pilots, aviation mechanics, other staff, check the fuel etc. You get the point. Most circumstances you can control, however, you have the 1% that you cannot. Don't concentrate what you cannot control, because that will leave you stranded at "getting by" island. There should be no ambiguity here. Focus on your day to day actions that will keep you productive and consistently growing toward your vision.

To be effective and a badass at life, concentrate on what you have can control, and take ownership.

Knowledge is not power

You heard me. What a crazy thing to say. You've heard knowledge is power your whole life. When I first had inspiration to walk a different path of life and follow in the footsteps of the wealthy, I said to myself, that my first step is to get some knowledge. I see so many people that complain about not making enough money. I sometimes ask, how can you make more money when you never learned how? I ask how many books they've read about money. Usually the answer is none. So why do I say, knowledge is not power? When I started my journey I looked up the top books about real estate. I read them thoroughly, I took it very seriously, summarizing the books, and taking notes. I knew I was destined to have a different life. I was so inspired and had a little more knowledge than the average person. However, as time went on nothing was happening. I was walking around every day at the peak of inspiration. Surely victory was around the corner, because now I was armed with the power of knowledge, which gave me monstrous hope. So what was the problem? The newly found knowledge did not push me hard enough. I was an inspirational deer in headlights; still scared to take action until I was around the right people that were doing the very thing I was after. Then action ensued. That is when I realized, the **APPLICATION OF KNOWLEDGE IS POWER**.

It seemed knowledge is power worked for the non-investor world. Go to school, get some knowledge, present your knowledge to employers, you get hired, show up, and get paid. However, that does not seem to apply in the entrepreneurial world. After acquiring knowledge, you have to brand, know customer segments, marketing, sales, form relationships, handle competition etc. You get the point. You can't just show up to a place and make an income.

Environmental Framework

Speaking of being around the right people. I did not take action until I surrounded myself with the people that were where I wanted to be. This is called environmental framework. I modified my environment to be around successful investors, like Charity. She was there to basically hold my hand so to speak, through every step of the process. Having that support gave me the final push I needed to use this awesome inspiration I had acquired. She was there to answer every question I had that stopped me from taking any action.

That is when I had my epiphany. Some people can read books and move forward which seemed rare in my experiences. Most people will need to set the framework for the environment. They have to have a person or people in place that they can turn to that will answer questions. Not just answer questions, but give hope, steer in a purposeful direction, avoid mistakes they've made which reduces risk, and have enormous value to your expectations of the outcome.

If you're not willing to set up the framework of your environment you will most likely fail. Get out of your comfort zone and meet people that will encourage and influence you to make the precise decisions, toward explicit action, required to cause a substantial desired outcome.

Wealth Warrior Success Model

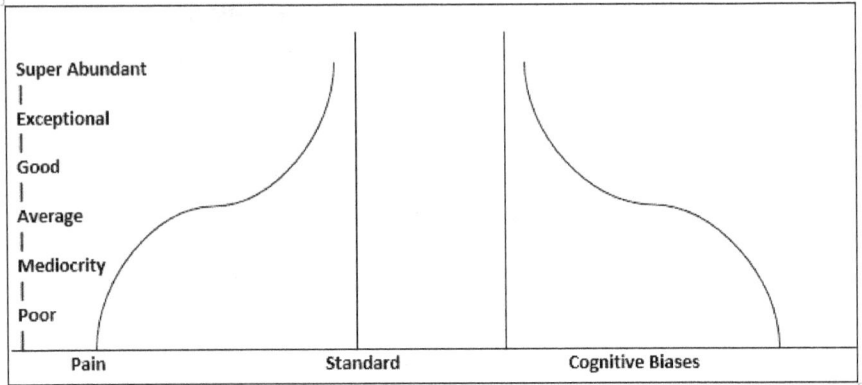

Pain	Standard	Cognitive Biases

(vertical axis labels: Super Abundant, Exceptional, Good, Average, Mediocrity, Poor)

This is the Wealth Warrior Success Model. Let's break it down.

Standard

Our living quality is determined by the standard we set for ourselves. You get what you tolerate in life. So if you tolerate low income you will have it, if you tolerate people treating you like crap, guess what, you'll have it too. You have to raise your life quality bench mark. Raising your bench mark is one of the best ways to have a better life. Know what you want and don't accept anything less. Period. Your standard, along with your knowledge and resistance of your cognitive biases and what you associate pain with determines your results in life.

Everyone has cognitive biases. A cognitive bias, from Wikipedia, refers to a systematic pattern of deviation from norm or rationality in judgment, whereby inferences about other people and situations may be drawn in an illogical fashion. Individuals create their own "subjective social reality" from their perception of the input.

Cognitive Biases

Basically, cognitive biases cause us to make irrational decisions that are sometimes against our own best interests based on our perception of our experiences and environment. Daniel Kahneman who is a psychologist known for his remarkable work on the psychology of judgment, decision making, and behavioral economics, who was awarded the Nobel Prize in Economic Sciences in 2002. Discusses in his bestselling book, 'Thinking fast and slow" about the enormous impact cognitive biases affect our lives and basically cause us to be irrational beings. There are dozens of biases, and they affect your thoughts, decisions, habits, social behavior, and memory. The best example to use is stereotyping. We expect a person or a group of people to have certain characteristics without have accurate information. The bandwagon effect is a cognitive bias that causes your belief in something to increase based on the number of people to hold that belief. I see the band wagon effect a lot with clients. They have friends and family that watch real estate reality tv shows; they all discuss it and pretty much form a collective opinion without reading any books or interacting with any investors. I was guilty of this as well. I was listening to so many people about real estate except the real investors. Before my real estate journey started and acquaintance of mine named Bob asked, "What will you do if the tenant stops paying the rent? Because I know someone that bought a duplex, he lived in one side and rented out the other. He almost got the house foreclosed on and got into big trouble, as a result of the tenant not paying. I responded, well, I would evict them. Bob said, well, they went to court and the judge sympathized with the tenant because there were kids involved and they lived rent free for almost 9 months. Can you afford a *mortgage for 9 months? See it's too risky. My answer was, holy crap."*

My real estate dreams basically came to a halt. I did not know what to do if the tenant stopped paying and could not get them out. I thought, wow, this is risky; this is only for people who have a lot of cash to be able to hedge this risk. As time went on and I received massive education in investing, I realized my lack of education led me to believe such things. I fell into this trap of believing uneducated opinions because I had zero education in real estate. After receiving just a little education, I realized the person purchased the property needing the rent from the tenant to afford the mortgage. The person took on too much house and did not follow smart investment principles or was being a wealth warrior. Further, familial status is not considered by the judicial system. If he was unable to evict, he was not following the proper processes.

Pain

Let's talk about pain baby. You want more on your plate so you have a better life, you must be a masochist. Sigmund Freud came up with the pleasure principle. You will procrastinate and avoid whatever you associate pain with and gravitate toward whatever you find pleasurable.

Researchers at University of Chicago found that people who were anticipating math problems had activity in a part of the brain that reacts to bodily threats or physical pain. Most likely due to association with a bad past experience. However, the brain did not react when they actually did the math work. Other studies suggest, the brain reacts to pain with stressful events as well. So it's not the actual act itself that causes pain, it's the thought of it.

What I found was that people associate lots of pain with success. If someone is working a full time job and wants to make the transition to be an investor that means; more work, pain, sacrifice of your favorite tv shows= pain, can't social media surf = pain, missed time with friends and family = pain. Get comfortable being uncomfortable. Make pain your friend; I guess masochists do have the right idea. The study suggests the thought and anticipation of what is about to happen soon or later causes pain, and there is no pain with the actual work. So get started first.

Raising your life quality benchmark, your standard of what you accept, knowledge and resistance of the cognitive biases, and associating tremendous pain to your lack of success, and all your actions contributing to lack thereof, and associating massive pleasure to the path of success and all activities conducive. This is the Way of the Wealth Warrior.

In summation of John's advanced perspective to what stops us from reaching our goals is us and our environment. We are the ones who chose our destiny, we choose our path. We, each moment of each day, make the decision to move forward or remain stagnant.

Action Items to Get Started

When I left my full time job to be a real estate investor one would think it would just be more of the same. Not the case at all!!! I realized that I had to really step it up and make enough to match my former income. This realization is a scary one. I had to send out more letters, make more signs, print more flyers, go to more networking events, and so on. I also formed a new LLC. Don't ask me why…

I realized that when I took a step back to look at the big picture it was overwhelming. I had to eat the elephant one bite at a time. I do wish someone had told me which bite to take first but I will tell you now. Many of these action Items are the same as the ones in the Before You Get Started section. The others will appeal to investing generally.

- **Create your LLC**
- **Get an EIN from the IRS**
- **Have an Operating Agreement**
- **Open a company bank account**
- **Have business cards made**
- **Write your mission statement**
- **Take a Fair Housing Class**
- **Create your Professionalism Packet**
- **Purchase a domain name (web address)**

- **I recommend getting a web based phone system**
- **Find networking groups in your area and attend**
- **Find your team**
  - Contractor
  - Attorney
  - Realtor
  - Hard money lender
  - Accountant
- **Create a Private Lender Packet**
- **Look for private lenders**
- **Start building a buyer list**
- **Order Yellow Signs**
- **Once you have your signs, begin getting your message out**
- **Figure out what method you will use for direct marketing and implement it. (Buy a list or create one)**
- **Start responding to craigslist and other site ads with homes for sale and rent**
- **Begin creating a list of home managed by a management company or realtor. Do not forget to record the month.**

- **Begin setting up your budget and determine how you want to do your accounting.**
- **If you are flipping or wholesaling, begin writing blind offers with a realtor.**

Once you have a property pending your next steps are outlined in the sections based on who you chose to invest in this property. For example, if you are flipping you will be contacting your contractor and planning the rehab; however, if you are planning to wholesale the property you will be going down your buyer list to find who will be taking it off of your hands. I am happy to leave you now full of knowledge and enthusiasm.

Happy investing my real estate junkies!!

I bet you thought I was done....Not yet but almost.....

Now, I just want to take a moment to be a classic narcissist...sidebar, my social worker friend, Jess, lets me know that I am using this term medically incorrect. But what about slang Jess? Am I right now?

I want to hear your feedback so please review the book online. Love it, hate it...IDC. Just talk about it. There is no bad press....well there is but as long as more of you like it then not I'm in the clear. Right? Gosh I hope so!

Also, if you do like the book and like free stuff... subscribe to my blog and get all kinds of free stuff. Over two thousand free words a week. Over 100,000 free words a year of good shit. I elaborate on all of the topics in here and will also create a blog to specifically answer a question. So subscribe and ask away!!! ThatFlippingGirl.com

Finally, if you are not a Wealth Warrior already, go to wealthwarriors.com. We offer seminars, coaching, mentorships, and more to supplement what you have learned in the book to assist you in maximizing your real estate potential; basically making you a real estate badass. Don't worry the tag line is "building your fortune shouldn't cost one."

If you just want to follow me, you can go to charitywoods.info, facebook.com/charitywoodsREI (or just search "that flipping girl"), Instagram.com/charityhowardwoods, Snapchat is charityhwoods, and you can link to all my other stuff from there.

The end!!! For real this time!!!